Caroline Webb graduated in History from the University of London and studied Italian and Art History in Cambridge and Verona. She has worked as a historical researcher and teacher and is co-author of *The Earl and His Butler in Constantinople: The Secret Diary of an English Servant among the Ottomans* (I.B.Tauris, 2008).

'*Visitors to Verona* is a rich compendium of travellers' impressions of Verona in the eighteenth and nineteenth century. It is lively, amusing and extremely instructive as to the checkered history of the city (for example, its conditions under French and Austrian occupation), thus reminding us of how much Verona has endured. (The twentieth century was to be no less dramatic.) From Shakespeare to Napoleon, from Dickens to James and Ruskin – the characters and comments in this book are endlessly fascinating. After reading it we very much want to return to Verona with renewed interest and knowledge. Caroline Webb has done a service to the visitor who wants to appreciate more deeply all that Verona means and has meant to its citizens and guests.'

Massimo Bacigalupo, Professor of American Literature at the University of Genoa

'This is a richly informative cornucopia of travel accounts of one of Italy's most fascinating cities.'

Edward Chaney, Professor of Fine and Decorative Arts at Southampton Solent University

'The author has certainly discovered a great many reactions to Verona, most of which are unfamiliar to me and many very amusing and enlightening. She writes fluently and with assurance about the historical background.'

Sheila Hale, author of *Verona and Titian: His Life*

'This book is a delight to read and provides a charming and fresh picture of Verona's daily life in past centuries. The author combines facts and travellers' accounts with masterly skill in a cohesive and lively framework.'

Professor Giandemetrio Marangoni, Universities of Verona & Lugano

'*Visitors to Verona* brings together a fascinating collection of writings, offering all kinds of insights into the national characters of both the Italians and the British, how they changed over centuries of travel and tourism and how each reacted to the other, whether with prejudice or admiration, or both. It's an intriguing slice of history and rich food for thought. Those who want to go that way will find Brexit in the making.'

Tim Parks, author of *Italian Neighbours* and *A Season with Verona*

Visitors to Verona

LOVERS, GENTLEMEN and ADVENTURERS

CAROLINE WEBB

BLOOMSBURY ACADEMIC
LONDON · NEW YORK · OXFORD · NEW DELHI · SYDNEY

BLOOMSBURY ACADEMIC
Bloomsbury Publishing Plc
50 Bedford Square, London, WC1B 3DP, UK
1385 Broadway, New York, NY 10018, USA

BLOOMSBURY, BLOOMSBURY ACADEMIC and the Diana
logo are trademarks of Bloomsbury Publishing Plc

First published in Great Britain by I.B. Tauris 2017
Paperback edition published by Bloomsbury Academic 2020

Copyright © Caroline Webb, 2017

Caroline Webb has asserted her right under the Copyright,
Designs and Patents Act, 1988, to be identified as Author of this work.

All rights reserved. No part of this publication may be reproduced or
transmitted in any form or by any means, electronic or mechanical,
including photocopying, recording, or any information storage or retrieval
system, without prior permission in writing from the publishers.

Bloomsbury Publishing Plc does not have any control over, or responsibility for,
any third-party websites referred to or in this book. All internet addresses given
in this book were correct at the time of going to press. The author and publisher
regret any inconvenience caused if addresses have changed or sites have
ceased to exist, but can accept no responsibility for any such changes.

A catalogue record for this book is available from the British Library.

A catalog record for this book is available from the Library of Congress.

ISBN: HB: 978-1-7845-3647-3
PB: 978-1-3501-7425-2
ePDF: 978-1-7867-3080-0
eBook: 978-1-7867-2080-1

Typeset in India by Integra Software Services Pvt. Ltd.

To find out more about our authors and books visit
www.bloomsbury.com and sign up for our newsletters.

 CONTENTS

	List of Illustrations and Plates	vii
	Acknowledgements	ix
	Map of Verona	x
	Preface	xi
1	The Aims of Travel	1
2	The Practicalities of Travel	7
3	Accommodation and Food in the City	20
4	L'Arena di Verona	30
5	Travellers' Opinions of the City	40
6	The City's Civic Architecture	58
7	The Veronesi	67
8	The French Occupation	78
9	The Austrian Occupation	83
10	Shakespeare, Romeo and Juliet	94
11	Scipione Maffei	101
12	Verona's Many Churches	107
13	San Zeno Maggiore	115
14	Religion through Tourists' Eyes	122
15	The Scaligeri Monuments	131
16	Piazza delle Erbe	137
17	The Giusti Gardens	143
18	Local Artists and Aristocratic 'Collections'	148

19	Music and Theatre	158
20	Matters of Health	166
21	Visitors' Views on Local Agriculture and Industry	171
22	The Dress of Local People	179
23	English Views of the Italians	185
	Postscript	193
	Appendix 1 *History of Verona Timeline*	196
	Appendix 2 *Biographical Notes*	198
	Notes	211
	Bibliography	229
	Index	239

LIST OF ILLUSTRATIONS AND PLATES

Illustrations

Illustration 1: Map of Verona   x
Illustration 2: Map showing places of entry of visitors from the north into Italy   7

Plates

Plate 1   Scipione Maffei (1675–1755), by Giuseppe Ghislandi
By kind permission of Associazione Chiese Vive on behalf of the Museo Canonicale, Verona

Plate 2   James Silk Buckingham (1786–1855), attributed to Clara S. Lane c.1850
By kind permission of the National Portrait Gallery

Plate 3   William John Bankes, MP (1786–1855), by George Sandars, 1812
By kind permission of The National Trust

Plate 4   Johann Wolfgang von Goethe (1749–1832), by Johann Heinrich Ramberg, 1791–2
By kind permission of King's College London Archives

Plate 5   John Ruskin (1819–1900), by George Richmond, c.1837
By kind permission of the National Portrait Gallery

Plate 6   Hester Lynch Piozzi (1741–1821), by an unknown Italian artist
By kind permission of the National Portrait Gallery

Plate 7   The River Adige at Verona, showing floating watermills, by Bernardo Bellotto, (1720–80)
By kind permission of The National Trust

Plate 8   Ponte Pietra, engraved by J. Godfrey, after Myles Birket Foster c.1870, published in *Picturesque Europe*, 1875, hand coloured

Plate 9   Castelbarco tomb and gate, next to Sant'Anastasia, by Robert Charles Goff, c.1900
Author's collection

Plate 10   Female costume and hairstyle in Verona, 1825, from an anonymous sketch book
By kind permission of Eton College Archives

Plate 11   A rehearsal for *La fida ninfa*, with text by Maffei and music by Vivaldi, in the Teatro Filarmonico, 1732, pen and ink wash by the architect Francesco Galli-Bibiena and the set designer Jean-Joseph Chamant
By kind permission of the Royal Collection Trust/© Her Majesty Queen Elizabeth II 2015

Plate 12   Map of Verona by Saverio Avesan, published in Scipione Maffei's *Verona illustrata*, 1732

Plate 13   The Arena, Verona, engraved by W. Miller, after J.M.W. Turner, *c.*1833, published in *Drawing and engraving* by P.G. Hamerton, 1892

Plate 14   The interior of the Arena, Verona, engraved by J. Sands after W.H. Bartlett, *c.*1840, published in *Fisher's drawing room scrap book for 1845*

Plate 15   Verona, with Castel San Pietro in the foreground, engraved by Mattheus Merian, from Martin Zeiller's *Itinerarium Italiae…*, 1640; edition of 1688

Plate 16   'Lungadige alle Regaste di S. Zeno', engraving published in Da Persico's *Descrizione di Verona e della sua provincia*, 1820

Plate 17   'Ponte delle Navi caduto l'anno 1757', showing the flood damage that year; engraving, published in Da Persico's *Descrizione di Verona e della sua provincia*, 1820

Plate 18   Piazza delle Erbe, etching, published in Da Persico's *Descrizione di Verona e della sua provincia*, 1820

Plate 19   'Porta di Borsari', drawn by Lady Henrietta Fortescue, 1821
Author's collection

Plate 20   San Zenone (San Zeno Maggiore), lithograph from *The ecclesiastical architecture of Italy …*, by Henry Gally Knight, 1844

Plate 21   'The amphitheatre at Verona', woodcut by Edward Whymper, published in *Italian pictures drawn with pen and pencil* by The Reverend Samuel Manning, *c.*1885

Plate 22   'The war – Austrian lancers passing the tombs of the Scaligers, Verona'; wood engraving after T.R. MacQuoid, published in *The Illustrated London News*, 1859

ACKNOWLEDGEMENTS

THE AUTHOR would like to thank, for their patience and helpfulness, the staff of the British Library; Burghley House, Stamford; Cambridge University Library; Dorset History Centre; College Archives, Eton College; Fitzwilliam Museum, Cambridge; Lincoln Record Office; The National Archives, Kew; National Records of Scotland; the National Library of Scotland; Nottingham University Library Archives; the Smallbone Library, Oakham School; the Sir John Soane Museum; the National Art Library, Victoria and Albert Museum; the historical archive of the Biblioteca Civica di Verona.

Dr Edward Chaney, Professor of Fine and Decorative Arts at Southampton Solent University, and Sheila Hale, author of *Verona* and *Titian,* kindly read a pre-publication draft of this book, and provided many valuable suggestions. Thanks are also due to Professor Giandemetrio Marangoni of the Universities of Verona and Lugano, Professor Massimo Bacigalupo of the University of Genoa, Tiziana Marangoni, Anthony Earl, Russell Jones, Darryl Toerien, and David Wootton of Chris Beetles Gallery.

For all their patience and helpful support, the author would like to thank Joanna Godfrey and Sophie Campbell at I.B.Tauris and Samantha Town at Integra Software Services.

Finally, the author would also like to express her heartfelt thanks to Brewster Kahle whose free-access Internet Archive (www.archive.org) has saved her many hours of research time as well as travel expenses, and provided access to many books not otherwise available to her; she is also similarly grateful to Google Books and HathiTrust.

References, in the form of endnotes, are grouped together, under the heading Notes, after the Appendices. Every attempt has been made to gain permission, where necessary, for the use of the quotations in this book. Any omissions will be rectified in future editions.

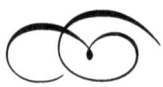

MAP OF VERONA

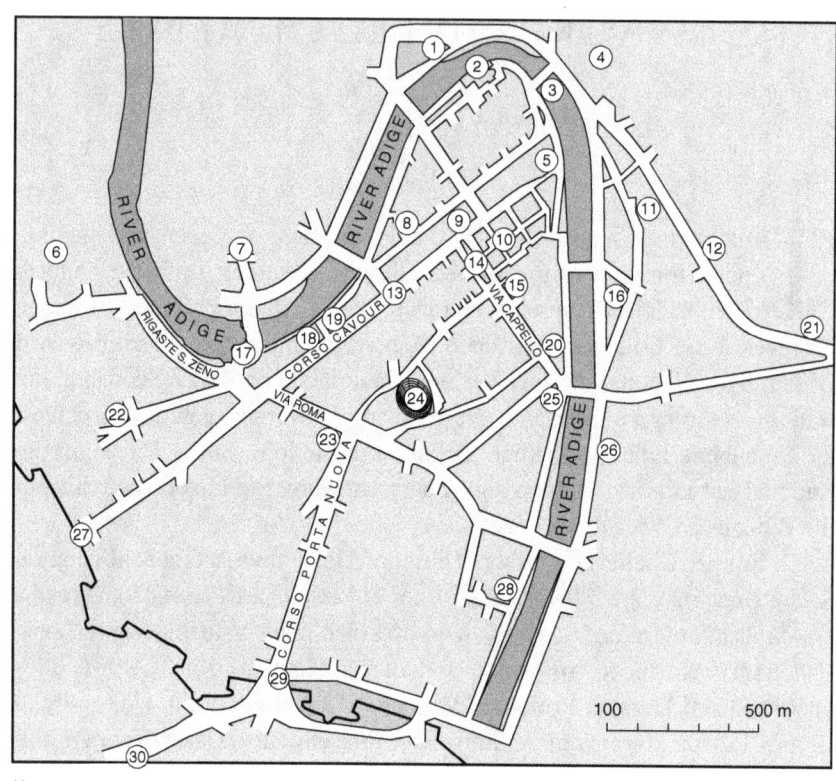

Key

ROMAN VERONA

Piazza delle Erbe market place	14
Roman theatre	4
Arena or amphitheatre in Piazza Bra	24
Arco dei Gavi	18
Porta Borsari	13
Porta Leone	20
Ponte Pietra	3

VERONA AS A COMMUNE

Piazza dei Signori	10
Palazzo della Ragione	10
Torre Lamberti	10
San Zeno Maggiore	6
San Lorenzo	19
The cathedral or Duomo	2

VERONA UNDER THE SCALIGERI

Scaligeri tombs	10
Castelvecchio and its bridge	17
San Fermo	25
Sant'Anastasia	5
Sant'Eufemia	8
Juliet's House	15
Juliet's Tomb	28

VENETIAN VERONA

Loggia del Consiglio	10
Santa Maria in Organo	11
San Giorgio in Braida	1
Palazzo Maffei	9
Giusti Gardens	12
San Tomaso	16
SS. Nazaro e Celso	21
San Bernadino	22
Porta Palio	27
Porta Nuova	29

OTHER PLACES OF INTEREST

Castelvecchio museum	17
Museum of Natural History	26
Gallery of Modern Art	10
Maffei's Lapidarium	23
The Arsenale	7
Railway station	30

 PREFACE

'Why Verona?' Verona is perhaps the most beautiful city in north Italy. The church of San Zeno is the ultimate perfection [...] Dante wrote a good deal of the Divina Commedia in Verona [...] Why Verona? Why Italy? [...] I happen to like Verona.[1]

Ezra Pound

THE EXPERIENCES OF VISITORS to Venice, Rome, Naples and Florence over the centuries have often been described. It is now time Verona had its due: this book is an exploration of which tourists chose to visit this city, how they described what they saw, and how their opinions changed over the course of the period from approximately 1500 to the years following the incorporation of the Veneto into the new Kingdom of Italy in 1866. This endpoint coincides very roughly with the growth of mass tourism, brought about by easy railway access, but allows inclusion of early railway travellers. The views of a few visitors from the late nineteenth and early twentieth centuries have been allowed to creep in where they seem particularly apposite.

It is, however, likely that the opinions of visitors about Verona, its monuments and its people, in over 500 quotations included in this book, are a very un-representative sample.

In the first place, only those visitors who found the time and inclination to write down their thoughts and memories, and whose writings were published or are still accessible in manuscript form, are represented.

Secondly, for the most part, only those of the above group who wrote in English or whose books were translated into English are represented. Certain British publishers of the nineteenth century were, however, always on the lookout for the opportunity to publish, in English, foreign travel literature that had proved popular, particularly in France or German-speaking countries.

Finally, from well over 400 books and manuscripts, covering visits to Verona but restricted as above, a selection of quotations was made primarily on the basis of their interest or entertainment value, the latter criterion often resulting in inclusion of unusual or extreme views.

Despite, then, the potential unreliability of the evidence selected for illustration, some generalizations that the reader may wish to bear in mind can be made about these visitors.

The majority of English visitors between about 1670 and 1760 were young members of the aristocracy, accompanied by tutors, who arrived on their way to or from Rome, as part of a 'Grand Tour' intended to provide some 'finish' to their classical education. There were, however, other such visitors well outside this period. They included Verona in their itinerary primarily in order to see the Arena and other Roman remains. Their contact with the Veronesi was very limited and usually restricted to members of the Veronese aristocracy.

There was also, over the centuries, a scattering of scholar-travellers whose accounts were influential on the contents of guidebooks and hence on the expectations of later visitors. Such a one was Richard Lassels who visited Italy several times; his *The Voyage of Italy* was published posthumously in 1670. Other travellers were fluent in Italian, such as Fynes Moryson, in Verona in 1595, or Thomas Coryat who travelled extensively in Italy in the early 1600s. Following the Reformation and England's split from Rome, there were sundry visitors' accounts that showed an innate prejudice towards the Catholic religion, obviously very visible in Italy.

With the increasing wealth of the upper middle classes, owing particularly to the Industrial Revolution, the number of British visitors to Verona increased from the mid-eighteenth century onwards, halted only briefly by Napoleon's invasion of Italy in the late 1790s. Many such tourists were interested in classical remains as a result of their education, but they were also alerted to a wider range of architectural and artistic attractions. As the eighteenth century progressed, increasing numbers of upper middle-class travellers from other European countries – both male and female – also found their way to Italy.

After 1815 and the allied victory at Waterloo there was something of a flood of British visitors, previously deprived of the opportunity of continental travel during the Napoleonic wars. Their expectations depended on their backgrounds, now more varied, and on what guidebooks and travel literature they might have read. As the nineteenth century progressed, the arrival of the railways brought an increasing number of visitors from Europe. Few tourists from North America seem to have reached the city before 1815 but those that came later often made up for this by their enthusiasm, particularly for its romantic aspects.

Many of these travellers came through Verona, which they often tended to regard as no more than a staging post on their way to or from Venice but, if they allowed themselves enough time in the city, they soon realized how mistaken they had been. Over this period, there was a growing awareness, for instance, of the merits of the city's architecture from the Middle Ages, and of the work of Verona's most famous architect, Michele Sanmicheli.

By the 1860s the Italian peninsula was in the final stages of becoming a unified country. The Veneto, which included Verona, was ceded to the Kingdom of Italy under King Victor Emanuel II of Savoy in 1866; this left only the Papal States outside this new unity until 1870 when they too were incorporated. These later political events seemed to have little real influence on the continued growth of Italy's tourist industry.

For Nigel, with infinite thanks

 CHAPTER 1

The Aims of Travel

> The degree of preparation necessary for travelling depends upon the motives which induce us to travel. He who goes from home merely to change the scene and to see for novelty; who makes amusement his sole object [...] has no need of mental preparation for his excursion.[1]
>
> *The Reverend John Eustace, 1815*

FOR THE ENGLISH, Italy always held the lure of the classical world, with memories of ancient Rome strong in the minds of those who had been educated in Latin and Greek at Oxford or Cambridge. From the Middle Ages onward English scholars had attended universities such as Bologna, Pavia or Padua, while other travellers had made their way to Rome on pilgrimage. In the years after the Reformation in the sixteenth century and the ensuing hostility between Catholic and Protestant in Europe, travel by Englishmen became more complicated, with a visit to Italy becoming suspect because of the perceived dangers of exposure to Catholicism. This resulted in warnings about the dangers to young Englishmen from Italian travel, well summarized by Roger Ascham in 1570 in *The Scholemaster*. He declared that not only would they encounter papistry, but they would also be influenced by the perceived bad habits of Italians, bringing back with them 'varietie of vanities, and chaunge of filthy living'. For him, an Italianate Englishman was a devil incarnate: *Inglese Italianato e un diabolo incarnato*.[2] The idea of Italy as a danger, particularly for religious and political reasons, was one that lingered on in the minds of the English for many years.

It was not until the seventeenth and eighteenth centuries that increasing numbers of young men from upper-class English families went on what became known as the classical Grand Tour, accompanied by their tutors or 'bear leaders'. Writing earlier in the sixteenth century, the philosopher and politician Francis Bacon had already given some positive advice to a nobleman about the aims and benefits of travelling abroad.

> Your Lordship's purpose is to travel, and your study must be what use to make of your travel [...] you shall have great help to attain to knowledge, which is not only the excellentest thing in man, but the very excellency of man.

This study should extend to knowledge of the country to be visited and the people therein, 'their buildings, their furnitures, their entertainments, all their husbandry and ingenious inventions in whatsoever concerneth either pleasure or profit'.[3]

So the aim of travel was to learn more, but there were dangers to be avoided. A young man should not be 'given to affectation (a general fault in most of our English travellers), which is both displeasing and ridiculous'. He should profit by association with the best of the local people, and 'restrain your affection and participation from your own countrymen of whatever condition'.[4] This was general advice directed to any visitor to Europe, but was particularly pertinent to Italy, a country very much the focus of travel from the sixteenth and seventeenth centuries onwards because of its classical associations.

It was not just young aristocrats in search of the ancient world who went to Italy. There were two Englishmen visiting Verona around 1600 who were driven, rather, by simple curiosity and a desire to see the world. For Thomas Coryat, an early English traveller and author, 'Of all the pleasures in the world travell is (in my opinion) the sweetest and most delightfull.'[5] This was because he felt it enabled a man to see other countries, to meet other scholars and to learn new languages. A few years later Fynes Moryson, student, skilled linguist and inveterate traveller, declared that his intention was 'to enable my understanding, which I thought could not be done so well by contemplation as by experience'.[6]

These two had clearly not been deterred by the perceived dangers of Italian travel, which were later enumerated by John Raymond, who went on the Grand Tour with his uncle in 1646–7. His *Itinerary contayning a Voyage*, sometimes described as the first comprehensive English guidebook to Italy, was an attempt to dispel the principal fears as Raymond saw them:

> There are three evitable dangers that divert some from this Voyage; the first is the heates of the Climate; a second, that horrible (in Report) Inquisition; the last, Hazard of those merciless Out Lawes Banditas.
> The first may be allayd by Moderation, the second prevented by Discretion; the last avoided by the defence of those States you pass through.[7]

Undeterred by such possible hazards, there were young Grand Tourists visiting Verona by the later seventeenth century. One such was John, 5th earl of Exeter, who visited Verona on his second trip to Italy in 1683–4, accompanied by his steward, Culpepper Tanner. James, 1st duke of Ormond, chose Francis Misson, a Protestant refugee from France, as tutor and guide to his grandson, Charles Butler, later earl of Arran. These two undertook their grand tour in 1687 and 1688, travelling to Italy over the Brenner Pass, and visiting Verona on the way to Venice. In 1691, Misson published an influential account of their trip which was translated into English as early as 1695; this work, *A new voyage to Italy*, has been described as 'resoundingly modern, comprising the sequential exposition of first-hand factual observations, nonetheless augmented by the critical perspective of a protestant travelling through a Catholic country'.[8]

The early to middle years of the 1700s saw the peak of the Grand Tour phenomenon of young English aristocrats and their tutors spending months or even years visiting the principal classical sites in places such as Rome and Verona. Its aim, according to Thomas Nugent, Anglo-Irish traveller, translator and writer, was 'to enrich the mind with knowledge, to rectify the judgement, to remove the prejudices of education, to compose the outward manners, and in a word form the complete gentleman'.[9] So, in the 1740s when Nugent was writing, the objectives of the Tour were still very much both instruction and development of character.

Since the education of such young men had been based largely on Latin and Greek, for their tutors the purpose of any Italian visit was to deepen their charges' understanding of the Roman world. This would certainly involve visiting Rome itself with its impressive remains that included the Coliseum, the Forum and Trajan's Column. It could also involve a visit to Verona, whose antiquities were perhaps not as notable, but were nevertheless varied and of great interest, particularly its Arena built in about AD 30 and in a fine state of preservation internally. In 1730, Alexander Gordon had published *A complete history of the ancient amphitheatres*, a translation of a treatise on the subject by the illustrious Veronese antiquarian, Scipione Maffei; this had helped to spread the fame of the Arena amongst English-speaking travellers.[10]

These well-born young Grand Tourists included Charles Sackville, eldest son of the duke of Dorset, who was in Italy from 1731 to 1733 with his tutor Joseph Spence, a clergyman and Oxford professor. They spent four or five days in Verona in November 1731 en route to Venice; in a letter home, Spence described how the first sight of the Roman Arena 'strikes one with such an admiration that one does not care to speak for four or five minutes'.[11] On the other hand, those who had seen Rome first found Verona's ruins of little consequence, as Marianne Colston, artist, author and traveller, noted later, in 1820. 'We visited the celebrated Roman amphitheatre in this place; it is far inferior in magnitude, and (as well as we can now judge) in architectural beauty, to the noble Coliseum in Rome.'[12] Few other visitors were so dismissive, with most ready to admire the excellent state of preservation of the Arena's interior, which contrasted with the more ruinous state of that of the Coliseum.

The Roman Catholic priest, The Reverend John Eustace, did not publish his influential guide *A tour through Italy* until 1813, but in it he still held the principal aims of the Grand Tour in mind. He gave perhaps the most succinct account of what 'a man of a liberal and active mind' should do before embarking on an Italian tour.[13] He should be instructed in the works of Latin poets and historians as well as in Italian history from the time of the Romans onwards. He should have a general knowledge of the principles of architecture, sculpture and painting, as well as a sufficient knowledge of the Italian language, that 'nothing may be wanting to complete his command of it but practice and conversation'.[14] Finally, he should be of 'an unprejudiced mind'.[15] Eustace was harking back to the days when the classical past was the focus of Italian travel, but in fact the world of tourism was already changing in nature.

From the mid- to late eighteenth century onwards travel to Italy was becoming increasingly a middle-class activity, with visitors to Verona including businessmen, artists, writers and women. These people might well take in the classical sites deemed the most significant, such as the Arena in Verona, but they were also interested in other matters, such as the customs and characteristics of the Italians themselves, buildings to be found in Verona from later periods, designed by architects such as Michele Sanmicheli and – inevitably – the city's Shakespearean connection with Romeo and Juliet. Many came to realize that Verona deserved more time than they had allowed. In 1820, for instance, Thomas Pennington and his party arrived in the city:

> [...] our intention was to have proceeded on our journey on the following day, but this town is so interesting from its antiquities, and from its being celebrated by our immortal bard, that we held a council on the subject, and the result was, a determination to stay the next day, by which means we should have a day and a half here.[16]

Travel to the Continent was becoming easier, with steamships crossing the Channel by the 1820s, and railways being built from the 1840s onwards; this enabled more people on limited budgets to explore France and Italy.

Travel was also much faster, resulting in tourists spending less time in each place, but visiting more of them. The political situation across Europe generally became much more secure after the defeat of Napoleon in 1815, making the idea of travel to places like Verona or Venice more acceptable. Even those who were unable to travel enjoyed reading guidebooks: in the ten years from 1819, an average of seven travel books a year about Italy were published in Britain.[17] Another source of interest and information was the publication of works illustrated with prints of foreign cities with their principal sights; these would have included the widely known *Landscape annuals* published in the 1830s and covering Italy, France and Switzerland.

Women travellers in particular commented in their letters and journals on the practical details of their journeys; these might be the comfort or otherwise of their lodgings, the state of the pavements or the works of art to be seen in public galleries. The growth of what might be called the guidebook industry was useful to women who often lacked the extensive classical education of their male counterparts but still wished to take full advantage of the opportunities now open to them. Some also wrote accounts of their travels that were tantamount to guidebooks, and which enjoyed considerable success. These included Hester Piozzi, married to an Italian musician, the author Mariana Starke and the Countess of Blessington, society beauty and friend of Byron. They were less likely to be didactic about recommending itineraries than, say, Murray's *Hand-book for travellers in Northern Italy* of 1842 which stated firmly that 'The principle of describing not what *may* be seen, but what *ought* to be seen has been strictly followed by the author of the present work […].'[18]

As Britain became an increasingly urban society in the nineteenth century, tourists displayed a particular interest in city life in Italy as well, which they could compare with their experiences at home. The range of city guidebooks now available was considerable, and the information they provided was bound to influence what tourists aimed to see, for instance, in Verona. One recent historian has described this development thus: 'Guidebooks were powerfully constitutive of the experiences of sightseeing; they determined what was seen and in what order, and shaped what judgements were made.'[19] Once a family had decided to visit Italy, the relevant guidebook could be studied at home before departure and, on arrival, the advice on essential places to visit could be followed, perhaps with the assistance of a *cicerone* or local guide. The resulting conformity is reflected in the accounts left by travellers, who repeatedly visited the same sights in Verona; it was a rare tourist who aimed to explore the back streets of the city.

Europeans, too, became more frequent visitors to Italy from the late eighteenth century onwards, often leaving accounts of their travels. The German author and polymath Johann Wolfgang von Goethe, for instance, had always wanted the opportunity to visit the country, and described his time in Verona in the 1780s with delight, showing a particular interest in the Veronesi and their way of life. French travellers in the 1830s included the indefatigable Antoine Pasquin, who visited almost every building in Verona, describing his researches in his guidebook. Travellers' interests now extended to a wider range of sights in the city that included the fortifications and *palazzi* built by the Veronese architect Sanmicheli, the Gothic Scaligeri funeral monuments in Piazza dei Signori and the contents of the many local churches.

There were also many more American travellers in the nineteenth and early twentieth centuries, all seeking to explore Europe now that this was easier and more affordable. So far as Verona was concerned, most were intent on making their way to anything that could be linked with Shakespeare's *Romeo and Juliet,* but they also commented on many other features of the city's life. So it was that changing opportunities for travel enabled tourists from across the world to come to a city that had much more to offer than classical sites such as the Roman Arena, and did not deserve in any way to be thought of as merely a stopping-off point on the way to or from Venice.

CHAPTER 2

The Practicalities of Travel

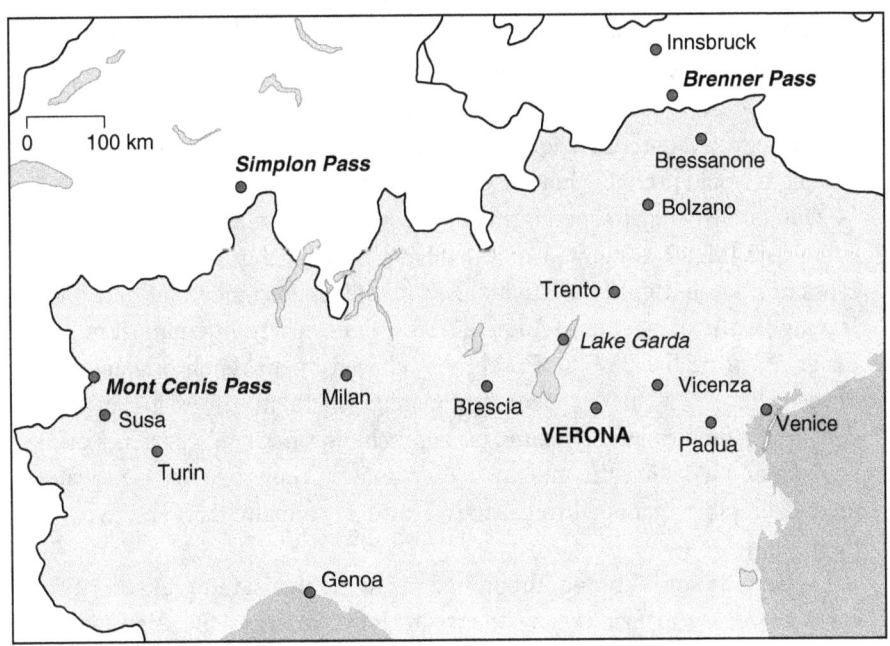

Map showing places of entry of visitors from the north into Italy, in relation to Verona

> At ten at night we started in the mail for Milan passing through Padua in a torrent of rain [...] Breakfasted in deserted Vicenza [...] our dinner was discussed at Verona, where we remained five hours.[1]
>
> *Andrew Clarke, 1841*

ONE OF THE FIRST preoccupations of any English or Scottish traveller setting out for Italy was to decide how to get there. It was possible to travel by sea to the south of France and then continue overland, but this took some time and was subject to the hazards of storms and pirates in the Mediterranean. The most popular choice until about 1814 was to cross the Channel and then proceed by road across France to the Lanslebourg-Mont-Cenis Pass over the Alps towards Susa in Italy; after that date the Simplon Pass became the preferred route, a proper road having been constructed at the behest of Napoleon. Another possibility was to use the Brenner Pass from Austria, now on the border with the Alto-Adige province of Italy, a route long controlled by the Holy Roman Empire as its means of access into Italy. Most of our seventeenth-, eighteenth- and early nineteenth-century English travellers would probably have used the Mont Cenis route.

One family, later to spend time in Verona, had an alarming experience when using this traditional route involving nothing more than a Channel crossing. Sarah Bentham, stepmother of the philosopher and reformer Jeremy Bentham, set out in August 1793 with her party, but, almost immediately, 'During the day the Packet was chased by a French privateer for Seven Hours.' As the privateer was gaining on them, the ship's captain declared it time to jettison some cargo, including her son's coach, stored on deck and blocking the gun ports. Fortunately, though, a breeze sprang up and the ship managed to escape.[2] There were many dangers, even in the Channel.

So Sarah's son, Charles Abbot, had made the decision to take his own carriage across to France and thence to Italy. To cross the Alps by the popular Mont Cenis route into Italy, the traveller would have to have his vehicle dismantled and later reassembled; to avoid this complication, many travellers chose the alternative of hiring the transport they required first in France and then again in Italy. Hiring was not the best option, however, according to William Patoun, Scottish connoisseur and experienced traveller to the Continent; in about 1766 he opined that it was always better for a traveller to take his own carriage from home on the grounds that the time and money involved in repairs to a second-hand vehicle purchased abroad would outweigh the costs of transporting one's own. 'I scarce ever knew an English Gentleman that did not regret his not having brought a Carriage with him from England.'[3] Three years later the Honourable William Fitzwilliam did bring his own carriage, recording in his diary how it was first disassembled and later put together again after the Alpine crossing so that he could begin his Italian tour. Such a traveller would then have needed to hire a local coachman and horses at the posting stations along the way.

Lord Drumlangrig gave a graphic account of how his party crossed Mont Cenis into Italy in 1680:

> We agreed with a people here, whom they call Marons to carry us over the hill upon open chaires made in the forme of our barrowes upon which criples are carryed through the countrey. Here we were necessitate to quit our horses, and some on mules, and others on the chaires we wrestled up hill till we came to the top, where we found a large plaine of two miles length and a fair lake of water wherein they told us there were fish [...]
>
> All the tyme we were on the plaine it snowed excessively so that we could scarcely see one another. We refreshed our selves and the men who carryed us, in a poor house here called a post house, where taking each of us a glass of wine, ill as it was, we made hast to get down the hill as we had gotne up. Here we all of us took the help of these Marons, who by a wonderfull adresse and nimblenesse of foot carryed us down such precipices and over such rocks that we were affraid to see our selves hanging over them in mens hands, and far more to look back againe from whence we had passed.[4]

On making the reverse journey from Italy into France by the same Mont Cenis route in 1770, soldier and author George Ayscough found a different method in use. Instead of being carried in a chair across the plateau, he was conveyed in a horse-drawn sledge. On arrival at the final precipice, the horse was unharnessed from the sledge in which the guide then seated himself; he 'gave it a shove, and we descended swift as an arrow shot from a bow, so that in about six minutes we reached the bottom'. Ayscough did not feel too nervous because the guide was able to steer and 'by means of an iron chain which sticks in the snow underneath the carriage, he is able to stop it at pleasure'.[5] One wonders at his calm belief that the iron chain would hold should the need arise.

Once across the Alps by this route, most travellers went on to Turin before deciding on the rest of their itinerary; they might choose initially to go southwards towards Florence and Rome, returning by Venice, or to go eastwards first towards Verona and Venice, and then travel south. Unless they were possessed of their own carriage, onward travel could either be by *vetturino* or by *cambiatura*. If they chose the first option, they made a contract for a fixed itinerary with a *vetturino* who drove his own carriage, saw to the horses and could, if required, make arrangements along the way for the tourists' accommodation and food. This was a good option for a group of people travelling together, although progress was fairly slow by this means, and did not allow for changes of route or extra stopping time. By English standards, the horses were badly treated and were often slow. Patoun had further thoughts here for the unnamed 'eldest son of an English peer' for whom he had drawn up a lengthy schedule of advice.

> Your Lordship will find this Manner of travelling by Veturino extremely tedious & disagreable, as they never exceed a foot pace. Nor will it signify to urge them to strike a trot when the road is plain & good. They are inexorable.[6]

An anonymous Scotsman, on the way to Verona in 1830, observed how his party's *vetturino* 'inspirited his jaded cattle with a couple of bottles of wine which he mixed with their oats'.[7] Unfortunately, our traveller did not report the effect of this on the horses.

It was assumed that, if using a *vetturino* or private coach, passengers should make provision for food to be eaten during the day. Patoun, as ever, had practical advice:

> In making long Journeys thro Places where there is nothing remarkable to be seen, a Cold tongue, or a Peice of roast beef in the Chaise will prove an Excellent Companion, save you time and Money and often indeed on Maigredays, nothing can be had on the road. [...] When you find good Bread at any place, carry some along with you, as you will find in General the Bread most disagreably sour and bitter.[8]

Charles Abbot recommended in his 1788 diary that travellers should always take biscuits and sugar with them, and (somewhat curiously) that 'For want of Milk fresh eggs will do as well in Tea.'[9] The idea of raw eggs in tea seems distinctly unappealing.

What tourists needed to take on their travels obviously required planning before departure. Access to funds was essential: the best method was to get letters of credit from one's English bankers to one's contacts abroad rather than to risk carrying quantities of money. The Scotsman Henry Cockburn, Scottish advocate and reformer, provided an example of this when in Verona;

he made mention of a 'Mr Martinelli the banker to whom we had a letter from Coutts.'[10] In any case, the fact that a traveller passed through so many different jurisdictions, each with its own currency, made it necessary to change money frequently; it was therefore more convenient to apply to one's banker for the local currency in each of the major cities visited. Patoun cautioned against carelessness in respect of money:

> Consider yourself in Money Matters as entering a hostile country where every individual almost has a design upon your Pocket. Draw for as little Money at a time as possible: both because the Exchange may rise in your favour, and that the Command of Money always lays a temptation in a Young Mans way to spend it.[11]

As to other items, once again Patoun was on hand with suggestions, from items for carriage maintenance to packing:

> Ropes, Lynch Pins a jack and drag for the Wheels &c are always to be at hand, in case of Accidents, and the Carriage to be examined carefully every Morning. [...]
> An Ecritoire which will hold your Money as well as paper [...]
> A tea equipage, or what is still more useful Chocolate and a Chocolate Pot are very Necessary Articles, as you can get very seldom either Milk or Butter on the road [...]
> Cloaths are often spoiled in the jolting of a long Journey by improper packing [...] Books and other hard Matters to be pack'd at bottom. The Linnen in a detached cover that fits at the top.[12]

Coxe's *Picture of Italy* of 1817 contained an extensive list of items considered necessary by the early nineteenth century. These ranged from pistols to a leather belt with pockets for valuables, as well as a stout trunk or two and a *sac de nuit*, soap and razors, a strong box for jewellery and money, writing materials, a barometer, an English corkscrew and a 'good steel table-knife'. He noted that some people took 'a large sack, made of the most impenetrable leather, containing a complete travelling bed' with mattress, pillow and sheets, and occasionally even a bedstead 'made of iron but extremely light'. This must have made for a very bulky collection of luggage. Coxe's final recommendation was very practical. 'A tin sandwich box, to hold cold tongue, ham, sausages, &c and a small bottle, covered with wickerwork, to contain about a pint of brandy, will be found useful for pedestrian excursions and short voyages [...].'[13]

Gaze's *North Italy and Venetia: how to see them for 15 guineas, etc.* of 1867 was a lot more down to earth, given that travel by train was now the preferred option of many. He suggested Murray's 1842 guidebook to northern Italy, an up-to-date copy of *Bradshaw's continental railway guide*, passports as necessary, a portmanteau and knapsack ('Do not encumber yourself with a needless ounce of luggage'), a telescope, shaving equipment and, finally, 'Pocket knife; nail scissors; wax matches; pocket comb; paper and envelopes; pens and portable inkstand; nail and tooth brushes; extra socks and handkerchiefs; shirts and collars; night dress; stout purse, soap.'[14] This was certainly a very practical list for someone travelling by train.

Once a traveller got underway, there were invariably problems. Complaints were frequently made about being cheated by innkeepers, postilions and *vetturini*, with the postilions a particular source of aggravation, as they often demanded extra money. Elizabeth Wynne, travelling with her family in March 1796, complained that '[...] we entered the Venetian territories, and came into the country of the cheating, cunning and good for nothing Italians. We were plagued to death by the postillions who are never contented with the *buona mano* which is given them.'[15] Patoun was again at hand with advice.

> The English give three Pauls to each Postillion per post. They are the most resolute ruffians in all Italy, and your Servants must be cautioned to avoid quarrels with them, as it is not a Word & a Blow, but a Word & a Stab. Several accidents of this kind happened whilst I was in Italy, which makes Me mention it particularly to your Lordship.[16]

T. Baring had his own way of dealing with these difficulties in 1814, by keeping a low profile.

> As I was travelling alone, I did not wish to be taken for an Englishman, supposing I should hear more of the people's real sentiments [...] for the Italians [...] think all Englishmen, to use a vulgar phrase, 'are made of money'; and they say any thing by which they may extort it.[17]

When in Verona in 1817, the artist and floor-cloth manufacturer John Samuel Hayward noted in his diary the arrangements for his *vetturino* travel onwards to Milan. Knowing it was always deemed essential to have a written copy of any contract, he 'entered into an engagement with Alessandro Zarra the same veturino who had brought me from Padua – to conduct me and Michele – to Milan – on the 3rd day – departing tomorrow – and allowing half a day at Desenzano – for 80 Lire d'Italia [...]'.[18] This precisely phrased contract, running to over 150 words of Italian, is signed with an X by Alessandro Zarra and witnessed by Hayward's companion, Michele Simone. In 1854, the Baltimore attorney Orville Horwitz found that bargaining with a *vetturino*

> [...] is no trifling matter; it requires considerable skill and some experience, and even then, you may rely pretty surely on being cheated. [...] What an honest country this must be, where so many precautions are required in hiring a carriage for forty miles – but, then, horse-jockeys and cabmen are the same species every where![19]

The widely travelled James Silk Buckingham and his party had an unfortunate accident in about 1846 while travelling by *vetturino* towards Verona. He described how

> [...] suddenly one of the wheels of the carriage flew off, and the carriage itself was thrown flat on its side. It was with great difficulty that we could extricate ourselves through the window, which, after many struggles, we at length succeeded in doing. We were both much bruised, but fortunately received no serious injury. With the help of some peasants passing on the road, we succeeded in getting the carriage up again, replacing the wheels, and reloading the baggage; but as Verona was near, we preferred walking the remainder of the way. A female peasant, who was in a gig driving into the city, kindly offered to take us with her: and a lady of elegant dress and manner, accompanied by her daughter, about ten or twelve years of age, who were taking an airing in a handsome carriage-and-pair, seeing our vetturo overturned, came instantly to our assistance, and were most kind in their enquiries and offers – while a bishop, riding by at the very moment of the disaster, and quite alone in his carriage, never turned aside for a moment to see whether any injuries had been sustained, or any aid was needed.[20]

By the 1870s, Augustus Hare, a long-time resident of Italy, was already feeling nostalgic about the passing of this traditional method of travelling, comparing it favourably with the frantic rush of train travel.

> The old days of Italian travel are already beginning to pass out of recollection – the happy old days, when with slow trotting horses and jangling bells, we lived for weeks in our vetturino carriage as in a house, and made ourselves thoroughly comfortable there, halting at midday for luncheon, with pleasant hours for wandering over unknown towns, and

gathering flowers, and making discoveries in the churches and convents near our resting-place.[21]

The other option for travellers was to make use of public methods of transport, which could be by *cambiatura* or diligence; here the traveller paid for each stage of the journey. This was a faster option, and gave him more freedom to decide his length of stay in each place; on the other hand, he had to share the diligence with the general public, which could be a disadvantage, and made this method suitable for men or for women with travelling companions. William Patoun had tried the *cambiatura* himself and declared he

> [...] never had such trouble in My Life. They are not obliged to travel after a certain hour in the Evening, nor carry above a certain Weight of Baggage. They give you their worst jaded Horses, and their best Curses, in short, even to Me who spoke their Language easily, and knew the Customs of the Country, it was the most disagreable task imaginable; judge what it must prove to young travellers.[22]

On the other hand, Thomas Barlow of Leeds, touring Italy with his family, found nothing to complain of when in 1835 they left Verona

> [...] about eight o'clock with our German companion, in a comfortable closed conveyance holding four persons, travelling by relays of horses: at the office from which we started, we were furnished with a time-paper, in which, at each change, the postmaster entered the time of our arrival and departure, thus ensuring us the proper speed.[23]

Others less fortunate would have agreed with Patoun's assessment. An anonymous Scotsman in Verona in 1841

> [...] saw the diligence start for Milan [...] Lady, Fat Priest and all, not to mention a basket of fine Pigeons, two of ditto quails and sundry of dead fish, the ice from which kept running off the top of the coach in a small stream all the way [...] The Baggage too looked [...] like a miniature Haystack – truly a diligence is a rum turn out and I am glad I am out of it.[24]

One night, in about 1847, Simon Lacklustre (a pseudonym) – who described himself in the preface to his book as 'a mere idler' – left Verona, where he had become

> [...] forgetful of present Italy in past Italy – a forgetfulness most speedily and rudely dispelled, by finding myself almost unconsciously deluded into 'a nice inside place for the night' – such an inside place! So cramped, so hard, so be-basketed and cloaked, so stewed in unwholesome heat, so peppered and served up (thus hot) with dust – I hope never to be again. There were two Germans, one Italian, one Muscovite, an American and myself, each and every one of us with a vast superfluity of coats, and furs, baskets and sacs de nuit, stowed into a rotonde that would have been small for four lightly-accoutred people. We tried to laugh at it, but 'twas really too uncomfortable, and one by one we relapsed into a cross silence, broken at intervals by peevish groans.[25]

Any idea of opening a window had, of course, to be balanced against the resulting clouds of dust or squalls of rain that would envelop the passengers.

The River Adige was navigable for part of its length, and was used for commerce. It could also be used for passengers, something noted by the German academic and tutor John Keysler in the 1730s.

> There is a very commodious water-carriage from hence to Venice. The passage in a barge takes up but three days and a half; but the return is more tedious; for the barge is drawn by oxen, so that it is not performed in less than eight days.[26]

It seems that this option was not popular with tourists, as it was rarely mentioned. On the issue of time taken for a journey, a 'Travelling lawyer' noted in about 1833 that going by post could be advantageous if one was in a hurry: 'There is a malle-poste which goes from Venice to Verona three days in the week, carrying four, which sets off at night, and arrives at ten next morning.'[27] This would certainly have been a highly convenient method, but again suitable mainly for male travellers.

There were always complaints about the endless inspections of passports or luggage as tourists moved from one jurisdiction in Italy to another, with customs officers often expecting bribes. In earlier times things had been easier for some. Fynes Moryson was clearly impressed in 1595 by the way he was able to avoid paying tolls in the Venetian territories.

> I rode fifteene miles to the Castle Peschiera, built by the old Lords of Verona, and seated upon the Lake Bennacus, vulgarly called Il Lago di Gardo, where they demanded of me two quatrines for the passage of a bridge: but when I shewed them my Matricula, that is, a paper, witnessing

> that I was a scholler of Paduoa, they dismissed me as free of all Tributes. And in like sort by the same writing, I was freed at Paduoa from paying six soldi, and at Verona from paying eight soldi.

He was a skilled linguist and inveterate traveller, explaining that from his 'tender youth [... he] had a great desire to see foreign countries'.[28]

By the beginning of the nineteenth century, however, things had become much more difficult. August von Kotzebue, German lawyer and novelist, had occasion to enter Verona at a time in 1805 when the River Adige formed the boundary between those parts of the city under either French or Austrian control. He found the larger and older section was in French hands, with the smaller part of Veronetta ceded to Austria. 'On a bridge which crosses the Adige, are stationed the sentinels and custom-house officers of both nations. The stranger is bandied about like a shuttlecock from one to the other.'[29] Matthew Todd, a gentleman's gentleman travelling with his master in 1815, described how they

> [...] arrived in Verona at the Doo Tours Albergo, about 8 o'clock in the evening [...] Here we were obliged to stay all night as the Police Office was shut and we could not get our passports signed. However, we got a soldier to get it signed for us by giving him 2 franks – and went to bed with the hopes of starting at 5 o'clock for Milan – but at 5 the waiter came to say that we must obtain an order from the police, to get horses, or we cannot go. Therefore were compelled to wait until an order could be got – oh! the comforts of travelling on the continent.[30]

The matter of correct documentation was always a fraught issue for travellers. It was necessary to prepare oneself for the fact that Italy was divided into many different jurisdictions, each with their individual requirements. Travel guides invariably warned tourists of the need to get their paperwork in order before leaving England, particularly if they were proposing to visit areas – such as Verona – under control of Austria in the years after 1815. The point can be illustrated by the unexpected problem experienced in about 1842, by Mrs Mary Shelley, widow of the poet.

> A sad disaster happened on our arrival at Verona. We had each our passport, and the whole was consigned to the pocketbook of one of the party; and when they were asked for at the gates of Verona, the pocket book was not to be found. Except our passports, and Coutts' *lettre d'indication*, it contained no papers of importance; but still, after all the annoyance the Austrians give about passports, it was rather appalling.[31]

They were promised a document to get them to Venice where the British Consul would sort matters out for them, but even that took the whole morning to obtain.

One other hazard faced the unwary traveller: the outbreak of disease locally, which could detain them in quarantine. Thomas Cholwick and his companions set out for Verona from Mantua in May 1743, 'but on entering Veronese territory they were taken to the *lazzaretto* at Verona as a precaution against plague, and not released for 14 days'.[32] Almost a century later, quarantine could still be a problem. Lieutenant-General Sir Herbert Taylor, aide-de-camp to Queen Victoria, was in Verona en route for Rome in 1835, when he heard that the frontier between the Austrian and Roman territories was closed, following an outbreak of cholera in Venice. Some tourists were advised they would have to spend two weeks in quarantine in the Lazzaretto nearest the border of the papal states, but the accommodation there was 'so filthy, so wretched, so horrible' that they returned to Verona. The reputation of the Lazzaretto towards Bologna was even worse; it had been a prison and was situated in 'the most unwholesome spot in the country'.[33]

Once arrived in Verona, the visitor could either go about on foot, or hire a carriage. On arrival there in about 1870, the American journalist Junius Henri Browne decided on the latter method.

> I found myself surrounded by a score or more of the most ragged and garlic-perfumed vetturini I had encountered in all Italy. They each and all invited me to ride in their cabriolets behind the worst-looking beasts I had seen on the Continent. Poor quadrupeds, I pitied them. They seemed ashamed of themselves. [...] The breathing skeletons stood together in the warm sunshine, with the hope of casting a shadow; but they could not. A shadow was impossible to any combination of such thinnesses as theirs. [...] I engaged a cabriolet after making an agreement with the vetturino not to make me pay for the forlorn quadruped if he should happen to run (I use run for rhetorical effect) against a shadow and kill himself. So we started at a snail-like speed, and with difficulty passed three large buildings, which we shouldn't have done, if the buildings had not been too old to get out of the way.[34]

Many other tourists preferred to walk, often employing a local guide or *cicerone* to take them around; this method, too, had its hazards, as will become evident.

Travel became much faster with the arrival of the railway. The first train from Venice through Verona to Milan ran in 1846, and the station outside Porta Vescovo in Verona opened in 1849. Yet there were still problems; an anonymous traveller in 1864 encountered the usual difficulties when his train entered Austrian territory at Peschiera:

> [...] here the train was stopped for an hour, in order that our Passports & Luggage might be examined. We had to open all our packages for inspection, and were kept standing for a whole hour in a dirty uncomfortable station, innocent of the most remote attempt to consult the comfort of travellers; – when the Austrian Authorities insist on giving one so much unnecessary trouble, they might at least provide seats, and the ordinary accompaniments of the meanest stations – but the stations along the whole line appeared to be very poor, and we found on arrival at Verona at 6.9. that the station there was no exception to the general rule.[35]

The increased speed of travel meant tourists were already spending less time in Verona. Thomas Cook's first conducted tour of Italy took place in 1864, making use primarily of the train. John Latrobe from Philadelphia arrived in the city one evening in 1868.

> It had been intended to remain a whole day at Verona, but, after the next morning had been devoted to the amphitheatre, the most perfect in its interior of the known Roman ruins, the tomb of the Scaligers, the Pinacotheca, the Roman gateways and the churches, it was found that nothing prevented the party from taking the train at 2.25 p. m. for Milan.[36]

It was most unlikely he and his party did real justice to the city in the course of one morning. Latrobe was a lawyer for the Baltimore & Ohio Railroad, who was perhaps more interested in the train service than in the city of Verona.

The arrival of American tourists in Italy resulted in a good number of published accounts of their travels, which often included visits to Verona. These authors included Catharine Sedgwick, William Dean Howells – at one time the American consul in Venice – or the author Henry James, journalists like Theodore Child or Junius Browne, lawyers like Nathaniel Carter or Orvill Horwitz from Philadelphia, and pastors like Henry Martyn Field from Massachusetts. Catharine Sedgwick was a relatively early visitor in 1841 and, travelling with a lady friend, found herself having to dispute a hotel bill in Verona. She was philosophical about this, but regretted having to pay charges to which the English had become accustomed. 'But we have in truth little to complain of. The inn-charges are seldom extravagant [...] We poorer Americans must pay the rates which luxurious English travellers who "lard this lean earth" have introduced.'[37] One other American lady visitor in the 1850s was Madame Octavia Le Vert, a socialite from Georgia, who described the city as presenting 'a charming aspect as we approached within its serrated walls and high towers'.[38]

Early in the twentieth century trams were installed in Verona, running from Porta Vescovo in Veronetta to Porta Nuova. When the service began, to great public acclaim, it was so popular initially that only the Veronesi were allowed to use it; foreign visitors still had to walk into the centre of the city.[39] The author and journalist Arnold Bennett did not visit Verona until 1926, but his remarks on this occasion showed how transport methods were continually changing within the city. 'At the lunch hour there is an enormous rushing outbreak of bicycles, which though dangerous to limb are less so than automobiles and belong more to the historic past.'[40] It would not be long, however, until the car came to dominate as the preferred method of transport. So far had travel options in the north of Italy, and more particularly in Verona, changed over the centuries since the days of Fynes Moryson or the Bentham family.

 CHAPTER 3

Accommodation and Food in the City

I think it not impertinent to observe that the most grievous Tax upon the pleasures of travelling in such parts of France and Italy as I have seen, is the want of Cleanliness in their Houses and Cookery [...] the English for universal Cleanliness perhaps excel all other Nations in Europe.¹

Lancelot Temple aka Dr J. Armstrong, 1771

ACCOUNTS OF TRAVEL in Italy paid particular attention to the availability and quality of accommodation en route. Security was always a worry outside the bigger towns, even if these fears were often exaggerated. Louis Simond, French by birth but an American citizen, summed up the general attitude on his tour in 1828.

> Italy is not a country like England, where you may stop at any out of the way place and find as good accommodations, if not better, and be as safe, as in large towns. A village here is thought to be (how truly I cannot say) little better than a den of thieves and cut-throats, where you run no small risk of never rising from the bed in which you go to rest at night.²

Once they reached Verona, however, most travellers found adequate or even good lodgings, but matters could certainly be less satisfactory en route. Shortly before arriving in Verona in 1793–4, Sarah Bentham and her family had an unhappy experience when the better hotels in the northern town of Trento were full:

> [...] we were obliged to submit to stay the night in a most miserable apartment, the windows broken, the beds and rooms so dirty that I could not venture to undress but stretched myself on the outside of the bed with my cloathes on.³

Guidebooks often suggested that travellers should take their own sheets to mitigate such conditions.

Verona had a number of hostelries used by travellers. In earlier years both the French and English favoured the inn called Il Cavaletto (now Il Cavalletto), near the Scaligeri tombs. This is where the famous French essayist and statesman Michel de Montaigne stayed in the 1580s: he said of 'the Nag' that it 'is a very excellent house, where we were entertained in superfluous abundance, for which we had to pay three times the cost of tavern-living in France'. He was also somewhat surprised to find that 'the people there had perfumed our beds, and we ourselves were asked into an apartment where were rows of vials and earthen vessels, containing different sorts of distilled waters, with which they perfumed us.'[4] The author and diarist John Evelyn also stayed here in 1646 but made no mention of perfumes or scented beds.[5]

By the eighteenth century Due Torri in Piazza Sant'Anastasia had become the hotel of choice for most English tourists. The building had once been the Palazzo dell'Aquila belonging to the Scaligeri rulers of Verona, and was generally described as being very comfortable. As early as the 1680s the 5th earl of Exeter had stayed there with his steward, Culpepper Tanner, who carefully recorded the costs they incurred, including payment for a broken glass.[6] By 1793, however, Sarah Bentham did not think 'the Due Torri or in English the Two Towers' was good enough for English aristocrats.

> Lord and Lady Palmerston, who with Three Children and three Maid Servants and also Six Men Servants, had been there a Considerable Time; And tho the House may be good for Italy as the Rooms were Large and Lofty; yet the Brick Floors & Dirty Furniture made me wonder that an English Family could like such a Residence.[7]

Traces of the hotel's past glories as a *palazzo* were still to be seen: 'The apartments are extremely grand, and the doorways finely carved marble in patterns, wreathed and billeted.'[8] There was a central courtyard, with the rooms giving off the first-floor balconies. The Scottish church reformer Henry Cockburn's entries in his 1823 diary included some unexpected art appreciation: 'We are at the two Towers, a clean & splendid Inn. There is more painting, well conceived & well executed in our parlour than in all Edinburgh, Ayr & Glasgow to boot.'[9] Another visitor ('J. W.') in 1862 described how 'Our bedroom floors were of marble, and our beds were supplied with mosquito curtains, for here one is obliged to sleep with windows and doors wide open', due no doubt to a spell of hot weather.[10]

Sarah Bentham felt that in most respects Due Torri was 'a good house, though the floors were brick, and beds without curtains, and no rooms to sit in without a bed in it, and charges extravagant [...] we found upon our beds cotton coverlets, instead of feather or down beds which we had throughout Germany'.[11] In 1815, Dr Herman Friedländer, a Prussian physician, was happier, describing Italian beds as 'very comfortable, being wide and soft. A palliasse of maize-straw, which is shaken every morning, a mattress, pillow and a light coverlid, form all the component parts of which they are made.'[12] An anonymous Scottish traveller provided this curious account in 1841: he noted that in Trieste it was customary for a man and wife to have separate single beds, but 'here [Verona] each bed is apparently made to contain not only the married couple but all their progeny and the nursery maids to boot'. His companion found himself in a bed 'about 10 feet broad, long enough for him [...] and high in proportion, innocent of posts and containing about a dozen straw matrasses: truly it is the grandfather of all beds'.[13] There could sometimes be unforeseen dangers in the bedrooms; Misson had asserted that, back in 1687, the Veronese locals placed their iron bedheads at some distance from the walls to prevent scorpions climbing onto the beds; however, he believed that 'the stinging of scorpions is not mortal in Italy', so he felt there was no great reason for concern.[14]

In the mid-nineteenth century, John Ruskin, author and art critic, and his wife Effie always stayed at Due Torri when they were in Verona. John was particularly attached to the medieval tomb of Guglielmo Castelbarco in Piazza Sant'Anastasia, and so expected always to have rooms at the front of the inn that overlooked it. On their visit in 1852, however, the Ruskins were assigned rooms at the back. Effie betook herself to her acquaintance, the Austrian Count Wrbna, occupant of a front room, and

> [...] told him that with his permission I would order his bed to be carried out as I knew he didn't care in the least for any Monuments in Verona & would prefer the comfortable sofa in the other room where he could smoke after dinner at his ease.[15]

She got her way, and so John was able to keep his favourite view of 'this pure and lovely monument, my most beloved throughout all the length and breadth of Italy'.[16]

Ruskin later sent his mother an account of his daily routine at Due Torri in 1869.

> I enjoy my *mornings* here immensely. I get up at quarter to five and dress quietly, looking out at the morning light on the tomb of the Count Castelbarco (my favourite old red one); then at quarter to six I go to the

café on the corner of the square and sip my cup of coffee, looking at the lovely old porch of St. Anastasia; then by six o'clock I am at my work, as I used to be in 1845 [...] Then I come in to breakfast at half-past eight and read a little – then draw again till eleven, when I come in to write my letters – then I rest till three – then get a couple of hours more work – and then my walk before dinner. I dine at eight, just now – for else I should lose the sunset (but seven is better) – and get to bed at ten.[17]

By this time his marriage to Effie had long since ended, so Ruskin could apply himself entirely to his work, determined to complete as many drawings and watercolours as possible of this city he loved so dearly. His was clearly not a routine likely to be followed by any visitor less devoted to Verona.

The English author and travel writer Louisa Costello was effusive in 1845 about her stay at this inn.

The hotel of the due Torre is, besides being interesting in an historical point of view, an excellent inn, where everything is most comfortably served, and where, as is universal in the North of Italy, great civility is met with. A beautiful bouquet of flowers was placed upon our breakfast table, which one might fancy gathered in the gardens of the Capelletti, and extreme attention was shewn to our slightest desire.[18]

A Scottish traveller of 1864 was less enthusiastic:

We found an omnibus ready to drive us to the Hotel 'Due Torre' where we got tolerable rooms, and a Table d'hôte dinner which proved better than we had anticipated from the general appearance of the Salle à Manger [...] tho' the hotel was far from being A1 and our comfort not very perfect [...][19]

The American John Latrobe felt at home in a rather particular way in 1868:

Rooms had been engaged at the Hotel delle due Torre, and lights were burning on the arrival of the party, weary with the length and excitement of the journey. The parlor had once been the salon of a palace, and two candles did little more than make darkness visible. It was not surprising, therefore, that the first who entered started back in surprise, for there, in a dim corner, stood a negro, his foot advanced and hand raised, while the whites of his great eyes shone fiercely in the gloom. Nor was he alone; a companion was starting apparently from another corner, as if to come to the assistance of his companion. The surprise, however, was but momentary; the figures were a part of the furniture of the apartment, and went some way to Americanizing it, after all.[20]

There could, however, be no pleasing everybody when it came to accommodation, then as now. A few years later another American, J. Henry Coghill, a businessman with interests on both sides of America, and travelling with his family, complained that this hotel, 'although the best in the place, we found to be anything but comfortable. The rooms all open upon a piazza running around the court, the lower part of which is used as stables.'[21] This was bound to mean powerful odours rising to the first-floor rooms. Henry Cockburn had already commented in 1823 that the arrangement of a central courtyard 'makes the good inns noisy, for it leads every body – ostlers & waiters & every creature, to hold their conversations within hearing & besides this it makes [...] a convenient place for dung hills'. As for Verona's public baths, he mentioned that, at the end of his party's stay, they 'departed in the evening, after taking a hot bath – The baths very bad'.[22] By 1841 another Scotsman 'took a hot bath after dinner for which I had to walk nearly a mile'. On a second visit there, however, he 'had a most delightful wash and then ate ices at the caffe till bed time'.[23] The idea of a hotel bathroom was still a distant dream.

Once guidebooks came into common use, travellers could find recommendations for a variety of places to stay. Murray's 1842 guide described Due Torri as 'a remarkably good and comfortable inn, with a table d'hôte at 1 o'clock, which, after all, is the most convenient hour. The master of the hotel presides at the table: a good old-fashioned custom now going fast out of use.'[24] Black's guide of 1869 echoed these opinions, even though Gaze's guidebook of 1864/7 had described the place as 'rather dear'.[25] Other guidebooks suggested La Torre di Londra, Il Gran Parigi or La Colomba d'Oro as alternatives. In 1835, the Barlow party from Leeds

> [...] proceeded to the Hotel du Grand Paris, and having duly refreshed ourselves after our long sojourn in the diligence, made a hearty breakfast of the rather incongruous medley laid out for us, viz., tea, bread, butter, mutton chops, cheese, apricots, and wine of the country.[26]

Not everyone chose to stay in a hotel. Elizabeth Vigée Le Brun, the well-known French artist, visited the city in 1789/90.

> During my eight day stay in Verona, I moved my lodgings twice. First of all I installed myself in a small apartment, after asking whether it was quiet. 'Yes, indeed,' replied my hostess. But at six o'clock the next morning I heard an almighty rumpus above my head, with sounds of jumping about to the accompaniment of a violin. On making enquiries of my hostess, I was assured there was nothing to worry about. The town's dancing master lived

above me, and every day the young people came for their two-hour dancing lesson. That was enough to make me decide to move on.[27]

Unfortunately, she did not reveal where she went next.

When it came to payment for accommodation, things could become complicated, because of the wide variety of currencies prevailing in different parts of Italy. In about 1766 the ever-practical William Patoun gave some general advice about the matter of payment for board and lodging:

> With regard to Dinners and Suppers on the road: The prudent English order each Meal at five or six Pauls a head which is half a Crown & three Shillings. Where you lie you give something for the Servants Beds, and often will be obliged to pay a Paul or two for your own. You pay over and above for Fire &c and often there is a separate Article in the Bill per l'incommodo for the trouble you put them to. If you order your Meals at so much a head, and bargain before hand for your Beds &c, you will seldom have any disputes.[28]

In 1796, Elizabeth Wynne calculated the family's costs in Venetian lire: 'We arrived safe and lodged at a good Inn where we have an apartment of 5 rooms for 20 Venetian lires a day, we give 6 lires a head for our dinner and supper for 5 lires a piece a day.'[29] This may or may not have been Due Torri, where they lodged in 1791.[30] About ten years earlier the architect John Soane had recorded in his diary paying 8 lire daily at the same establishment;[31] by 1817, John Samuel Hayward paid, for candles, lodgings, breakfast, lunch, wine, wood and an amount for the waiter, a total of '35f' for a stay of two days.[32]

These examples, using pauls, lire and 'f' (probably francs), demonstrate some of the various currencies that travellers mentioned having to use, and there were others; for instance, in 1595 Fynes Moryson specified that, in Verona, 'Here I paid forty soldi for my supper, and sixteene soldi for the stable, (that is for hay and straw) and eighteene soldi for three measures of Oates.'[33] There were also Venetian gold sequins and French Louis d'or in circulation, as well as Austrian paper notes. With each city or region often having its own currency, travellers were obliged to change money frequently, making it hard for them to compare one lot of costs with another. William Patoun advised thus: 'In general look upon a Sequin as half a Guinea and Pauls as Sixpences.'[34] Arthur Young, the English agriculturalist, also provided a comparison about ten years later, in 1787:

> My expences […] at Verona are, dinner, 3 *pauls*, supper 2, chamber 2; which, at 5d English, are 2s 11d a-day; and as I have rooms not at

all bad, good beds, and am well served at the meals as I require, it is remarkably cheap.[35]

As well as specifying what they had to pay for food and lodging, travellers often complained about being overcharged. Innkeepers could be avaricious; regarding his experience in 1814, T. Baring grumbled that 'They do not scruple to ask three or four times the value of what you have had, or of what they would take were you so disposed to bargain with them, but which few Englishmen have the patience to do.'[36] In 1839, the American Catharine Sedgwick, travelling with a female friend, found the business of disputing costs stressful:

> K. and I returned from a truant stroll in the morning in time to swallow our breakfasts, and to remonstrate against an over-charge in our bill: a hateful charge that falls to my share, and often makes me regret the days when I went on *like a lady*, quietly paying prices and scarcely knowing them.[37]

In 1866, with Verona still under Austrian control, the English author and journalist George Sala may have exaggerated his experience at 'a most infamous hostelry, called La Colomba d'Oro, where I remained until six in the morning, a prey to bugs and anxiety as to how I was to proceed on a journey'.[38] He hated all things Austrian and was most anxious to be allowed to leave Verona; permission achieved, his landlord then 'presented us with *his* permission to quit the Austrian territory in the shape of receipted bills, – whose amount, so far as my own was concerned, led me to the conviction that the Clarendon in Bond-Street is not such a dear hotel after all [...]'.[39]

Food and wine were, of course, essential matters for all travellers. Henrietta, countess of Pomfret, in about 1741, rather damned the local food with faint praise: 'considering it is Italy, we have supped very well at Verona'.[40] Others fared better. In 1780, the author William Beckford and his tutor or bear leader John Lettice stayed at an unspecified Veronese inn,

> [...] a lofty, handsome-looking building; but so full, that we were obliged to take up with an apartment on its very summit, open to all the winds [...] and commanding the roofs of half Verona. Placing our table in a balcony, to enjoy the prospect with greater freedom, we feasted upon fish from the Lago di Garda, and the delicious fruits of the country.[41]

This could well have been Due Torri where, in 1791, the Wynne family also had 'a very good dinner of fish from lake Garda', but 'only some punch for supper'.[42] There were plenty of good local fruits and vegetables to be had, especially at the market stalls in Piazza delle Erbe where in the season peaches, plums, grapes and artichokes abounded. Henry Cockburn noted happily in his diary, in 1823, that 'We got a plate of excellent fresh figs to breakfast.'[43] Andrew Clarke, a Scotsman from Culross travelling in 1841, had 'an elegant repast at La Torre di Londra' enjoying 'the delicious trout of the Lago di Garda'.[44] Praise for fish from Lake Garda was a recurring theme in travellers' accounts.

Anything outside a tourist's normal experience might come in for negative comment. Philip Skippon, travelling with his tutor Philip Ray, found it strange in 1663 that there was 'at meals only a dark coloured salt, like brown sugar, which they bring always in a plate. The white sort is prohibited.'[45] In Verona in 1707, Henri de Blainville, Huguenot refugee and tutor to the Blathwayts, teenage sons of a senior English politician, complained about the bread: 'it is very bad, being heavy and hard, tho' the corn of the country is very good; the reason of this is, that they don't know how to bake it, and they over-heat their ovens'.[46] However, Louisa Costello had different ideas by the mid-nineteenth century when she found some bakers' shops 'filled with singular-shaped loaves, long, short, and round and flat, of every possible variety, the bread being remarkably white and good here'.[47] It seems that travellers usually ate in hotels, as places more likely to cater to their tastes. The Reverend David Drummond from Edinburgh, visiting in 1852, certainly believed they should do so:

> Let travellers beware of inns frequented by Italians. I dined in one of the latter out of curiosity. The filth was abundant – the waiting wretched – the food like nothing else I ever saw before or after, and the charges exorbitant.[48]

Some tourists could not bear to be without all traces of home comfort. In 1857, Kate Crichton and her mother tried to make sure the tea in their hotel was to their liking.

> Here we found the chief-waiter arranging the table, an elderly, stiff, pompous person, who had nothing Italian about him except his over-flowing politeness. But when, anxious lest any accident should befall our favourite beverage, I requested that the milk might not be boiled for the tea, a look of injured dignity assailed me as he replied, 'Signora, of course I know perfectly well how to make tea. I am not like a young boy who does not understand these things. If I had been like Piccolo, there,' he flung his thumb back over his shoulder in the direction of a youth, who was busy brushing boots in the yard, 'then I might have required instruction.'[49]

Much embarrassed, the Crichtons tried to make up for their faux pas by leaving a large tip.

The Honourable William Fitzwilliam, journeying in 1769, made a perceptive observation about the general eating habits of Italians. He noted that much outdoor eating went on in 'all the great Towns of Italy, by many a Man who by his Dress looks as if he had got a Dinner at home'. At every corner could be seen 'Extemporary cooks, Frying & Fricassying a Variety of Things, Sausages, Fish, Eggs, Macaroni etc etc Savoury Food, that comes at a very Easy Rate & saves them the Expence of both Cook and Kitchen'.[50] Eating in the street was clearly perfectly acceptable, even by the more affluent citizens who might have been expected to eat their meals at home; the climate, of course, made this an agreeable and sociable experience.

Tourists also sampled the local wines. In 1595, Fynes Moryson praised Verona for various reasons:

> The territorie of this Citie is most fruitfoll, abounding with all necessaries for life, and more specially with rich Wines, particularly the Retian wine, (much praised by Pliny, and preferred to the Wine of Falernum by Virgill), which the Kings of the Gothes were wont to carrie with them as farre as Rome. It is of a red colour and sweet, and howsoever it seemes thicke, more fit to be eaten then drunke, yet it is of a most pleasant taste.[51]

Henri de Blainville remarked on 'a Glass of a Kind of very good Red Wine from our Landlord, but all the other Wines in that Country which we tasted were either very flat, or rough, and disagreeable to a Stranger not used to drink them'.[52] But by about 1740 Sacheverell Stevens, Gent., found the local Veronesi inns 'in general pretty tolerable, where you meet with plenty of that famous wine called Vino Santo, remarkable for its delicious flavour and sold exceeding cheap'.[53]

By the end of the nineteenth century things had apparently gone downhill again, if The Reverend Charles Williams is to be believed; he asserted that 'The wines of Verona were celebrated in ancient times [...] but their reputation at present is very low, as is that of almost all the wines produced on the northern side of the Apennines.'[54] But, much later in 1938, the Irish travel writer Walter Starkie was having none of that; for him, the local area produced a 'wine for every hour of the day – Soave, Bardolino, Raboso, Vin Santo, Recioto, Valpolicella'. This last he called 'the wine for such Epicureans who sit in shirt-sleeves under the pergola of a small inn with their companions and gaze dreamily at the River Adige flowing beneath the Bridge of Boats'.[55]

These accounts across the centuries inevitably demonstrate a wide variety of attitudes. Sarah Bentham was critical of the facilities at Due Torri, expressing her surprise that an English Milord should tolerate dirty rooms. Others, such as Henry Cockburn, found the hotel clean, so it was not just women who noticed such details. High charges came in for much criticism, but Arthur Young found his accommodation satisfactory and cheap. Naturally, anything strange or different gave rise to particular comment, be it hard bread, unusual mattresses or well-to-do Veronesi eating street food. Most travellers stayed at hotels where, for instance, tea might be properly prepared for someone like Kate Crichton; others like Elizabeth Vigée Le Brun were brave enough to try out rented lodgings. It was inevitable, then as now, that food, accommodation and drink were matters likely to produce a wide spectrum of opinion among travellers from so many different countries and backgrounds.

 CHAPTER 4

L'Arena di Verona

Of the Roman Arena, the architect Sebastiano Serlio (1475–1554) said:

It stupefies me even to think of it. And it is understandable that the Romans built like this in Verona: because it has in my view the most beautiful situation in Italy.[1]

THE ONE PLACE that all travellers were sure to visit was the Roman Arena, situated in the heart of the city in Piazza Bra. The Romans founded Verona in about 49 BC, as evidenced by an inscription on one of the city gates. Its site was chosen for being both on the Via Postumia that ran across Italy from Genoa to the northern Adriatic, and on the route from northern Europe from South Tyrol down the valley of the River Adige into Italy. The most impressive of Verona's civic buildings was undoubtedly this Arena, or amphitheatre, which dates to about the year AD 30 and was built just outside the original city walls. There, in about 1818, the Englishman James Wilson (travelling to Italy 'in search of health')[2] was clear that this building demonstrated Verona's importance to the Roman state: 'We do not find such amphitheatres except on the sites of the largest and most renowned cities of antiquity.'[3] It was formed originally of four oval sections, but only a small part – the 'ala', or wing, as the Veronesi still call it – of the exterior section is still standing, following a severe earthquake in the twelfth century. Some of the stone was apparently reused later for construction work within the city, but the inside of this vast structure is largely intact, with its stone benches still in use today for performances of opera and popular music.

The Arena, second in size only to the Coliseum in Rome, was always the focal point of interest to visitors. Bernardino Barduzzi, a Franciscan preacher at San Fermo in the 1480s, found the building in a poor state of repair, 'partly ruined through neglect, partly decayed by the passage of time, while some areas are wholly destroyed and levelled to the ground, and from others the great stones have even been removed to reinforce other buildings in the city'.[4] A hundred years later some Frenchmen, including the influential writer Montaigne, were more impressed.

> The finest thing we saw in this place, and, indeed, that M. de Montaigne said he had ever seen in his life, was a place they call the Arena. This is an amphitheatre of an oval form which the eye embraces entire at one view, with the exception of the extreme end; and the remains are sufficient to give a vivid idea of the whole of the original edifice, and of the purposes to which it was applied. The [Venetian] seigneury employ a few convicts in doing odds and ends of clearings and repairs, but the restorations thus carried on are far from adequate; and, indeed, M. de Montaigne doubted whether the whole town together could effect the great work. The form is oval; there are forty-three rows of seats, rising one above another, and each about a foot high, or somewhat more; the diameter at the top is about six hundred paces.[5]

Fynes Moryson, with the eye for detail this ex-bursar of a Cambridge college had doubtless needed, described the Arena in 1595 as a 'stately monument', and gave his version of its measurements, using 'walking paces' as a scale.

> The inner yard is sixety three walking paces long, and forty eight broade, where the lowest seates are most narrow, whence the seates arise in forty foure staires or degrees [...] and they so arise, as the upper is still of neater circuit then the lower.[6]

Later tourists also felt the need to describe dimensions and architectural features, as well as an estimate of how many people could be accommodated therein. This last figure varied wildly; William Withrow, a Canadian journalist, put the number as high as 100,000 in 1880. Genevan historian Jacques Galiffe noted in 1816 that a local guidebook, *Notizia delle cose più osservabili della Città di Verona*, gave the seating capacity as 23,484, a figure slightly higher than his own estimate.[7] Moryson himself had stated that 'the seates within the same, are said to bee capable of twentie three thousand one hundred eightie and four beholders, each one having a foote and a halfe allowed for his seate',[8] a pretty accurate estimate. In addition to those who were seated, about 12,000 could stand in the central area.

When Thomas Coryat visited the Arena early in the seventeenth century, he, too, noted that some stone had been removed 'partly for the garnishing of the private houses of the citie and partly for other uses'. Many of the marble benches inside had also been carried off, but various 'gentlemen of Verona' had paid out 'threescore and sixe thousand crownes' for repairs to the interior.[9] This issue of repairs intrigued later tourists, including the English politician William Bromley in 1691.

> Here is an Amphitheatre built by the Romans, the most entire of any in Italy; they are now repairing it, to which use they employ the Rents they receive for the Ware-houses under it, and besides this, raise more Money by fining the young Gentlemen of the Town when they have committed any Extravagancy to contribute more or less, according to the Quality of their Offences towards these Repairs. They were when I was there at work and he that shewed it me told me, that there were Fines lately laid sufficient to finish it.[10]

The English architect Joseph Woods had done further research by 1816.

> As early as 1228 we find that its preservation had become an object of public attention, as the Podestà (the governor or mayor) engages to spend five hundred lire in its restoration. In 1475 penalties were decreed against any one who should remove any of the stone. In 1545 a special officer was appointed to take care of it. In 1568 a voluntary contribution was raised for its support, and in 1579 a tax was imposed for its reparation.[11]

The care of this, Verona's principal glory, was clearly important to local administrators, but finding the necessary funds for its upkeep must have been an ongoing problem. It seems, however, that the authorities generally took great pride in the maintenance of their city, as Montaigne had noticed in 1580:

> There is no lack of inscriptions here, for not a gutter is mended but they stick up a memorial of the event, setting forth the why and the when and the name of the mayor for the time being, and of the person who did the work.[12]

The uses to which the Arena was put had changed fundamentally over the centuries, from Roman times when it was used for contests between men, or men and beasts. In the first century AD, Pliny the Younger wrote to a friend, apologizing that 'the African panthers which had been largely provided for this purpose did not arrive in time enough [...]' for a gladiatorial contest.[13] In 1620, the Cornishman Peter Mundy recalled the 'inhuman spectacles' of Roman gladiator fights and contests with wild beasts that had taken place there.[14] Memories of former times led Baron Carl Theodor von Uklanski, visiting in 1807, to remind his readers that in ancient times the

Arena had a water channel which 'swept away the blood of the slain animals and men, together with their mangled limbs'.[15]

By the time early visitors were recording their personal experiences, the Arena was apparently used for less bloodthirsty activities like jousting, as reported by both Montaigne and Coryat. In 1609 Henry, prince of Wales, was in Italy; 'while he was at Verona, a magnificent tilting was performed by the noblemen of that city, where the flower of Lombardy was assembled'.[16] There were also reports of the space being used for bull baiting with dogs and bull fights on into the nineteenth century. By this time the floor of the Arena had been cleared; by order of Napoleon, the debris that had accumulated up to the level of the first row of seating had been removed, thus increasing the central space available for performances. Joseph Addison in 1701 had noticed this build-up: 'the Area is quite fill'd up to the lower Seat, which was formerly deep enough to let the Spectators see in Safety the Combats of the Wild Beasts and Gladiators'.[17]

Tourists often remarked on the performance of plays and shows of one sort or another on small stages or booths within the Arena. Sacheverell Stevens, Gent., reported a fatal occurrence there while in the city in 1740. A comedy was performed,

> [...] at which an incredible number of people were present, and the stone benches of the amphitheatre entirely filled, making a most glorious appearance; after the comedy was finished a dance succeeded, which was finely performed; but this comedy ended most tragically; for as the head dancer was retiring out of the amphitheatre he was shot dead at the door by a villain, with whom he had had some trifling dispute the day before, concerning a mistake he had made in a dance; the delinquent was soon taken and conveyed to prison, he did not seem to be under the least concern, but rather rejoiced at what he had done; to such an height do the Italians, tho' in many respects a worthy sober sort of people, carry their revenge [...][18]

Fortunately, not all performances ended as tragically as that one had done. In 1770, Charles Burney, musician and author, did wonder if the era of gladiatorial contests was truly over as he neared the Arena,

> [...] for the roaring and noise which assailed my ears, seemed to proceed from nothing human: when, behold upon a nearer approach, I found it was only *Pantalone* and *Brighello*, who had been baited and beaten by Harlequin; indeed, this gentleman's wit had great force to-night, and, I believe, had contributed more to the happiness of the spectators than ever the elephants, lions or tigers did in former times [...] The stage was erected

in the middle of the *arena*; there were only two boxes, one on each side [of] the stage: the area before the stage made a kind of pit, where the better sort of company sat on chairs. The next best places were on the steps, about twelve deep, railed off from the rest of the steps [...][19]

Much to his surprise, in 1815 Dr Herman Friedländer

[...] saw a booth erected in the Arena of this astonishing edifice, where Punch promised to amuse the populace in the evening, when, as the playbill, printed in very large letters, promised, the famous play of *Maria Stuarda difesa dai Carbonari* (Mary Stuart defended by the Coal-burners) was to be performed. Astonishing![20]

Astonishing, indeed. By contrast, in the following year Joseph Woods 'saw there an exhibition of horses and horsemanship, of dancing on the tight rope, and of dancing dogs'.[21] The experience of Antoine Pasquin, author of *Travels in Italy*, first published in 1838 in French, under the pseudonym of M. Valéry, was even more bizarre.

After witnessing a puppet show, I afterwards attended a rather childish spectacle in this same arena: pigeons had been trained to perch themselves on a pistol and sit motionless while it was fired; they also discharged a small cannon, and then let off crackers while soaring in the sky. The intrepidity of these pigeons, carrying thunderbolts like the eagle (which is said to be cowardly), was little to my taste; boldness is not becoming in graceful beings, and I preferred the tender and unfortunate pigeons of La Fontaine to these warlike ringdoves.[22]

There are few recorded comments on the players who took part in performances in the Arena, but 'A Yankee', writing in about 1850, did note how sorry he felt for one girl during a rehearsal.

Through a chink in the tent we had a glimpse of their proceedings. A young girl in a short frock, with bare neck and shoulders, was standing before the dancing-master rehearsing her part in the ballet. The teacher sat astride a chair, facing the back, and had a small cane in one hand with which he occasionally switched the poor girl's legs, instructing her to raise them higher and keep them extended longer. By her side sat an elderly lady with a bonnet on, who seemed to be her mother, and two or three of the 'Verona dandies' were walking about smoking and quizzing the performance. The poor girl, who seemed not to have lost all her modesty, looked ashamed and fatigued; and the perspiration streamed down her face and neck. I pitied her with all my heart.[23]

The elderly lady was there as a chaperone, no doubt, but it was hard on the girl not only to be caned but also peered at by the 'Verona dandies'.

There were different opinions expressed about the use of this venerable building for such shows. Some, like James Wilson about 1816, thought it was degrading to see strolling players making use of 'a paltry wooden theatre. That such a hovel, assuming the name of a theatre, should stand in that vast and noble amphitheatre, which served for the diversion of the antients, conveys, though unintentionally, a bitter sarcasm upon the moderns.'[24] The travel writer John Eustace was particularly vociferous in his condemnation of the French for encouraging such performances, saying the Veronesi themselves had compared this to the vandalism of the Huns and Lombards.[25] This, however, was unfair: the Arena had been used as a playhouse for many years before the coming of Napoleon in the 1790s.

Hans Christian Andersen found his 1833 visit depressing.

The Veronese sat upon the stone benches of the amphitheatre, where their fathers had sat before them. In this little theatre was acted 'La Cenerentola.' [...] Aurelia performed the principal parts of the opera. The whole was miserable and melancholy to witness. The old, antique theatre stood like a giant around the fragile wooden booth. A contredance completely drowned the few instruments; the public applauded and called for Aurelia. I hastened away. Outside all was still. The great giant-building cast a broad, dark shadow amid the strong moonlight.[26]

Others, such as George Sala, there in 1866, argued that the locals relished such spectacles, and 'flocked to the edifice, and paid their soldi to see the show'. He had himself seen and enjoyed 'a horse-riding circus in one corner, and a company of *zanni* and pantomimists in another, and Doctor Dulcamara, in his red coat, powdered wig, and topboots, drawing teeth and selling vials of the elixir of love in the centre [...]'.[27] In 1872, Henry James, American novelist, critic and travel writer, attended a play on a sunny August afternoon.

It was all deliciously Italian – the mixture of old life and new, the mountebank's booth (it was hardly more) grafted on the antique circus, the dominant presence of a mighty architecture, the loungers and idlers beneath the kindly sky and upon the sun-warmed stones. I never felt more keenly the difference between the background to life in very old and very new civilisations.[28]

Occasionally the amphitheatre had been put to other uses. In 1785, the Emperor Joseph II of Austria, together with his Empress and noblemen, visited Verona and was treated to a bullfight; as Eustace has it, 'a Roman Emperor was once more hailed in a Roman amphitheatre with the titles of Caesar and Augustus, by spectators who pretend and almost deserve to be Romans [...]'.[29] It was apparently a very hot day, so that part of the Arena was nearly empty, but the shadier parts were very crowded; music was provided, together with ice cream and flowers for the visitors.[30]

On another important occasion in 1782, Pope Pius VI who was passing through Verona

> [...] was requested by the magistrates to give the people an opportunity of testifying in public their veneration for his sacred person: He accordingly appeared in the amphitheatre, selected on account of its capacity as the properest place, and when the shouts of acclamation had subsided, poured forth his benediction on the prostrate multitude collected from all the neighbouring provinces to receive it.[31]

Pasquin, there in about 1826, surmised that 'this Father of the Faithful, blessing twenty thousand Christians from the top of this arena of some Roman emperor, must have been a grander and more affecting sight than all the pomps of worldly princes'.[32] It was estimated that 70,000 to 80,000 people were crammed into the Arena on this occasion, presumably with standing room only, given that the seating capacity was in the order of 23,500.[33]

An unusual event took place when the Irish writer and art historian Mrs Jameson was in the city in 1845, and reported thus:

> At Verona I saw a balloon ascend from the interior of the ancient amphitheatre, crowded with 15,000 people – a spectacle which I shall always remember as one of the most magnificent I ever beheld in itself, and from the inevitable associations connected with it, and the comparison between ancient and modern times. For example, they carried on the chemical processes for preparing the gas and filling the balloon in the very receptacle from which the wild beasts used to spring out upon their victims.[34]

Unfortunately, she did not recount what happened to the balloon. She did note, though, that she had climbed to the top of the Arena and walked round the summit, an activity that Murray's 1842 *Hand-book* had declared 'should in no wise be neglected'.[35]

Although many visitors remarked approvingly on the way the city fathers had cared for the Arena's interior fabric, some were less happy with what was allowed to take place under the outside arches. Coryat was one of the first to condemn the way that these 'are now converted to very base and sordid uses. For they serve partly for stables to put horses and hay in, and partly for tipling houses for poore folkes to sell wine in, and other necessaries.'[36] In 1805, Kotzebue remarked that

> Officers called conservators are appointed to take care of these ruins. In my opinion these conservators have done both too little and too much: too little, because they have permitted all the arcades on the outside to be occupied by the shops of blacksmiths, locksmiths, and other trades, or by storehouses of wood and hay, which of course greatly disfigure the edifice; too much, for they have repaired the whole of the interior of the amphitheatre, consequently the antique can no longer be distinguished from the modern, and it appears as new and neat as if it had recently been erected.[37]

In his journal of 1817, artist John Hayward noted that he had entered the Arena through one of these shops, 'paying the owner a gratuity (which was voluntary in amount) as I returned'. He was also offered prints of the Arena for sale, and a guide to show him round the city.[38] His contemporary, the artist Henry Sass, was unhappy with what he saw.

> The lower arches or vomitores on the outside, are now let out to blacksmiths, farriers, and such like trades, under the miserable plea, that the trifling rent they pay may contribute to the preservation of the building. The disfigurement of this noble pile by these black and dirty vocations, is another instance of Italian feeling; while the interior is *ornamented* with a trumpery theatre, as an emblem of their taste.[39]

Louis Simond, the French American, also noted the squalor in which the poor lived in 1817: 'the rain penetrates into these wretched tenements; and when we saw it, from all the windows ragged garments were hanging out to dry', thus detracting from the grandeur of the building.[40] About ten years later, though, Pasquin was more positive.

> The outside of the amphitheatre is inhabited by the poorer classes of the town. It appears to me however that travellers are sometimes too indignant against the occupying ancient monuments in this manner; for it detracts less from the picturesque of these ruins than would the residence of classes more

elevated or the practice of genteeler trades: the forge, with its flame sparkling at night in the bottom of the amphitheatre of Verona, has a finer effect than the lights which illuminate brilliant apartments, or the gas of some new shop or coffee-house.[41]

Other visitors enjoyed the romance of the Arena, reflecting eighteenth-century sensibilities. Writer and art collector William Beckford made a point of going there at twilight in 1780, and found he had the whole vast interior to himself. But, as the sun set, 'the wind blew chill and hollow, and something more than common seemed to rise from the withering herbage on the walls'. This unnerved Beckford so much that he fled and 'arrived, panting, in the great square before the ruins'.[42] In 1819, author and journalist John Scott walked round the exterior, where his imagination was stirred by the sight of

[...] poor artisans and tradesmen at their occupations by candle light, in small cells below the vast empty arches, through which there was an indistinct view through the gloom into the scene of melancholy ruin [...] the cells and prisons where human agony and brutal ferocity suffered and roared [...]

He found it unsettling

[...] to walk under this ruin at night [...] a stranger [...] knowing no one in Verona [...] surrounded by these signs of human mutation. &c [...] All is fleeting [...] what then are we, that we should hope to remain stationary?[43]

An anonymous Englishman, visiting in 1822, felt that the authorities' care of the Arena detracted somewhat from its atmosphere, especially when compared with the Coliseum.

Yet this very care, so laudable, destroys that veneration with which we are wont to approach, and explore the productions of antiquity. When viewing this theatre, apparently so new with modern work, it seems an effort for the mind to revert to its hundreds of years of age; and we, involuntarily, contrast it with its parallel, the Coliseum, those ever venerable, shattered ruins, so picturesque in their fall; o'ergrown with ivy, and the moss of centuries, so silent and so dignified; reminding us, amid such wrecks and desolation, of the furrows, and grey hairs of old age which need the tale to tell how many years have passed away.[44]

Three or four years later Edward Baines agreed, wanting the inside to be 'more ruinous' and therefore 'much more picturesque', while also describing the outside as 'a dull, uniform, unsightly pile, though with something of stern grandeur'.[45] Such remarks show a more emotional response to the Arena, very different to observations from earlier times about its exact measurements and details of its construction.

There was general agreement over the centuries that the Arena was indeed a noble pile, if smaller than the Coliseum in Rome and less impressive, at least from the outside. In 1732, Joseph Spence, later professor of poetry at Oxford, was not easily able to put his thoughts about it into words: 'A poet would say that its grandeur strikes you mute with admiration, but I choose to tell it you in plain prose, just as I felt it.'[46] Visiting in 1787, Adam Walker, lecturer on 'Natural and Experimental Philosophy', had no such difficulty, calling it

> [...] one of the most perfect specimens left, of the great things the Romans did in architecture! This wonderful and stupendous fabric must be immortal, for it is built of hard petrifaction, which defies the tooth of time [...] Every stone in this vast edifice, is of a size and weight, to defy the present puny race, and all their engines.[47]

Mrs Trollope wondered to herself in 1841:

> Why is it that with all the accumulated science of so many ages to help us, we can no longer rear such works as this? [...] so beautiful in its grand simplicity, and at the same time so completely fulfilling the purpose for which it was planned [...][48]

After all these serious thoughts, it is rather refreshing to find James Silk Buckingham, after having climbed to the top to enjoy the view in about 1846, able to afford himself some relaxation:

> We took an ice in one of the coffee-houses of the Piazza; and there was something strange and impressive in sitting to take refreshments in a public square, then filled with people, carriages, and vehicles, all in active motion, while this magnificent relic of the past lay unoccupied in all its silent grandeur close before us. The past and the present were never more strikingly united.[49]

CHAPTER 5

Travellers' Opinions of the City

Verona is an exceedingly odd town, but not pretty [...]
The Adige is a pretty, lympde river;
otherwise there is no sort of beauty in the situation of Verona.[1]

Henry Bankes, 1779

Verona, 'this last and most lovely of all the Italian States & Towns'[2]

Hester Piozzi, 1786

VISITORS TO VERONA, including Hester Piozzi, often praised both the city's situation and its appearance, while the more negative remarks of Henry Bankes of Kingston Lacy in Dorset, later a politician under the younger Pitt, were something of an exception. As early as 1489, Bernardino Barduzzi – the visiting preacher from Florence – could not speak highly enough of a city which not only received 'eloquent tributes from the whole of Italy, but is also held in the highest regard among different nations and foreign peoples all over the world'.[3] The city's inhabitants, its buildings, its industries and its environs were all praised, although his final – and predictable – assessment was that 'Florence would undoubtedly be judged by all as superior to Verona in the magnificence of her buildings, the elegance of her streets, and the rich variety of her merchandise.'[4] About a hundred years later, Adriano Valerini, author and leader of a company of actors, devoted an entire book to the beauties of the city, called *Le bellezze di Verona* (1586). He agreed with Barduzzi's favourable assessment, declaring that Verona contained so many virtues that, as a city, it epitomized excellence, just as Aristotle epitomized the philosopher and Homer the poet.[5]

The highly observant Fynes Moryson, visiting in 1595 after having already seen an arcaded city like Bologna, noted that Verona

[...] is not built with the houses cast out towards the streetes, and supported with Arches to avoid raine, as other Cities are in those parts: but the building of the houses is stately, and the Cathedrall Church is remarkeable for the antiquity, as likewise the Church of Saint Anastacius for the great beauty thereof; and towards the wals the ground lies void of houses, as the manner is in strong Townes. It hath a pure aire, and is ennobled by the civility and auncient Nobility of the Citizens, who are indued with a chearefull countenance, magnificent mindes, and much inclined to all good literature.[6]

His near contemporary, Thomas Coryat, thought Verona 'a very delectable, large, and populous citie, and most sweetely seated'.[7] In 1646, John Evelyn particularly admired Verona's environs:

[...] for in my opinion the situation is the most delightful I ever saw, it is so sweetly mixed with rising ground and valleys, so elegantly planted with trees on which Bacchus seems riding as it were in triumph every autumn, for the vines reach from tree to tree; here, of all places I have seen in Italy, would I fix a residence.[8]

The English author and Grand Tourist John Raymond gave a curious analysis of the origins of the city's name; there was a

[...] vulgar Criticisme on this Name, that if it bee syllabizd, it comprehends the first letters of the three head Cities of Italy Ve-Venetia. Ro-Roma. Na-Napoli. Others leave the verball dirivation, and more strictly interpret it, that whatsoever is contain'd in those three Cities may bee found in Verona. Her wealth may be compar'd to that of Venice; Her Monuments of Antiquity equall even those of Rome, neither is the delightfull situation inferiour to that of Naples.[9]

Like Evelyn, he would have been happy to return: 'Thus much I needs say, were I to see Italy againe, I should make my Station at Verona, for I know no place more agreeable or commodious for a stranger.'[10] These somewhat exaggerated claims for the city appeared in Raymond's 1648 guidebook to Italy, described as the first of its kind in English.

In about 1600 an anonymous Scotsman called it

[...] a noble and hansome towne beautified with an excellent Amphitheatre and the home of the Signori di Scala [...] Its an ancient towne, enioying good ayre, hansome streets and buildings and is full of good company; which makes it a sweet dwelling place.[11]

In his *Voyage d'Italie*, published in 1681, the Huguenot Jean Huguetan compared Verona's location to that of his hometown of Lyons, calling her one of the strongest cities in the Venetian state, and one of the best situated.[12]

Inevitably, there were dissenting voices. In 1687, Francis Misson expressed his disillusion:

> By what we saw at our entrance into [Verona], we judg'd it to be but thinly Peopled. There are great void places on that side, and Grass growing in the Streets, and the greatest part of them are not paved: 'Tis true, the rest of the City is not like this part; but putting all together, Verona looks like a poor place; and indeed there is but little Trade in it, and those who live on their Estates make no great Figure. If there be some fine Buildings, 'tis certain, that the Houses in general are very low and uneven. [...] The Streets are dirty, and almost all narrow. In a word, This City is not at all fit to please the Eyes of a Traveller; nevertheless, it is very large, in a good Air, and its Situation is admirable.[13]

Misson was one of the first to comment on the extensive unoccupied areas within the city walls; this was due to the drastic fall in the population during the outbreak of plague in 1630 when 33,000 deaths reduced the total of 54,000 inhabitants to about 20,000.[14] Little wonder that 50 years later there were still empty stretches of land within the walls.

Italy was often spoken of as a dangerous place to visit, with Verona being no exception to this general state of affairs. In John Raymond's account of 1648 he declared that the sort of people travellers were most likely to have problems with were *vetturini* or innkeepers, who

> [...] are very peremptory and crosse, which if you menace they wil repaire with double insolence; knowing that if in the contest their Stilletto should do mischiefe, the next Church may be their Asylum, where no Law or violence can attempt them.[15]

In 1720, the Englishman Edward Wright was not happy with Verona's security, noting that

> [...] the People of all Conditions have the Office of the Sbirri (whose business is to arrest Criminals) in such hatred and contempt, that no Man, that is not one of them, will do any thing that is reckon'd a part of their Function, or any way to belong to it; so that a Man may kill another at Noon-day, in the open Street, and no body will lay hands on him.[16]

Twenty years later, in 1740, Sacheverell Stevens, Gent., had witnessed a fatal shooting in the city, making him critical of the way Italians took revenge against an alleged opponent: 'it is sufficient if they only think themselves injured, and so for any affront, whether real or imaginary, they either villainously assassinate him themselves, or basely procure it to be done by others [...]'.[17] After seeing about 50 roadside crosses on his journey from Brescia to Verona in 1787, Arthur Young also deplored the prevailing lawlessness:

> When a person is murdered, they set up a cross for the good of his soul. They had better institute a police for that of his body. What a scandal to the government are such proofs of their negligence! yet that of Venice is called a wise one. – Impassable roads, towns unlighted, and a full harvest of assassinations; with men counting their beads, and women crossing themselves, are the chief signs of wisdom I have yet seen.[18]

The 1700s saw increasing numbers of visitors arriving in Verona from different parts of Europe. These included Henri de Blainville and his English charges, William and John Blathwayt. As their party approached the city in 1707, they found its prospect from afar most impressive, but on arrival they had to pass through an area which 'is no more than a mean Suburb, which is only inhabited by the Rabble'; once through the Porta Borsari gate, however, de Blainville allowed that 'the Houses are magnificent, mostly consisting of three Storeys'.[19]

The tutor later wrote an extensive account of their visit, including a vigorous contradiction of the views expressed by Francis Misson in the 1680s. For him, Verona was definitely not a poor place with little trade, as Misson had said; on the contrary, it was 'a fine large City' where 'great Crowds are seen almost every where in the Streets, especially on the Side of the Square, upon the Exchange, and the Bridges'. So far as trade went, de Blainville asserted that

> [...] there are here a great many rich Bankers; that the Goods sent from Germany to the Fairs of Bolzane, in order to be transported into Italy, generally come thro' Verona by the Adige; that there are besides a vast Number of Silk-weavers, together with Swarms of Jews who carry on large Dealings.[20]

The German John Keysler, there in 1730, also noted how varied some aspects of the city were:

> [...] as to its beauty, it will not bear a comparison with most of the large cities in the southern parts of Italy. Most of the streets of Verona are narrow, winding, and dirty, and the houses are meanly built; and, as it stands in a very pleasant country, when viewed from a neighbouring eminence, it appears much more beautiful than it is really found to be upon entering it.[21]

Twenty years later, Thomas Broderick agreed: 'When we come up to it, we find the buildings irregular. The houses are in general low and mean, and the streets are dirty and very ill paved.' However, he did concede that 'The public buildings, which are not thinly scattered in it, are as remarkably august and elegant, as the private ones are mean and contemptible', and that 'I am far from dissatisfied with the time I have spent in looking over its curiosities and antiquities.'[22]

Not only male tourists visited the city in the eighteenth century. An early arrival was Lady Mary Wortley Montagu who, in 1754, was entertained in the house of Scipione Maffei, the famous Veronese antiquarian; as a well-known British author and aristocrat, she would have found the doors of the best houses in the city open to her. Hester Piozzi, Welsh, but a fluent Italian speaker, loved the place, writing to her daughter in 1785 that 'Verona is an exquisite Spot, I hated ever to leave it, tho' fatigued to death with posting up & down to see the Antiques, Amphitheatre, &c.'[23] A French poetess, Madame du Boccage, wrote of the kindness she received during her visit.

> M. ZENOBRIO, Governor of Verona, that I might have the pleasure of seeing the whole country at one view, was so obliging as to accompany me to St PETER's Castle, built upon the ruins of an ancient Theatre, from whence we discovered the Adige, which runs through the town and waters a fertile plain.[24]

Elizabeth Wynne's grandfather had married a Venetian, so, on her extensive travels with her parents in 1796, Elizabeth found herself mixing socially with Italian friends and relations. She was not impressed with the Veronesi she met because they 'all talk at once laugh make no scruple of swearing like waggoners and make a most dreadful noise'.[25] Women travellers such as these were very fortunate to be able to engage with people from the upper levels of Veronese society; ordinary tourists had to be content with more mundane contacts with the likes of Italian servants, innkeepers or the dreaded postilions.

On arrival in the city, travellers would usually find themselves in the broad Corso, now known as Corso Cavour. This was Verona's principal street and originally the Decumanus maximus, one of the two major Roman roads through the city. Keysler was taken by an annual event that took place there during *Carnevale*.

> The best street in the city is il Curso, where the carnival diversions conclude with foot-races, etc. Formerly common prostitutes were permitted to enter the lists, and to run for the prize; but this custom has been justly abolished, and altered to a horse race.[26]

That was in 1730; the last Corsa del Palio apparently took place in 1795.[27]

Others noted the use of the Corso for social gatherings. When printer and bookseller James Robson 'arrived at V. in the Evening' in 1787,

> [...] it being Sunday, many carriages were crowding in and out of the Gates on airing; and also the Corso, the great Street at the Entrance, was gay and brilliant; here it is fashionable for the Quality to have running footmen.[28]

In 1826, Thomas Hogg, barrister and biographer of Shelley, described it as

> [...] a wide and even street, paved with slabs of marble, which are so large at the sides as to be quite sublime; and out at the gate to the end to an avenue of horse chestnuts, that have been lately planted: in returning we enjoyed a most lovely view of this finely situated place; and of the snowy mountains that back it.[29]

A few years earlier, the artist Marianne Colston had extended her approval to other parts of the city, although she could not resist a comparison to home. 'Many of the streets of Verona, are of a breadth unusual in continental towns [...] The neatness and convenience of the pavements for foot passengers, remind the English traveller of his own country.'[30] Perhaps reflecting the tourist's general unease with the foreign and also reminding himself of home, Henry Sass noted in 1817: 'Verona, from its clean appearance, reminded us of England.'[31]

The River Adige provided a picturesque touch as it wound its way through the city. This caused Louisa Costello to become lyrical during her visit in 1845:

> The colour of the water of the Adige was, on the bright sunny day when I gazed upon it from the parapet of the Palazzo Canossi, of a rich clear green, and every one of its waves was crested with pearly foam as they danced and whirled along over the rugged rocks that must cover the secret depths

with caverns bristling with pinnacles and spires. To live in a house on the extreme verge of such a powerful torrent seems bold in the extreme, and yet beautiful balconies filled with flowers are hanging gracefully over its raging course as if smiling at the commotion: it comes roaring and tearing through the town, dividing it in half, and all along its rocky borders stand these magnificent dwellings as far as the eye can reach.[32]

This very subject of Verona's balconies had been a source of worry to Misson in 1687: 'The greatest part [of the houses] have Balconies of Wood, so loaded with little Gardens full of Pots, that it seems dangerous to walk under them.'[33] The French writer Charles de Brosses agreed about 50 years later:

Here the houses are closely built, the windows and balconies of iron, having terraces upon which flower pots are ranged, full of plants and orange trees, these giving the streets the appearance of being the gardens of Semiramis; but the drawback to this custom is that if there is much wind one is liable to receive one of the pots upon one's head.[34]

By the mid-nineteenth century, John Ruskin took a much more romantic view:

[…] the chief city of Italy, as far as concerns the strict effect of the balcony, is Verona; and if we were once to lose ourselves among the sweet shadows of its lonely streets, where the falling branches of flowers stream like fountains through the pierced tracery of the marble, there is no saying whether we might soon be able to return to our immediate work.[35]

Beautiful as the Adige was, it was liable to flood, causing much inconvenience and, sometimes, terrible damage. Coryat, there in 1608, was told that 'this river Athesis doth sometimes so extremely swell, that it hath utterly overwhelmed all the bridges, and much annoyed the citie'.[36]

In 1793, Sarah Bentham noted that:

The Town of Verona is sometimes overflowed, and in the year 1776 the Water was Many Feet high in the Streets, and consequently the Lower Apartments of the House were under water, the want of Sewers make the streets often very Offensive from the Stinck of Filth.[37]

There had also been bad floods in 1757, but those in 1882 were so severe that the authorities later had to take drastic action to renew damaged bridges and buildings, and to construct embankments to contain waters which, on that occasion, had risen 4.5 metres above road level.[38] To this day these embankments by the Adige can clearly be seen from Ponte Pietra, running towards the church of San Giorgio and beyond. William Devereux, in Verona in 1883, heard an account of the 1882 flooding of Due Torri from its landlord: 'the courtyard was found to be some six or seven feet deep in water; the cellars and lower rooms were completely swamped, and the horses had to be brought up to the first floor'. The 40 or 50 visitors were unable to leave the hotel for a week, so 'gondolas and other boats [...] were employed for the conveyance of food etc.'.[39] That quarter of Veronetta near the church of San Tommaso, previously an island, had to be evacuated in the floods that same year. It was finally joined up to the main part of the city in 1895 after further severe flooding; there is a street named Interrato Acqua Morta in Veronetta, serving as a reminder of the course of the river before the canals were filled up.

There was always some commercial use of the Adige. In 1608, Coryat observed:

> This river yeeldeth a speciall commoditie to the citie. For although it be not able to beare vessels of a great burden, yet it carrieth prety barges of convenient quantitie, wherein great store of Merchandise is brought unto the city, both out of Germany and from Venice it selfe.[40]

Keysler noted that it was possible, in 1730, to get to Venice by water in three and a half days, but that the return journey took nearly three times as long.[41] The river continued to be used as a commercial waterway into the nineteenth century; in 1828, Richard Hollier was watching his friend, the artist Charles Brockendon, sketching by the river when 'there came down the stream, with great rapidity, a raft, with several men on it conveying timber, etc., towards Verona'.[42]

Another curiosity was the sight of the floating watermills on the Adige. Coryat saw 19 of these operating, and in the 1590s the Belgian lawyer known as Francesco Scoto – an Italian alias for Franciscus Schottus, a lawyer from Antwerp – remarked that 'There are many Mills with and without the City, and other Edifices for the Mecanicks.'[43] These mills had been in use since about 1000, both for grinding corn and for raising water.[44] In 1817, the observant and widely travelled William Cadell described their use for irrigation as well:

> On the river are seen some wheels that lift water for watering the gardens. The rim of the wheel is hollow and divided into compartments. Each

compartment plunges in the water of the river, is filled when at the bottom of the circumference, and empties itself into a trough when it comes to the upper part.[45]

By the mid-nineteenth century there were as many as 62 mills on the Adige, but the number gradually reduced with the introduction of more modern technology. These heavy wooden structures had always been liable to damage by floods; indeed, in 1882 one broke loose, crashing against the Ponte Nuovo with drastic results.[46] In the same year, the American author Laura Collins was fascinated by

[…] one feature I have not seen elsewhere, that of its innumerable mills on wheels to be run into and out of the rapid Adige. Just fancy a line of these queer-looking structures some distance from shore, working away with all the impetuosity that swift current can give, and as steadily as is their wont.[47]

The rise of Napoleon and the subsequent wars with France in the late eighteenth century meant that opportunities for British travel to Italy were interrupted; should a British subject be detained, he could be imprisoned for many years. The Scotsman Joseph Forsyth had taken advantage of the brief truce provided by the 1801 Treaty of Amiens to visit Italy, where he remained until 1803; however, on his way home, he was seized in Marseilles and was not released until 1814. Gentlemen prisoners were, however, allowed some degree of liberty, and he was able to use his time in captivity to write his *Remarks on antiquities, arts, and letters, during an excursion in Italy*, a work much used by tourists in later years. Once Napoleon had been defeated in 1815, many tourists quickly took the opportunity to travel abroad again, their number increasing rapidly. Living was said to be cheaper in Italy, and of course the climate was better than in Britain. Verona was thought to have a particular advantage for health reasons; Albanis Beaumont had declared in 1786 that 'From its vicinity to the mountains, being nearly at the foot of the Alps, the air is both serene and healthy.'[48] However, this influx of visitors across Italy did not please habitual Italian devotees; Lord Byron wrote to a friend in 1816: 'The north of Italy is tolerably free from the English; but the South swarms with them, I am told.'[49]

The Prussian Baron von Uklanski (also styled d'Uklanski) had clearly been expecting something better when he arrived in Verona, then under French control, in 1807. Perhaps he did not make allowances for the upheavals that the city had experienced in the years after 1796 when it was occupied by either the French or the Austrians up until 1814. He declared that

> [...] the city made a disagreeable impression on me. Houses with windows in every story barricaded with cracked shutters, or with paper casements, the pieces of which flutter to the wind, or with round panes in lead, one half broken, and the other covered in dirt, so much so, as not to admit a sunbeam, excite on all sides the stranger's astonishment. [...] Verona resembles a coat of coarse cloth, in which some precious threads are interwoven. Crooked streets, houses at all angles, arches crumbled into dust, and palaces tumbling down, alternate with noble architecture, and the remains of Roman Herculean works. Verona boasts 50,000 inhabitants; and, to judge by the liveliness that prevails in its streets, the number is not exaggerated. Particularly populous is the Strada de' Birboni, near St. Zeno's; by the very outside of its houses you may perceive that their tenants are any thing but honest; and in fact it took its name from the bad people, called in Italian *birboni*, who live there.[50]

These observations by a tourist about a specific part of the city and its inhabitants were most unusual; d'Uklanski had clearly made a wider exploration of the less respectable back streets of Verona than most visitors did.

Verona fell under Austrian control in May 1814 and, after Napoleon's fall in 1815, became part of the Austrian Empire and a major military station. The Swiss Jacques Galiffe, visiting the following year, regretted the city's visible decline.

> We staid five days in Verona, and left it with real regret. This beautiful city, which has produced so many great men, and which has, through them, so far advanced the land-marks of science and literature, has, for the last five and twenty years, been falling to decay with the most alarming rapidity. The number of its inhabitants, which formerly amounted to fifty-eight thousand, is now reduced to forty-five. A great many houses are completely deserted, and the streets are crowded with beggars. What mind can contemplate unmoved the ruin of such a city? But let us hope that the present government will take effectual measures against the progress of this calamity; and will take them immediately, while it is yet possible to arrest the evil, if not to repair it.[51]

Clearly, Galiffe was optimistic about the possibility of improvement that would come with Austrian rule.

Within just two years, however, Major William Frye painted a quite different picture, commenting in 1818 on the expensive carriages filled with pretty women on the Corso, and on the delights of going to Rossini's *La Gazza Ladra* at the theatre.

> I should think Verona would be a very delightful sêjour; everything is very cheap; a fine country highly cultivated; a remarkably healthy climate; a society which unites much urbanity and a love of amusement with a taste for the fine arts and for the graver sciences, and a generous appearance of opulence and comfort. The shops in Verona appear very splendid, and the Bra, when lighted up in the evening, is a very lively and animating scene.[52]

It is difficult to reconcile two such different accounts of the city in the space of two years; contributory factors must have been both the expectations and experiences of the individual tourist, and perhaps comparisons provided by other Italian cities already visited. Worcester's *A geographical dictionary* published in America in 1823 settled for mixed reviews. It had 'a pleasant and picturesque situation'. On the other hand,

> The interior of the city does not correspond with the beauty of its situation, most of the streets being narrow and dirty; several, however, are spacious and paved. The houses are in an antique style, but of good appearance from the quantity of marble employed in their construction.[53]

The nineteenth century also saw women travellers from England, France and America passing through Verona and commenting on all manner of subjects. After the departure of the French, memories of their occupation lingered on; the Comtesse de Boigne, a well-connected royalist and society hostess, declared her dislike of Napoleon's libertarian views in her 1814 memoirs. She found her attitude shared by a Veronese postilion who told her, 'We have had our fill of liberty'; he even refused to accept a coin showing liberty's image.[54] By 1820, Marianne Colston had much to say in favour of the city, and in particular of the *passeggiata*, or traditional evening stroll by local citizens; perhaps surprisingly, she gave 'the improving spirit of Bonaparte' credit for having created a public drive and walkway as 'an innocent amusement, calculated to make people happy'.[55] For her, the Veronesi 'appear more opulent, more industrious, and possessed of more public spirit, and love of improvement, than are to be found through the greater part of Italy'.[56] Other women were pure romantics; the American Catharine Sedgwick was off in search of the city's connections with Juliet and Romeo within half an hour of her arrival in 1839. A year later the Countess of Blessington was equally smitten with the tale of the two lovers, declaring that Verona was 'a most befitting scene for those dramas by which Shakespeare has immortalised it, and every balcony looks as if formed for some Juliet to lean over'.[57]

Tourists of a romantic turn of mind often found themselves carried away simply by some aspect of the city; here is the writer and painter William Hazlitt describing a brilliant sunset over the city in 1825:

> The Adige foamed at our feet below; the bank opposite was of pure emerald; the hills which rose directly behind it in the most fantastic forms were of perfect purple, and the arches of the bridge to the left seemed plunged in ebon darkness by the flames of light that darted round them.

For him,

> Verona has a less dilapidated, pensive air than Ferrara. Its streets and squares are airy and spacious; but the buildings have a more modern and embellished look, and there is an appearance of greater gaiety and fashion among the inhabitants. The English sometimes come here to reside, though not in such crowds as at Florence, and things are proportionably less dear.[58]

Several Englishmen are known to have resided in Verona during the eighteenth and nineteenth centuries. These included William Henry, duke of Gloucester and brother of George III, and William Bankes, son of Henry and by then owner of Kingston Lacy in Dorset. In the 1770s the Duke of Gloucester was there briefly with his family for health reasons, after abandoning the damp climate of Venice. One of the Duke's attendants reported thus: 'I now think HRH will take a house near the Porta San Giorgio that formerly belonged to the Jesuits – it seems airy, and cool – north side of the River.'[59] However, the family was soon forced to leave the city when the Duke's health deteriorated yet further.

Following a sexual scandal in England, William Bankes lived in voluntary exile in Verona for long periods in the 1840s. His main purpose was the commissioning of stonework to be sent back to Kingston Lacy, the home he probably never saw again. The much-travelled Englishman James Silk Buckingham encountered Bankes in the city in about 1846; because the two men had fallen out many years before, Buckingham made sure to describe the miserable life the other man was enduring. Bankes had apparently been living alone in the hotel Due Torri for some months, never speaking to anyone when he went out. 'Even in walking the street, he seemed to hide his face with his cloak […] and sought always the narrow byways, where they exist, as if unwilling to be seen or known.'[60] Buckingham may not have realized that Bankes was fully occupied with his plans for the renovation of Kingston Lacy, a pursuit involving much negotiation with local Veronesi workmen.

In 1846, Buckingham described his own impressions of Verona thus:

> As a modern city, the impression that the traveller receives on first entering it from the south, as he passes across the Piazza di Bra, with the noble public edifices on either side, in the best style of modern architecture, and the venerable amphitheatre opening on his view to the right, the broad streets, clean pavements, [and] gay shops [...] is more favourable than that presented by almost any other provincial city in Italy [...] Exterior paintings on the shop-windows and fronts of houses were very frequent; all the shops appeared to be well supplied, and much visited; and there was an air of active business, industry, neatness, and good taste everywhere, which gave us great satisfaction.[61]

A few years later the author Elizabeth Sewell bemoaned the lack of time at her disposal in Verona:

> I have scarcely ever left a place with more regret; so many things were left unvisited; and seeing the buildings which had remained unchanged for so many years was better far than reading history. It was as if one had gone back to the times themselves. But there was nothing to be done but to try and be contented.[62]

In 1835, Thomas Barlow had a quite different opinion. He was quite emphatic in his view that 'Verona is decidedly the least interesting of any Italian city that we visited.'[63] This, however, could have been due to the speed of his travels through much of Italy. Others made more nuanced observations, making allowances for particular local circumstances. For instance, Louisa Costello, visiting in 1845, drew attention to the many changes that were taking place under Austrian rule.

> There is a great deal of building going on at Verona, and heaps of old houses are being cleared away daily [...] everywhere parts of every city I saw were in a state of confusion indescribable, disclosing bare walls and old gables of frightful antiquity. The most inveterate lover of auld-world wonders cannot regret the removal of such close dens as are swept away by these renovating acts, since modern people are still to live in the ancient cities, and it was amongst these haunts that were kept concealed the germs of plague and fever. The fine old piazzas of Verona, however, need not be

destroyed: the arcades may remain, and whole streets of curious houses: though every year part of its antiquity must disappear, it can never wear altogether a modern aspect, while the fine old irregular bridge, which divides it in two, still raises its forked parapets, its rugged old towers and venerable walls, jagged and looped, too strong to be beaten down, yet remain: and, above all, while the pride of its treasures, the magnificent Roman amphitheatre, stands conspicuously forth to tell how great and glorious it once was amongst the cities of Italy.[64]

Charles Dickens, of course, loved the romantic associations of the city, writing thus in his *Letters from Italy* to reflect his 1845 visit:

> I had been half afraid to go to Verona, lest it should at all put me out of conceit with Romeo and Juliet. But, I was no sooner come into the old Marketplace, than the misgiving vanished. It is so fanciful, quaint, and picturesque a place, formed by such an extraordinary and rich variety of fantastic buildings, that there could be nothing better at the core of even this romantic town: scene of one of the most romantic and beautiful of stories.[65]

He enjoyed the whole aspect of the city, too:

> Pleasant Verona! With its beautiful old palaces, and charming country in the distance, seen from terrace walks, and stately, balustraded galleries. With its Roman gates, still spanning the fair street, and casting, on the sunlight of today, the shade of fifteen hundred years ago [...] With its fast-rushing river, picturesque old bridge, great castle, waving cypresses, and prospect so delightful, and so cheerful! Pleasant Verona![66]

Dickens also made sure to visit Juliet's alleged house and tomb, though all the while maintaining a degree of scepticism about the veracity of the claims made for these buildings.

Sometimes a tourist would describe a particularly affecting moment. Here is The Reverend John Stoughton reminiscing about his arrival at the city gates in 1850:

> The entrance to Verona! It was about two hours after midnight, and the moon was very clear and brilliant when we reached the gates. The diligence paused awhile ere admission was allowed, and then – the silence after the thunder of the wheels had ceased, – the voices of the passengers, – the shout of the postilion, – the knocking of an eager friend at the huge portal, – the forked

battlements of the walls and towers standing up against the blue sky, – the opening of the doors at last, – and the flitting about of Austrian soldiers with lanterns, as under the hollow archway they examined the passports [...]⁶⁷

For The Reverend James Wylie, however, in the following year,

The gates of Verona opened, and the enchantment was gone. He who would carry away the idea of a magnificent city, which the exterior of Verona suggests, must go round it, not through it. The first step within its walls is like the stroke of an enchanter's wand. The villa-begemmed city, with its ramparts and its cypress-trees, takes flight, and there rises before the traveller an old ruinous town, with dirty streets and a ragged and lazy population.⁶⁸

Yet only five years earlier Buckingham had compared Verona very favourably with other Italian provincial cities, praising both the inhabitants and the broad, clean streets.

The Englishman who loved Verona the best was John Ruskin, who visited the city many times between 1835 and 1888. For him, it was 'my dearest place in Italy'.⁶⁹ In his opinion, there was no Italian city to rival it in terms of its art and architecture, or its location.

Verona possesses, in the first place, not the largest, but the most perfect and intelligible Roman amphitheatre that exists, still unbroken in circle of step, and strong in succession of vault and arch: it contains minor Roman monuments, gateways, theatres, baths, wrecks of temples, which give the streets of its suburbs a character of antiquity unexampled elsewhere, except in Rome itself. But it contains, in the next place, what Rome does not contain – perfect examples of the great twelfth-century Lombardic architecture, which was the root of all the mediaeval art of Italy, [...] it contains that architecture, not in rude forms, but in the most perfect and loveliest types it ever attained – contains those, not in ruins, nor in altered and hardly decipherable fragments, but in churches perfect from porch to apse, with all their carving fresh, their pillars firm, their joints unloosened. Besides these, it includes examples of the great thirteenth and fourteenth-century Gothic of Italy, not merely perfect, but elsewhere unrivalled [...] not at Rome, nor Pisa, nor Florence, nor in any city of the world, is there a great medieval Gothic like the Gothic of Verona. Elsewhere, it is either less pure in type or less lovely in completion: only at Verona may you see it in the simplicity of its youthful power, and the tenderness of its accomplished beauty. And Verona possesses, in the last place, the loveliest Renaissance architecture of Italy, not disturbed by pride, nor defiled by luxury, but rising in fair fulfilment of domestic service, serenity of effortless grace, and modesty of home seclusion; its richest work given to the windows that open on the narrowest streets and most silent garden. All this she possesses, in the midst of natural scenery such as assuredly exists nowhere else in the habitable globe – a wild Alpine river foaming at her feet, from whose shores the rocks rise in a great crescent, dark with cypress, and misty with olive: illimitably, from before her southern gates, the tufted plains of Italy sweep and fade in golden light; around her, north and west, the Alps crowd in crested troops, and the winds of Benacus bear to her the coolness of their snows.[70]

No one else has ever managed to provide quite such a euphoric description of the city's Roman, Gothic and Renaissance architecture, or of its geographical situation.

The 1850s saw a rapid growth in the number of middle-class tourists in Italy, due at least in part to the arrival of the railways that were to revolutionize travel throughout Italy. The first train from Venice through Verona to Milan ran in 1846, and the station outside Porta Vescovo in Verona opened in 1849. This development brought more tourists to Verona, but often contributed to a shortening of their stay. In 1852, Elizabeth Sewell bemoaned the constraints on her time which meant that

[…] all of Verona was to be seen in a few hours; and any person who has ever been there, would know that such an undertaking is no slight one. For Verona is even more full of curious and ancient buildings, and monuments, and churches, than Padua. […] The situation is extremely lovely; some persons say that it is the finest in the north of Italy.[71]

About ten years later an anonymous Scottish traveller had similar feelings: 'we enjoyed our short visit to Verona exceedingly and I very much regretted having to leave it so soon and with such a superficial idea of its many beauties'.[72]

Towards the end of Austrian rule in the 1860s, Verona was undoubtedly in decline, a fact reflected in the opinion of its visitors. It had been used as a fortified military station, with little regard apparently paid to the welfare of its local inhabitants. In 1864, the French critic and historian Hippolyte Taine found his visit depressing.

An hour more and we enter Verona, a melancholy provincial town paved with cobble-stones and neglected. Many of the streets are deserted; alongside of the bridges are piles of ordure descending into the stream. Remains of old sculptures and of tarnished arabesques run here and there along the facades; the once prosperous air of the city is evident but it is now fallen.[73]

Journalist George Sala, whose comments about the Austrians were invariably unfavourable, was in the city in 1866 just before its transfer to the Kingdom of Italy. Early one morning,

> I went into a *caffè,* the grandest one in Verona, but like everything else in this war-begone town, pitiably neglected and dilapidated; waiters without braces, slipshod, unshaven, and dirty; coffee-cups without saucers and without spoons, looking-glasses cracked across, columns split up the shaft, and chairs with three legs – it was all of a piece.[74]

By 1880, the situation had not apparently improved, although by this time the city had been part of the newly formed Kingdom of Italy for more than ten years, with the Canadian William Withrow still calling it 'a decayed and poverty-stricken place'.[75]

There were other later travellers to what was now the Kingdom of Italy who viewed the city in a more romantic light, despite its social and financial woes. The American journalist Theodore Child, on a visit in 1887, commented:

> Of all the old European towns that I have seen Verona most completely retains its mediaeval aspect; houses, palaces, churches remain just as they were in the days of the Capulets and the Montagues[76] [...] The great charm of Verona is that it has retained its mediaeval aspect. There are no modern buildings and no modern improvements, except a tramway and a few very discreet gas-lights.[77]

The lighting was, in fact, so discreet that William Smith, an Englishman touring Italy by train, had complained in 1880 that his evening walk had had to be curtailed, it being 'almost too dark to see our way home, for Verona is very badly lighted'.[78] The gas lighting was inadequate and the municipal authorities did not have electric street lighting installed until 1912.[79]

British journalist Walter Gallichan in 1909 was another romantic entranced by the city's past.

> Verona then is very beautiful; it is certainly one of the loveliest cities of Europe, both in its surroundings and within its confines. You will not soon tire of the Piazza della Erbe, with the flying lion on its column, the charming fountain, and the stately Municipio. Here you will watch the life of Verona

of today, and reflect that it has not wholly changed since the time of the Scaligers, the mighty rulers of the city. There is, of course, the modern note. But the old buildings stand, and in their shade people in the dress of olden days pass continually. It is inspiring and a trifle unreal when the moon lights the square, and the silence of night lends mystery to the scene.[80]

The final word can perhaps be left to Arnold Bennett, visiting much later in 1929 and very happy with the absence of tourists:

Verona is not a mean city. The first view of the vast old reddish Castle, with superb bridge to match, after you have passed through its triple enclosure of walls, is exceedingly impressive. Also the place is unspoilt. It exists now as it did exist. The hoof-marks of the globe-trotter are not upon it. The streets are narrow, with very few new monuments, and without vistas [...] The main street is forbidden to all wheeled traffic [...] I was pleased, too, to see that no concerted effort had been made to utilize socially or touristically the fearsome river Adige, on which the city is situated. Not a terrace on its banks; not a café with a river view.[81]

Many things have changed in Verona in the years since 1929, particularly with regard to the number of hoofmarks of globetrotters, but there are still almost no restaurants or cafés bordering the banks of the river.

CHAPTER 6

The City's Civic Architecture

Verona makes me lose my wits; it is so beautiful.[1]

John Ruskin, 1852

For the architect, the decorator, the scene-painter,
and the searcher after the picturesque and the romantic,
Verona is a mine of wealth, an inspiration.[2]

Theodore Child, 1889

AS WELL AS SPENDING TIME in the imposing Arena in Piazza Bra, travellers explored other Roman sites across Verona. Some visited the remains of the Roman theatre on the far side of the River Adige, reached by crossing Ponte Pietra, itself built by the Romans and the oldest bridge in the city. There were also various city gates to be admired dating from the Roman period, including Porta Borsari (also known as the Arco di Gallienus or Porta Jovia), Porta Leoni and the Arco dei Gavi.

These remains of antiquity were of particular interest to the classically educated Grand Tourist. Observations were often made, for instance, about the dates when the Romans might have constructed particular buildings. Breval pondered in 1726 whether Porta Borsari was from the reign of Flaminius or of Æmilius. As to the Arco dei Gavi, he declared that 'it is of too good a Taste for Gallien's Age', in contradiction of the views of some other authorities.[3] On a visit to the remains of the Roman theatre in 1786, the artist Albanis Beaumont displayed his knowledge of the architectural orders of its three triumphal arches: 'The first I took to be Corinthian, the second Composite, and the third Tuscan.'[4] The fact that the Latin poet Catullus was born in Verona and had a villa at Sirmione on Lake Garda also evoked much interest from those tourists who had had occasion to study his works.

In 1817 William Rose, poet and translator, saw Ponte di Pietra as being from 'the pure age of Roman architecture',[5] while a few years later William Webb noted that two of its arches 'are the work of antiquity, and one of their abutments is much worn away by the sheer action of the water: the portion besides these two arches has been repeatedly mended, or restored, in modern time'.[6] Once over this bridge, tourists could visit all that was left of the Roman theatre on the hill below Castel San Pietro. An anonymous Scotsman reported thus in his diary in 1841:

> Our guide a chattering old Italian now led us through the town and across a renovated Roman bridge to some excavations in another amphitheatre [...] of this I could make very little except that it seems to have been much larger than the other [...] it was built on the side of a hill facing the river and the whole has been covered with modern houses.[7]

It seems that, after purchasing this site in the 1830s, a wealthy local merchant, Andrea Monga, had begun excavations at his own expense, after the sudden disappearance of a local child down a hole in the area. The American consul in Venice, William Dean Howells, visited these excavations in 1865 but could still find little to see. That there had been a substantial Roman theatre on the site is clear from drawings by the artist Giovanni Caroto, made to accompany a 1540 book about Roman Verona entitled *De amplitudine et antiquitae civitatis Veronae*; at that date there must have been quite extensive ruins still visible. The theatre may also have included a *naumachia*, or facility for staging mock sea battles; in his 1728/9 travel diary, William Freman confirmed there were vestiges to be seen of both theatre and *naumachia*.[8] A century later, Thomas Pennington's guide showed him 'the remains of Ponte Emilio, the *naumachia*, into which part of the Adige was introduced'.[9] Of the theatre, it is now possible to see a substantial part after much excavation and reconstruction, and in the summer plays are performed here; of the waterworks there is no trace, probably because of the road and embankment that have been built in more recent times.

The Roman Porta Borsari situated in the Corso and built in the first century AD was later strengthened, together with the city walls, probably by the Emperor Gallienus during the third century AD. This gate was of particular interest to visitors because of its double arches, 'one archway being probably intended for those who entered, and the other for those who quitted the city', according to Murray's 1842 *Hand-book*.[10] Mariana Starke appreciated its antiquity: 'here is an Ancient double Gate, now called Porta dei Borsari, and similar to the double gates of ancient Rome'.[11] However, artist John

Hayward saw 'a want of proportion and misplaced ornament in this piece of antiquity' in 1817,[12] while some years later The Reverend Charles Williams expressed his disapproval that 'Each arch has its own pediment over which are two stories of building, with windows and pilasters whimsically disposed, without any correspondence to the gateways below.'[13] None of this criticism discouraged Lady Henrietta Fortescue from making a careful pencil sketch of the gateway in 1821 (Plate 19). Today the Porta still stands in the Corso leading from Piazza Erbe towards Castelvecchio, this roadway being the old Roman *decumanus maximus* that was revealed some years ago when major road repairs were being carried out in the city.

The Roman Arco dei Gavi also attracted attention from those of a classical turn of mind. This had originally served as a gateway for traffic at the Castelvecchio end of the Corso; it was built in honour of the Gavius family to a design (wrongly) attributed to the famous architect Vitruvius. It had stood the test of various barbarian invasions over the centuries, and, according to the guidebook writer Pasquin, visiting in 1826, 'was till some thirty years ago, another precious relic of antiquity,' with its 'fluted columns and elegant capitals'.[14] However, in 1805 the French under Napoleon had seen fit to destroy it during their occupation of the city; Murray's 1842 *Hand-book* declared that 'For this act there was no other reason assigned, except that the arch stood in the way of the baggage wagons.'[15] This desecration resulted in a French promise to repair the damage, but nothing was done until 1932 when the Arco was finally rebuilt in its present site on the riverbank near the Castelvecchio museum.

In the years after the decline of Roman rule, Verona experienced many changes of fortune, coming under the control of various rulers, including Theoderic, the Ostrogoth who is commemorated in a hunting scene carved on the front of San Zeno. In the eighth century, under the rule of the Franks, Charlemagne's son Pepin based his seat of government in Verona, with the city enjoying a period of economic prosperity. Later, as one of the self-ruling communes that developed in northern Italy in the eleventh and twelfth centuries, Verona owed a loose allegiance to the Holy Roman Emperor. During the commune, the city's rulers had the Palazzo della Ragione – now the city's art gallery – in Piazza dei Signori built as their seat of government. The Palazzo also incorporated the Torre dei Lamberti, one of those defensive towers found in many north Italian towns, with both structures built in red and white blocks. The church of San Zeno also dates from this period of the commune. Unfortunately for Verona, in the first half of the thirteenth century it came under the control of the tyrant Ezzelino da Romano who was such a byword for cruelty, torture and bloodshed that in his *Inferno* Dante consigned him to eternal torture in the Seventh Circle of Hell.

The Scaligeri family, also known as della Scala from their heraldic ladder emblem, then took control of Verona from about 1260 until the 1380s, during which time they undertook many building projects. In particular, they were responsible for the construction of the red brick castle with its forked battlements known as Castelvecchio – now the city's museum – as well as the Ponte di Castelvecchio, which crosses the Adige from the castle. This bridge, built as an escape route for the city's rulers in troubled times, was the subject of frequent comment. James Wilson in about 1816 saw it as 'a prodigious work of architecture in the early age in which it was executed',[16] because one of its three arches had the extensive span of 142 feet. William Rose stated that, in 1817, it was 'only a holiday bridge, having been opened formerly but once a year, on account of the danger which would have attended a greater wear and tear, and now being entirely shut up'.[17] Other travellers also remarked on the bridge's closure at different periods, and on the skill of its construction, with one of its arches having such an exceptionally wide span.

The Scaligeri built a further series of walls to protect an extended area of the city; they also built two forts in dominant hilltop positions, the Castel San Pietro and the Castel San Felice. The most famous member of the family, Cangrande della Scala, had a palazzo built in Piazza dei Signori where he entertained Dante, in exile from Florence, as well as the painter Giotto who was reputed to have executed some murals, now lost. Just next to Piazza dei Signori (also known as Piazza Dante) are the Gothic tombs constructed for various members of the family, unique monuments worthy of their own chapter, not least because of the varied reactions to them by generations of tourists.

Dante Alighieri spent time in Verona on two different occasions, first as the guest of Bartolomeo della Scala from 1303 to 1304, and then from about 1312 in Cangrande's household, well known at the time as a centre of culture and learning. Much of Dante's *Paradiso* was written in the city; as well as referring to both his della Scala hosts in this work, the poet finally dedicated it to Cangrande. However, the poet found the experience of his lengthy exile hard to bear, remarking on how bitter the bread was in other people's houses. His general disillusion with life may explain why his statue in Piazza dei Signori – and many others round Italy as well – represents him as looking so severe; that he was not an easy man was illustrated by an anecdote reported centuries later by the Frenchman Pasquin. Dante was alleged to have thrown the tools of a Veronese workman into the street, saying: 'If you do not wish me to spoil your things, do not spoil mine: you sing my verses, but not as I made them; they are my tools, and you spoil them for me.'[18]

Verona has few Renaissance buildings, but there is one outstanding exception in Piazza dei Signori; here tourists found the Palazzo del Consiglio or Loggia, built in the 1490s, perhaps to a design by Fra' Giocondo. Theodore Child described it in 1887 as 'one of the most beautiful early Renaissance buildings in northern Italy, most richly decorated and most perfectly proportioned'.[19] Some years earlier, Taine had particularly praised its 'sculptures twining around the coins and cornices of the windows; branches loaded with leaves, stately flowers springing out of an amphora, Roman cuirasses, cornucopias, medallions [...]'.[20] Along the Loggia's roof are statues of past famous Veronesi; in 1646, John Raymond named them as Cornelius Nepos, Emilius Marcus, Pliny and Vitruvius, 'all of which men graced their native Verona by their singular vertues'.[21] He failed to mention Catullus, whose statue is also there; the poet was, in fact, the only one of this group to be a native of the city. In 1745, Alban Butler noticed that over one of the exits to Piazza dei Signori 'Jerome Fracastor's statue is erected on an arch.'[22] Fracastoro was a famous Veronese doctor of medicine during the sixteenth century, and local legend had it that he would drop the stone ball in his hand on the head of the first honest man to pass beneath him; so far, the ball is still in position.

Once Venice had established its rule over Verona by 1405, further building work followed, especially for the strengthening of the city's defences. In 1608, Coryat commented that 'the wals of the citie are the fairest of all the Italian cities that I saw, and indeede fayrer then any I ever saw before in all my life', being 40 feet high in some places.[23] Raymond remarked on the fact that, although by 1646 the city was smaller than it had been under the Romans, 'yet the Venetians have with great expence joynd new bulwarkes and walls unto the old, and it is fenced with three castles, which make it as well impregnably strong, as delightfull'.[24]

The most important building works in the city during the Venetian domination from 1405 were defensive. One of the most renowned military architects of the sixteenth century was Michele Sanmicheli, a native of Verona, who was employed by Venice to strengthen the walls and construct gates at the city's entrance points. The most significant of these gates were Porta Palio, Porta Nuova, Porta Vescovo and Porta San Zeno, all of which still stand today. Vasari described them all in 1550 as 'those beautiful gates which have not their equal in any other city',[25] while for Heinrich Reichard in the early 1780s Porta Palio (or Porta Stupa) 'whatever may be its imperfections, rivals the works of the ancients'.[26] Sanmicheli was also famed for his skill as a military engineer; according to the architect Joseph Woods in 1828, 'to him we owe the invention of the modern system of fortification, where every part is flanked by some other'.[27] Sanmicheli achieved this by the use of angular bastions as part of Verona's defences instead of the old-fashioned round tower, which was employed for the last time at the bastion of San Giorgio in 1523.[28] These defensive walls largely survived until the occupying French armies demolished stretches of them in the late eighteenth century.

This architect was also responsible for designing many of the palazzi in the city, including Palazzo Canossa, described by Vasari in the sixteenth century as 'singularly beautiful'.[29] Unfortunately, by the time Buckingham visited it in about 1846, this building was in a poor state.

> The edifice is fine, the architecture in the best taste, and the situation beautiful, overhanging the swift stream of the Adige, with really magnificent views from its windows and balconies; but every part of the interior was in a dirty and neglected condition – the furniture scanty and decayed – the gallery filled with a number of worthless pictures, among which there were not half-a-dozen of any merit.[30]

Sanmicheli also designed Palazzi Bevilacqua, Mocenigo, Sparavieri and Pompei; according to William Rae Wilson in 1837, this last had a façade with 'an air of dignified simplicity […] to which no parallel can be pointed out in any of the structures of the same class erected by Palladio'.[31] It is now the city's outstanding Natural History Museum across the Adige in Veronetta, with an impressive display of fossils from Bolca.

William Wilson also thought Palazzo Bevilacqua 'has a commanding facade of rather unusual design',[32] albeit unfinished, but 50 years earlier Charles Abbot had condemned it as being 'built in bad taste'.[33] Charles Barry, architect, in the city in 1820, seconded this negative opinion: 'This has never been finished and would have been much better for the reputation of Sanmichele its architect had it never been begun. There are scarcely any beauties in it to set against its hideous deformities.'[34]

The English architect and antiquary John Soane showed particular interest in Sanmicheli's work, comparing it favourably to that of Palladio. In 1760, he observed that this architect 'seems to have had rather more genius than Palladio in the ornamental part of architecture & is sometimes bold & masculine in his decoration'.[35] Soane also made notes on the leper house, known as the Lazzaretto di Porto San Pancrazio designed by Sanmicheli, which he may have visited while in Verona. He may even have thought of publishing something on Verona's architecture, since a friend had advanced him money to work on measuring Sanmicheli's buildings.[36] The Veronese architect's reputation continued to be respected; in 1837, William Wilson stated:

> [...] his name is here held in as much estimation as that of Palladio is at Vicenza: nor is it undeserving the honour paid it; for his style was certainly as pure, and there is generally greater dignity in his designs than in those of the other.[37]

Later centuries saw alterations to the cityscape by successive rulers of Verona. Under the French, most changes were of a military nature; the old Castel San Pietro was levelled and the city's defences strengthened, especially after the 1797 Veronese uprising. Under Austrian rule after 1815, military building again took preference as Verona formed an important part of the Quadrilateral or line of defences maintained in north Italy by Austria. To this end the large Arsenale (or barracks) was constructed in the city in the mid-nineteenth century, just across the river from Castelvecchio, in a neo-Romanesque style using red, yellow and white brick.

One Englishman in the 1850s had rather different and unusual reasons for commenting on some of Verona's buildings. Henry Cole and his party were in Italy to find suitable architectural design ideas for the new Victoria and Albert Museum to be built in London. He was interested in the alternating layers of marble and brick on the *campanile* of San Zeno, an architectural feature quite common to Italian churches. He was also much taken by the Loggia in the Piazza dei Signori, 'where we stumbled upon one of the very prettiest buildings we have seen in all Italy and one very suggestive for South Kensington [which] was built in 1500 [...]'.[38] Quite what influence the architecture of a Renaissance loggia in Verona had on the final designs for the Museum is an interesting question.

The real centre of Verona lay next to the Arena where a large open space was known first as Piazza Armi and was later called Piazza Bra, a name apparently shortened from the word *braida*, meaning 'large'. Here markets had been held in the spring and autumn since the 1600s, by permission of the Venetian rulers.[39] Initially, the area had been unlevelled and muddy, covered with rubbish left by builders, carpenters and stonemasons; it was not until the early nineteenth century that it was substantially improved, just in time for the 1822 Congress of Verona when heads of state from all over Europe were in the city. The Liston, as it was called, was the walkway in front of the row of palazzi that faced onto Piazza Bra, and was paved over during the 1770s. This was a fashionable place for the evening *passeggiata* by the

Veronesi and visitors alike. The other large building that faces onto the Piazza is the Gran Guardia, begun in 1609 as a military academy, but not completed until 1821; its original design was attributed to various architects, including Sanmichele, but was actually the work of his nephew, Domenico Curtoni. Lady Blessington was right in her book of 1840 when she surmised it was not by Sanmichele: 'for though an imposing pile of building, it wants the perfect proportion and fitness that characterize his style, and of which the Porta del Palio is a very happy specimen'.[40] The Gran Guardia is now used for major exhibitions, and the steps in front of it as a place to wait for local buses.

Because Piazza Bra became the focus of Veronese life, tourists would often mention it. The Scotsman J. Sinclair gave an atmospheric account of an evening's entertainment there by an Austrian band in 1827, ending with a reminder of the Arena's dark past:

> The Parade, or Piazza d'Arme, is now an elegant public walk, of which the amphitheatre forms the centre; and which is crowded in the evening with ladies and gentlemen, thousands of whom are attracted after sunset, to enjoy the cool pleasant air, and to hear some beautiful pieces of martial music. There are several Cafes in the Piazza d'Arme, with awnings spread in front of them, under which coffee, ices, and other refreshments, are served to the numerous groups from the promenade. I took much pleasure in viewing the scene until a late hour. When the clash of the military band ceased, the company soon after dispersed, and I was left almost alone, contemplating, by the reflection of a few glimmering lamps, the massive dark walls of that vast fabric, so often stained with the blood of gladiators, and many other victims of the crimes and ferocity of the Imperial Romans.[41]

In 1837, William Wilson noted how much could be seen by those prepared to wander about the city slowly, especially if they indulged in the fashionable Victorian habit of sketching.

> Of middle age antiquities there are not a few. Exclusively of churches, many curious bits of architecture arrest the eye in various nooks and corners throughout the city – just the bits which one would imagine a draftsman would be eager to take; yet most of those who have lately visited Italy for the purpose of filling their sketch-books appear to have scampered through Verona without hardly vouchsafing a glance at it. At the most, they have given us but three or four subjects, whereas it would afford nearly as many hundred [...][42]

An earlier visitor, John Hayward, had indeed taken his sketchbook with him in 1817, leaving careful pencil sketches in his travel diary of the church of San Giorgio and of Ponte Pietra.[43]

Ruskin loved sketching the small architectural details to be found throughout Verona; some of his detailed drawings did appear in his *Stones of Venice*, but unfortunately he was never to achieve a companion volume on Verona's buildings. His wife Effie noted in 1849: 'John is engaged in some very elaborate and beautiful drawings from the Monuments of the Scaliger family.'[44] Twenty years later, in 1869, Ruskin was again at work drawing these monuments, where he was found up a ladder by his American acquaintance, the poet Henry Wadsworth Longfellow.[45] His long association with Verona over 40 years meant that he was always alert to any changes to the cityscape, many of which he deplored. In a letter of 1869 to his friend Charles Eliot Norton, he wrote:

> [I] must stay as long as I can and do all I can; they are destroying so fast and so vilely, not merely taking away the old but putting up new [...] They have pulled down the remains of Theodoric's palace on the hill [...] and they have built a barracks about the size of the Vatican.[46]

Theodore Child was another visitor who enjoyed strolling through the city in 1887, admiring small details as he went.

> In every narrow street you see houses decorated with now faded frescoes, balconies sculptured into the loveliest fret-work of stone, doors gorgeous with bronze knockers of splendid design, trefoliated windows, door-posts chiselled with ornaments that the pencil alone can render, street-corners crowned with statues, arcades decorated with colored bas-reliefs in stone or 'terra-cotta' a profusion of color and ornament which words cannot describe.[47]

From its Roman remains to its modern shop fronts in via Mazzini – innovations which Ruskin would have hated – Verona is still a beautiful city with many quiet corners to be explored at leisure, away from the hustle and bustle of today's tourist crowds. A glance upwards at windows and balconies or a glimpse of one of the many splendid marble doorways will reveal details of the kind Ruskin loved so dearly. He, of course, would have liked the city never to change: 'I wanted, and I still want, to buy Verona. I would give half my fortune to buy it for England, if any other people would help me.'[48]

CHAPTER 7

The Veronesi

This town is full of beauties, wits and rarities.[1]

Anon, The Geographical Magazine, *1790–2*

SCIPIONE MAFFEI, ONE of the city's most illustrious sons, was happy to share his views on the character of his fellow citizens. Writing in his *Verona illustrata* in 1732, he stated, 'The Veronese character is one of liveliness; the people succeed in most things, but particularly in study and literature. They are courteous and easy-going, and particularly friendly towards strangers, with whom they readily become familiar.'[2] He had his criticisms too, but would probably not have gone so far as to endorse the well-known North Italian saying which declared the people of Verona to be out of their wits, the 'Veronesi tutti matti', which was somewhat more complimentary than the description of those from Vicenza as eaters of cats, 'Vicentini mangia gatti'.

Foreign visitors to the city formed their own views about the Veronesi. A Grand Tourist, for instance, was probably more interested in antiquities than in local people, spending time measuring the dimensions of the Arena or looking at other notable Roman remains. As the years went on, however, travellers seemed more inclined to record their impressions of the Veronesi, favourable or otherwise. Some compared the local people to those in other cities such as Naples; others, such as Hester Piozzi, commented on the games played in the streets, or – like William Beckford – recounted tales of the guides who had shown them round the city.

In 1686, Careri, Italian adventurer and round-the-world traveller, had described the city's 40,000 inhabitants as 'all of them ready witted and well behav'd'.[3] Visiting in 1707, de Blainville was equally complimentary: 'As to the Inhabitants of Verona they have always passed for a very industrious People, and for having a very improvable Genius for every Thing that is good or useful.'[4] In 1771, Lady Anna Miller believed them to be 'ingenious and more knowing in physicks, and the speculative branches of science, than the Italians in general', while admitting that she had not yet encountered many Veronesi.[5] As a member of the British aristocracy, her acquaintance was in any case likely to be restricted to the upper-class inhabitants of the city.

Several of the growing number of visitors during the nineteenth century found the locals agreeable company. In 1815, with Verona newly under Austrian rule, the Prussian doctor, Herman Friedländer,

> [...] met here a great number of living Veronese, who were either walking in friendly conversation on the comfortable brick pavements, or taking their ice before the open coffee-houses. We had already noticed with pleasure, some peculiarities of the people; their affability to strangers, their activity in business, the strong make of the men, and the agreeable shape of the women. There is much industry displayed in the shops, and a great bustle in the streets.[6]

William Wilson, describing himself as a 'veteran traveller', was able to make comparisons between Italian cities and their inhabitants, something he did to Verona's advantage in 1836.

> The Corso of Verona is gay; not, indeed, after the fashion of the Strada Toledo at Naples, which is by far too hurly-burly in its liveliness, but in a more sober and decorous style. The shops look inviting, and the cafes, with their silk curtains, still more so. There is quite stir and bustle enough without that incessant scampering up and down, and that furious pushing and scrambling along, which in more senses than one struck us so much in the Toledo. The people, too, seem far more good-humoured, obliging, and civil; certainly many degrees less indolent, as well as less boisterous: all which is to be taken into account in striking a balance between the two places: not, indeed, that they have ever been compared together, for they are in almost every respect antithetical. Were the alternative put, one would undoubtedly rather forego seeing Verona than Naples; but for a sojourn of any length, Verona would obtain my preference.[7]

James Silk Buckingham, author of several travel books, saw the Veronesi in about 1846 as 'well-dressed, ruddy, healthy, and cheerful-looking people [...] who appeared to us to be handsomer, healthier, better dressed and in greater comfort than any we had yet seen'.[8] Similarly, for The Reverend Charles Williams a few years later, the population 'appear healthy and well fed. Chubby and rosy children, with bright curling hair in profusion, attract the eye, and excite agreeable emotions. The women are tall and well grown.'[9]

The local women drew particular comment. The Italian playwright Valerini praised both the honesty and chastity of Veronesi women in 1586, adding with disarming honesty that, 'from my own point of view, I would rather that some of them were less chaste'.[10] However, on occasion it was felt necessary to warn young English gentlemen about the dangers of Italian women in general. The 9th Earl of Kinnoull, guardian to Thomas Graham who visited Verona in 1796, had advised him to be particularly careful of the 'bewitching sirens who fascinated young men if they were not upon their guard'.[11]

Fifty years later, the American Henry Maney was quite carried away by his experiences in both Venice and Verona. He must surely have been one of those zealous and over-romantic American tourists who went to pay homage at Juliet's so-called house and tomb in the city.

> The beauteous women, and total absence of beggars, contrasted agreeably with what we had just left in the squalid alleys of Venice. But one seeks in vain here for the golden locks and softened features of Titian's 'Bella Donna.' The women are dark, imperious and bewitching, with a dashy style and a wicked sparkle in their eye. The warm gaze of the Verona girl is passion's essence, and the pages of romance could scarcely exaggerate the deeds she dare do in her love's madness.[12]

Visitors' opinions were, however, by no means always favourable. The Frenchman Jean Gailhard had declared in 1669 that 'Those of Verona are accounted to be of a proud nature & of a fantastical humour.' He complained, too, of the number of murders committed in Padua, Vicenza and Verona, saying he believed this 'is chiefly caused by the example of some of the Nobles, and by the favours that they show to delinquents in such cases'. These nobles 'are of a High and Lordly carriage because they are very rich, but spend it very profusely, and often they run very deep into debts'.[13] Maffei himself criticized the Veronese character as being lazy, greedy and obstinate, while deploring the upper-class view that idleness was the first prerequisite of a nobleman. He also commented that many local craftsmen never worked more than three or four days in a row; outsiders, especially from Bergamo or Trento, tended to do any task that involved hard work.[14]

In 1750, the Englishman Broderick agreed with Maffei: 'There is a strange face of idleness at Verona, and of its consequence, poverty. I am less in humour with the generality of the people here, than with any I have seen in Italy.'[15] However, this poverty was nothing new; in 1728, the lawyer and political philosopher Montesquieu had noted:

> The Veronesi are poor. Everyone asks you for money; a cobbler from whom I had bought some shoes asked me for alms; the man who sells you a book asks for a tip, as does someone who gives you directions or the latest news. In Holland they ask for money to drink; here it's to enable them to live.[16]

Such unfavourable reports, particularly of the lower classes, continued into the nineteenth century. In 1807, d'Uklanski described how

> Grey-headed women without caps spin before their doors; shoemakers, tailors, comb-makers, and glovers work in the streets; hence the insufferable smell that pervades every quarter and affects the air. Instead of horses you see asses shod, beaux parade on mules, ladies on long-eared grizzles, and big fellows ride on heavy-loaded asini [donkeys] not much taller than a mastiff.[17]

Nevertheless, his description gave a real feel for a local street scene, despite his dislike of the smell of leather working.

In the 1840s, Louisa Costello thought Verona

> [...] full of dirty people – slovenly, shabby, ugly people: – its lower orders do not seem to know what neatness means; they are wild and coarse in their manners, not uncivil but savage, with none of the native grace and gentleness which had so pleased me hitherto, and sometimes made rags and dirt forgotten.[18]

George Sala agreed, describing 'the modern Veronese', in 1866, as being 'a dirty, lazy, good-for-nothing lot, generally speaking, who find it convenient to excuse their own sloth and uncleanliness by declaring themselves to be the lineal descendants of ancient Romans, cruelly oppressed by successive hordes of barbarians [...]'.[19] It has already been noted that by this time Verona was in decline under the rule of the Austrians who regarded the city as little more than a military fortress, and did little to encourage the growth of its economy or the well-being of its inhabitants. In addition, there was a general resentment by the local population towards the Austrians as an occupying power.

These visitors were merely passing through, but John Ruskin's association with the city spanned much of the second half of the nineteenth century. He never lost his passion for Verona's early art and architecture, but his opinion of the Veronesi seemed to undergo a radical change. During one of his earlier visits, he described them as 'quite a different race, evidently amiable compared to the southern Italians and more industrious & human – the children have sweet playful faces'.[20] However, by 1869 he was complaining of 'the vilest wretches of ape-faced children riding on my griffins' outside the Duomo.[21] Furthermore, he declared:

> This place would be too beautiful and delightful – if only it were utterly desolate. But the human creatures of it are horrible. They live in a perpetual anger with their neighbours, their cattle, and themselves, for they have all a discontented and downcast look [...] and they speak but in loud fury if the question be but of a cabbage stalk.[22]

The reason why he became quite so disillusioned with the Veronesi over time had much to do with any evidence he found of neglect or destruction to the fabric of a city he loved so dearly. As regards those responsible for this, he would like to 'put these Italians in a waterbutt with the top on, or roast them in sulphur a little'.[23]

Many appreciated the way that the local population took advantage of outdoor life in the city whenever the weather allowed. Goethe commented in 1768 on the way

> [...] the Italians come to life particularly in the longer evenings [...] the man who lives here in actual life cannot go wrong, because all the enjoyments of his existence are regulated not by the nominal hour, but by the time of day. About an hour and a half, or an hour before midnight, the nobility begin to ride out. They proceed to Piazza della Bra, along the long, broad street to the Porta Nuova, out at the gate and along the city, and when night sets in, they all return home. Sometimes they go to the churches to say their Ave Maria della sera; sometimes they keep on the Bra, where the cavaliers step up to the coaches and converse for a while with the ladies. The foot passengers remain until a late hour of night, but I have never stopped until the last.

He also found time to observe the Veronesi playing games in Piazza Bra or enjoying their leisure after work out in the streets, because for Italians 'everything possible is done in the open air'.[24]

In the 1820s, Heinrich Heine, German poet, essayist, journalist and literary critic, noted a similar attitude:

> As soon as daylight wanes, all the gay world of Verona promenades in the Piazza La Bra, or sits on low seats before the cafés sipping sorbet, and enjoying

> the music and the coolness of the evening. It is restful to sit there; the dreaming heart rocks itself upon the dulcet tones and echoes a response.²⁵

Ten years later, Thomas Barlow was positive about a different section of the population.

> The streets furnished a new scene of life for us, crowded as they were with ambulatory and stationary dealers in fruit and vegetables, butchers' meat, &c. On the shady side of each street were artisans working at their employment in the open air, anxious to catch as much breeze as was to be obtained; groups of children were munching away eagerly at the melons which form a main feature in their diet, and from their price caused by the great abundance of that fruit, a very cheap kind of food, quite as much so as the turnips in our less sunny land.²⁶

In 1845, Louisa Costello, now in a more tolerant mood, was

> [...] amused at observing the manner in which the inhabitants carried on their occupations in the crowded narrow streets as regardless of the shock of carts and carriages as of the wild uproar created by their rushing and dangerous river. At several doors I observed ranges of high stools perched on one of which a tailor with legs crossed would be busily engaged in his trade; his cloth and implements placed on a stool equally exalted, close behind him: women were stuck up in this same manner above the streets chattering laughing and working and reaching over to a twin seat for what they wanted. This custom may perhaps have arisen from the darkness of the houses and the wet dirty state of the streets in former days, but now all are as well paved as in the other Italian towns.²⁷

This scene had not changed much into the early years of the twentieth century. For Walter Gallichan,

> In Verona everyone strives to live and work in the open air. The streets are thronged on days of market, stalls are set up in the narrow lanes and in the piazzas, vegetables and fruit come in great store. The eternal garlic scents the street, but we learn to love its odour. In Spain a market is quiet and solemn; here the scene is gay and noisy. Voices are raised, and there is lively bartering of wares. There are subjects at every turn for the brush of the painter: stern old buildings, winding alleys, and groups of garishly dressed peasants.²⁸

Even as the number of tourists increased, Arnold Bennett could still describe the Veronesi in 1929 as 'unspoilt children of the Renaissance, ingenuous, provincial, violent in face and mien, unpolluted yet by their brief contacts with the touristic horde!'.[29] This horde was certainly on the increase, but Bennett noted that in his experience still only Italian was understood: 'Neither English nor French is spoken in the dark cavernous shops.'[30]

Sometimes visitors described local pastimes, revealing a real interest in how people amused themselves. After a visit to the Arena in 1786, Goethe

> [...] came to a modern public spectacle, about a thousand paces from the spot. Four noble Veronese were playing ball against four people from Vicenza. This pastime is carried on among the Veronese themselves all the year round, about two hours from night [...] The spectators seem to have amounted to four or five thousand. I did not see women of any rank [...] It seemed strange to me that they carry on this exercise by an old lime wall, without the slightest convenience for spectators; why is it not done in the amphitheatre where there would be such ample room?[31]

About the same time, Hester Piozzi saw people in the public areas

> [...] reciting stories or verses to entertain the populace; boys flying kites, cut square like a diamond on the cards and called Stelle; men amusing themselves at a game called Pallamajo, something like our cricket, only that they throw the ball with a hollow stick, not with the hand.[32]

Hester Piozzi and her Italian musician husband looked for more refined pastimes in the evenings. 'The Countess Mosconi [...] made Mr Piozzi and I pass the first Evening we came at her Conversation; when Abate Bertola made Improviso Verses to my husband's Accompanyment [...].'[33] Elizabeth Vigée le Brun, also in the city in about 1789, thought well of the social scene.

> Every evening while I was in Verona I went to the 'conversazione', which is what an assembly is called in Italy. Quite a number of us gathered together in a gallery, with the women sitting round the sides and the men walking about in the middle. The vivacity of the Italians and their gesticulations made these events very lively to watch.[34]

In the 1770s, the Italian Contessa Silvia Curtoni Verza held such a salon in her *palazzo* overlooking the Liston, which the local worthies such as the poet Ippolito Pindemonte attended every Thursday, as did important foreigners who were in town.³⁵ We do not know if Lord Byron ever attended a salon in the city, but he did meet Pindemonte. Writing to John Murray in 1817, he noted:

> Today, Pindemonte the celebrated poet of Verona – called upon me – he is a little thin man – with acute and pleasing features – his address good & gentle – his appearance altogether very philosophical – his age about sixty – or more – he is one of their best going.³⁶

There are occasional references by tourists to particular locals with whom they had more than casual acquaintance. Mrs Georgiana Hare-Naylor, second cousin to the Duchess of Devonshire, mentioned a Veronese banker called Alberto Albertini; she was then living at Valdagno near Vicenza in the 1790s, and gave her postal address as 'chez M. Albertini à Verona'.³⁷ Albertini himself wrote to Lord Bentinck in Genoa in 1815 in terms indicating a long-standing relationship between them: he thanked 'My most respected and beloved Lord' for the harp procured for his daughter, saying that 'My heart overflows of gratitude at the remembrance of so many repeated favours imparted on me, and on all my family.'³⁸ A visiting Scotsman described Albertini the banker as 'the politest specimen of the Old School I ever met with'.³⁹

William John Bankes, busy collecting items to send back to his home at Kingston Lacy in Dorset, dealt over several years with a number of Veronesi craftsmen, including Salesio Pegrassi the sculptor, Michelangelo Montresor the stonemason and Luigi Ferrari, a gilder from the Castelvecchio district. Bankes was particularly impressed by Pegrassi's ability to carve in stone.⁴⁰ The letters Bankes wrote to his sister in England gives a unique account of the way he interacted with these local craftsmen and the demands he made on them.

There was one group of Veronesi in constant contact with visitors to the city. Nearly all tourists employed a guide or *cicerone* to escort them to the principal sights. Murray's *Hand-book* suggested that initially a guide was necessary, but there were essential rules to be followed. 'Make him conduct you to every place you wish to see, not allowing yourself to be put off with *"non c'è niente da vedere"*, – that is, "there is nothing to see".' In addition, 'Go and see every object that he recommends, unless it should evidently be something quite absurd.' Even if he includes a visit to a friend or relative's shop en route, 'yet he will be quite as often the means of conducting you to some object [...] which you would have been sorry to have lost'.⁴¹ One other point to be borne in mind was that Italians involved in the lucrative business of looking after tourists often 'reflected back to the foreigners what they wanted to see or hear, the better to secure their custom'.⁴²

Before the ubiquity of the guidebook in the nineteenth century, visitors would have had their own ideas about what was required from local *ciceroni*. On his arrival in 1780, William Beckford wished to go straight to the Arena, and so requested a guide:

> The people of the house, instead of bringing me a quiet peasant, officiously delivered me up to a professed antiquary, one of those precise plausible young men, to whom, God help me, I have so capital an aversion. This sweet spark displayed all his little erudition, and flourished away upon cloacas and vomitoriums with eternal fluency. [...] But perceiving my inattention, and having just grace enough to remark that I chose one side of the street when he preferred the other [...] he made me a pretty bow, I threw him half-a-crown, and seeing the ruins before me, traversed a gloomy arcade and emerged alone into the arena.[43]

A few years later, Arthur Young also considered a guide a necessary evil:

> This morning I took a cicerone to attend me to view churches and places, an uncomfortable method, but when a traveller has one master pursuit, such secondary objects must give way. The great fault here, as everywhere else, is being carried to too many things.[44]

The Swiss Galiffe had mixed experiences in 1816. His first guide assured him that the Arena had accommodated 85,000 spectators on the occasion of a papal visit, when Galiffe's own research revealed its true seating capacity to be about 22,000. 'This is a trifling specimen of the degree of credit, which this sort of Cicerone deserves.' Later, however, his luck changed.

> A youth of fourteen, whom we met at the theatre, Mr. Gio. Battista Malenza, son to the Secretary of State, no sooner discovered from our inquiries that we were foreigners, than he immediately offered to be our Cicerone about the town. He called upon us early the next morning, and the following day accompanied us to every place that deserved attention; insisted upon paying the fees in spite of our endeavours to the contrary; and was almost offended upon perceiving that, on one occasion, I had anticipated him in this respect. I never met with a more obliging youth. We were happy to be afterwards introduced to his father, and to offer to him at once our thanks and our congratulations.[45]

The Reverend Thomas Pennington was equally fortunate in getting help in 1820.

> Passing over the river, on a bridge having still two of the Roman arches, we availed ourselves of the kind attention of a young priest, in pointing out to us some of the curious antiquities of Verona; he obligingly shewed us the remains of Ponte Emilio, the Naumachia, into which part of the Adige was introduced, and the walls of the ancient Roman theatre, which was one of the largest in Italy, and extended up the hill as far as the castle of St. Pietro, the venerable tower of which alone remains, and which we inspected. From hence is a most beautiful view of the extensive city of Verona, and the Adige almost under you, rolling its rapid waves.[46]

Six years later, however, American lawyer and journalist Nathaniel H. Carter was less than convinced by his guide.

> Our attention [in the Maffei museum of antiquities] was also attracted to a representation of the fall of Phaeton into the Po. We asked the cicerone into what part of the Po, the young charioteer was precipitated. He replied, 'It was near Ferrara, about 60 miles from Verona, where the place may still be seen.' These Italian showmen feel themselves bound in all cases, to give a positive answer to the inquiries of the traveller, whether they know any thing of the subject or not.[47]

An anonymous Scottish tourist wishing to do some sketching in Verona in 1841 put himself in the hands of a youthful guide.

> About four in the evening I scrambled up to the top of the clock tower by the most rickety wooden staircase I ever had the boldness to walk upon [...] the ledge at the top has no rail and it required a steady head to look down on the market place the people foreshortened into the size of big mice. My guide a cute boy from the inn told me a marvellous story about a miraculous fish of which I could make very little except that one of his ribs was hanging up in the arch of the market place and sure enough there hangs a rib big enough for a porpoise [...][48]

This rib – actually that of a whale – still hangs today over one entrance to Piazza dei Signori.

Shortly before Verona joined the new Kingdom of Italy in 1866, George Sala went in search of permission to leave Austrian territory, something involving application to several different levels of officialdom.

> I had retained, since six [a.m.], as a guide, an Italian lad who was a kind of ostler at the Colomba d'Oro. I think he must have been half-witted. In any case, he was so desperately afraid of the Austrian soldiers that he could

not approach a corporal without assuming the posture of adoration, or pass a sentry without quivering like an aspen. This lily-livered wight being an impediment rather than an assistance, I dismissed him in peace and prosecuted my further inquiries alone.[49]

After considerable time and trouble, Sala managed to achieve the necessary paperwork on his own.

Visitors continued to employ the services of *ciceroni* into the twentieth century. When in the Piazza dei Signori in 1925, the travel writer and art critic Robert Byron had a guide who pointed out

> [...] a low red-brick shell of a house, the ground floor of which was occupied by a wheelwright's shop. This, he said, was the palace of Romeo's family, where Romeo had actually lived. There is always an unreasonable humour about the reverence that foreigners display for Shakespeare. Simon and I burst into unthinking merriment, at which the guide took great offence. He angrily spluttered out long passages of Dante, which were intended to prove that Romeo's family was not merely an ornament of fiction [...][50]

The tale of Romeo and Juliet had always been – and still continues to be – a source of fascination to visitors to the city, with guides never failing to take advantage of any connection with Shakespeare that they could think of.

The *cicerone* Arnold Bennett encountered in the church of San Zeno in 1929 gave him the greatest satisfaction and – he felt – should serve as a model to others.

> But the most interesting phenomenon in the great church was the guide, who captured my affections to the extent of ten lire. This extremely unusual guide had learnt no lesson by rote. He talked vivaciously in both Italian and French, and at once communicated to you his personal passionate enthusiasm for the marvels under his charge. He begged you to stay as long as you liked in any spot you liked. He knew when to be silent. He had none of the usual guides' air of having designed, built and decorated the same with his own brain and hands. He talked as an artist might talk. Were all guides as the guide at the church of San Zeno, I would be ready to revisit every public monument in Italy.[51]

CHAPTER 8

The French Occupation

The French would have deserved the thanks of Europe,
had they only overrun the countries they did
for the sake of destroying the monks and making improvements.[1]

Young English Merchant, 1814

NAPOLEON INVADED ITALY in 1795, aiming first to take control of the Italian territories then belonging to the Austrian Empire, and thereafter to gain access to the passes leading northwards towards Austria itself. His armies swept through northern Italy in 1796, rapidly capturing swathes of the country and forcing the Austrians to withdraw from their possessions in Lombardy. The territories of the Republic of Venice were also in Napoleon's sights. He used alleged Venetian support for Austria as an excuse to threaten the destruction of Verona, something only avoided when the Serenissima agreed to allow the French entry to the city and passage across the River Adige; by 1797, Venice itself had fallen to Napoleon.

Napoleon actually entered Verona on 1 June 1796. Clearly, there had already been a great deal of destruction, given the opposition of the local populace to the advance of the French and their allies. The English visitor Thomas Ireland noted more than 30 years later one result of the fierce fighting around Verona involving the French: 'over our room door at "I Due Torri" was fixed a large shell, inscribed 26th April 1796, the day on which it was thrown into the town'.[2] In 1798, the Wynne family, journeying north towards Verona, bore witness to the aftermath of French conquest: 'Everywhere we found traces of the fury of the French: demolished houses, profaned altars and the hatred and fear of them still living in every heart.'[3] The architect George Tappen reported a further desecration, with serious economic consequences, in 1803. He explained that the main road from Verona to Milan

[…] abounds with mulberry-trees; but they were so much lopped by the French armies for fuel when they occupied this part of Italy, that the peasants, who formerly kept a vast quantity of silk-worms for spinning, have suffered a serious loss in their trade on this account.[4]

With Verona now apparently firmly in French hands, its citizens never really forgot or forgave the behaviour of their conquerors. Within the city, an innkeeper, one Valentino Alberti, kept a diary during 1796 and 1797 in which he recorded how the French vandalized churches, carrying away statues and breaking up pulpits, choir stalls and confessionals; they also used the church and convent of Sant'Eufemia as a hospital. Not only that: French soldiers came to his inn, Tre Corone, but left paying only what they wished rather than the value of what they had enjoyed. 'Oh che galantuomini! All'inferno ve ne sono dei migliori. [Oh what brave men! There are better men in hell than they are.]'[5]

As a result of this kind of behaviour, the French occupation was much resented by the Veronesi, and in April 1797 a popular uprising took place, known as the Pasque Veronesi. Four hundred French soldiers were captured and a number killed, with the rest having to take refuge in the military strongholds on the edge of the city, including Castelvecchio and Castel San Pietro. A large French force of 15,000 was then sent to relieve the city and to restore order, and later eight leaders of the revolt were executed by firing squad. Bonaparte inflicted severe punishment on Verona, including a substantial fine and the removal of many of the city's greatest works of art to France.

Items taken included Andrea Mantegna's altarpiece of the Virgin and child from the church of San Zeno, Titian's *Assumption of the Virgin* from the Duomo, Veronese's *Martyrdom of St George* from the church of San Giorgio, antiquities from the museum set up by Maffei in the 1730s, as well as bronze reliefs by Andrea Riccio from the Della Torre tomb in the church of San Fermo Maggiore. Some of these the Louvre was 'obliged to disgorge at the restoration of the Bourbons in 1814', in the words of one English visitor to Verona in 1833;[6] one such item was Titian's *Assumption*, which, according to the English tourist James Wilson visiting in 1816, 'was taken away by the French and had only been replaced a fortnight when we saw it'.[7] Some works of art were never returned, including the Riccio bronzes currently in the Louvre. Others were returned only in part; for instance, the three *predella* panels of the Mantegna altarpiece are still in France, those in San Zeno being copies. The Veronese author Da Persico described the behaviour of the French in this respect as descending into 'an abyss of public and private pillage'.[8]

In the years between 1797 and 1814, control of Verona oscillated between the Austrians and the French. In February 1801, by the Peace of Luneville, the city was divided between the two powers, with the French overseeing the main part of the city and the Austrians controlling Veronetta and its riverbank, on the east side of the city. Depending on the state of relations between the two, control of the city bridges was more or less securely enforced, to the exasperation of any traveller trying to cross from one side of the River Adige to the other. In June of that year, each side erected gates on the approaches to the bridges; these gates were coloured red, white and blue by the French, and yellow and black by the Austrians.[9]

The German traveller Kotzebue managed to preserve his sense of humour when faced with trying to go from the Austrian to the French side during 1805:

> On a bridge which crosses the Adige, are stationed the sentinels and custom-house officers of both nations. [...] I could not refrain from laughter, on passing over the bridge which separates the imperial states from the French republic, to find written in great characters these words: Circondario della libertà ('Free quarter of the town'), of which assertion the French sentinel presented me with the most striking confutation. We were here as much pestered with the passes as in the Austrian countries. In every town, at every gate, and at every public house, they were called for; and it was necessary on all these occasions to have them enrolled, copied, and signed, so that at last they contained a collection of fifty different hands and seals. At the gates we must wait a quarter of an hour, or even longer, before we can be let in or out. In many places we are obliged to repair to the police officer. In short, we should imagine that at this time the art of government consisted in a well-organised system of distrust.[10]

It was not until December 1805, by the Treaty of Pressburg, that the city was handed over in its entirety to the French and all these gates removed. This followed some fierce fighting between the French and the Austrians in and around Verona; the American minister William Berrian noted in 1817 that 'On the front of the church of St. George [in Veronetta] [...] and on an adjoining house, the marks of hundreds of bullets, from the musketry of the French, in their attack on the Austrians in 1805, are still visible.'[11] By this time, Napoleon had decreed that the republic of Italy he had established should now become the kingdom of Italy, and duly had himself crowned king, a state of affairs that continued until his final downfall in 1814. Thus the whole of Verona and the Venetia region became – at least temporarily – French territory.

In the course of the French military occupation, the face of Verona was changed, particularly following the unsuccessful uprising of 1797, after which parts of the old sixteenth-century fortifications built by military architect Sanmicheli were destroyed. In 1801, the ancient Castel San Pietro was levelled by the French to deprive the Austrians of its use; so were several towers of the Scaligeri fortress of Castelvecchio so as to give French troops a better field of fire. One change that upset both the local population and visitors was the destruction by the French in 1805 of the Roman Arco dei Gavi, situated in the Corso, the city's main thoroughfare. The pretext for this was that the gate obstructed the street, but the Veronese Da Persico deemed it to be 'a barbarous destruction' of a monument that had been admired by architects such as Palladio.[12] William Wilson, a Scottish antiquary, later claimed (1837) that, on hearing the news, Napoleon had been 'exceedingly displeased, and directed that it should be completely rebuilt on the very same spot; but delays intervened, and the subsequent changes in political affairs at length caused the project to be laid aside altogether'.[13] The Arco was only finally reconstructed in 1932.

Other changes imposed by the French included the destruction of many signs of Venetian rule, particularly the image of the lion of St Mark that disappeared from many sites round the city, including the stone lion on the column in Piazza Erbe. The statue of Madonna Verona in the Piazza was also pulled down, and a Tree of Liberty erected in her place. The French also saw to it that a number of churches were closed, as well as many monasteries suppressed. Nor did they have much regard for the care of important buildings; visiting in 1807, d'Uklanski described the Bevilacqua palace as 'a lofty structure and the oldest in Verona. It discovers many traces of architectural beauty [...] It is going fast to ruin, so much the more, as the French commander has taken up his quarters in it.'[14] However, some nineteenth-century visitors did credit Napoleon with having improved the Arena by ordering that rubble should be cleared from the central area of the interior. In addition, an anonymous young English merchant, travelling in 1814, observed that the French 'have made a military road between Verona and Mastre [Mestre, near Venice], that has no equal in the world'.[15] Usually tourists made negative comments about Italian roads, so any improvement would have been welcomed.

Naturally, any traveller's opinion of the French domination of the Veneto would depend on his own political viewpoint. The Reverend John Eustace, whose *A classical tour through Italy* became a handbook much used by British tourists, hated everything that the French Revolution stood for. He was in Verona in 1802 and declared that, for the Veronesi, 'the French are detested as the most cruel of the many barbarous tribes that have invaded their devoted country'.[16] His condemnation of the French for allowing the use of a wooden stage within the Arena was unreasonable, given that such performances – undoubtedly popular with the local people – had been commonplace for many years, and continued to take place well into the nineteenth century. For instance, Charles Burney had attended a performance in 1770; a century later Henry James, there on a sunny August afternoon, was able to see this tradition continuing, with some paying spectators of the play watching close by and 'a free-list of unauthorized observers' standing further away.[17]

Of course, there were those within Verona who had supported the aims of the French Revolution and the Jacobin notions of liberty, equality and fraternity, hoping perhaps that reforms would follow, with the power of the nobility being curtailed. There was, for instance, the so-called *La Società Patriottica*, said to have assisted in the destruction of images of Venetian power round the city.[18] As the years went by, however, even a French woman expressed her disillusion with Napoleon and all he stood for. In 1814, the French Countess de Boigne commented:

> I must ask pardon of that generation that has since grown up in admiration of the Emperor's liberal principles; but at that moment friends and enemies alike were suffocating beneath his iron hand, and felt a desire to rise against him with equal force.[19]

Many Veronesi had indeed had enough of French promises of liberty and freedom, remembering the treatment they had received in the years since 1796.

Verona was again occupied by the Austrians in May 1814; after Napoleon's final defeat in 1815, the city was to come under Austrian rule for 50 years, during which time its citizens would have other reasons for disliking foreign domination. In fact, there were tourists, later in the Austrian occupation, who even regretted the departure of the French. Here is the Englishwoman Louisa Costello, in 1845:

> One of the many fine palaces at Verona was all I had an opportunity of visiting; the Palazzo Canossi, famous as the place where Napoleon resided during his stay at Verona. The apartments occupied by the great conqueror are still shewn with considerable pride, for there is by no means a feeling of enmity towards him in Italy, as far as I could observe.[20]

Perhaps she had found that some 30 years later Veronesi memories of French rule had faded somewhat, and had now been overtaken by dislike of the city's current overlords. However, as the next chapter will show, there was very little love for Austrian rule by the 1860s.

CHAPTER 9

The Austrian Occupation

> [Verona's] situation on the Adige is pretty, and there seem to be pleasant environs; but being walled and strongly garrisoned by Austrians, the general aspect of the place is hatefull, and its dull, antique streets are seen with a degree of commiseration.[1]
>
> William Chambers, 1862

AFTER NAPOLEON'S FORCES swept through northern Italy, they moved on to take Verona in 1796 and Venice itself in 1797. Napoleon now had access to Austrian territory by means of the Brenner Pass, and took the precaution of maintaining a large garrison in Verona because of its strategic importance as a gateway to the north.

In the years that followed up to 1814, control of Verona now alternated between France and the Austrian Empire, something that caused particular difficulties for travellers. It has already been noted how the city was shared between the two powers, with the river used as a dividing line. Here is August von Kotzebue, wearily explaining the procedure on reaching the city in 1805.

> At length we arrive at Verona. Here, at the gate, in the first place, the trunks are examined; secondly, the pass is produced; thirdly, we must attend the police, where the pass is registered at two different offices; fourthly, we must proceed thence to the deputy captain, to have it signed; fifthly, from the deputy captain we wait on the mayor of the town, who only sets his 'Vidi' under the signature of the former. We now suppose ourselves at liberty to pass unmolested over the bridge which separates Austrian from Cisalpine [French] Verona: but even on the bridge we must, in the sixth place, produce our pass; and when we are confident that all our obstacles are overcome, the excise officer presents himself, in the seventh place, but is however much more easily dispatched.[2]

After Napoleon's defeat at Waterloo and the 1815 settlement in Europe, Verona became part of the Kingdom of Lombardy-Venetia within the Austrian Empire. As there were still outstanding matters to be resolved by the major European powers, it was agreed to attempt a final settlement at a Congress in Verona in the autumn of 1822. This was attended by a number of important heads of state, including the Austrian Emperor Francis I, Frederick III, king of Prussia, Alexander I, tsar of Russia, and Charles, king of Sardinia. Others present included Metternich, Austria's foreign minister, as well as the Duke of Wellington, victor of Waterloo, and the Duke of Montmorency as the French representative. Various of Verona's palazzi were assigned to these important statesmen, their Italian owners apparently profiting by demanding high rents; only the Austrian Emperor Francis I, as sovereign over Verona, was exempt from payment. Tsar Alexander was welcomed to the city with a special salute of 101 guns; he and his party were then housed in the prestigious Palazzo Canossa.[3]

Verona was by now a major Austrian garrison town, so security was tight, with 10,000 Austrian troops on standby and numbers of extra police being drafted in from Venice and Milan. This was in case any undesirable elements should cause trouble. It seems, however, that in general the Veronesi were content to enjoy the various public spectacles that took place in honour of their illustrious visitors; for instance, one night all the main streets and squares were illuminated, with the shops remaining open. The *podestà*, or mayor, Giovanni Battista Da Persico – already encountered as author of an important guide to the city – had organized other entertainments, including a performance in the Arena and another at the Teatro Filarmonico. Gioacchino Rossini had written a special *cantata* entitled *Il vero omaggio* for the latter occasion, with words by the Veronese Gaetano Rossi, about shepherds assembling on the banks of the Adige to welcome the arrival of their Sovereign. Rossini himself appeared for the performance; at the end he picked up his music and left, much to the consternation of the Chamber of Commerce whose members had paid for the score. Continued efforts were made to recover it, but without success; in fact, it seems that the score has disappeared without trace.[4]

The authorities also made use of Verona's most outstanding monument, the Arena, to entertain its important guests. John Cam Hobhouse, a frequent travel companion of Lord Byron, wrote later of his visit during the Congress, noting that

> [...] nothing could pass off more peaceably than the concert and the ball with which their imperial majesties were regaled in the amphitheatre. [...]
> In the middle of the Arena stood a gigantic figure, half plaster, half drapery,

of Madonna Verona. [...] A few days after the concert [...] the allied sovereigns attended the performance of a cantata composed for the occasion [...][5]

It must have been relatively hard to maintain security for the Russian emperor Alexander, who enjoyed the Congress immensely, if not for the most obvious reasons. The American Presbyterian pastor Henry Martyn Field, writing later in 1859, summarized a contemporary account:

> Of the Sovereigns at Verona, the Emperor Alexander took the most pains to ingratiate himself with the Veronese, by rambling about in pretended incognito, and seizing the hands of the ladies whom he happened to encounter in the streets, or giving sequins to the boys at play. He one day amused himself with carrying up the coffee to his brother of Austria, and it was some time before Francis discovered that he was waited upon by an emperor in disguise.[6]

On another occasion Alexander, still in disguise, went into a lowly bar and ordered a glass of brandy; he then left, apparently without paying, much to the landlord's disgust. However, further investigation revealed a gold *zecchino* beneath the Emperor's empty glass.[7]

For all the grandeur of the Congress and the attendance of so many important players on the European stage, very little was achieved, with formal meetings of the Congress held infrequently in Palazzo Broilo near the Duomo. Field quoted thus the opinion of John Hobhouse, who had been present at the Congress:

> Whilst looking at the cluster of crowned heads, it was impossible not to remark that the absolute lords of so many millions of men had not only nothing to distinguish them from the common race of mankind, but were, in appearance, inferior to what might be expected from the same number of gentlemen taken at hazard from any society in Europe.[8]

On a lighter note, in 1826 the American Nathaniel Carter was shown the seat in the Accademia Filarmonica where the Russian Emperor Alexander used to sit. Carter's guide

> [...] coolly added with an air of pride and exultation that 'the Emperor took such a fancy to one of his sisters, as to induce her to accompany him to St. Petersburg, where she still resides.' Such was the occupation of the Holy Alliance, while convened in Italy to settle the pacification of Europe. Happy would it have been for the world, if its members had passed still more of their time at the opera, in recruiting mistresses.[9]

The Irishman William Webb, commenting on the Congress in 1823, did at least appreciate the good sense of the Powers in agreeing to meet in such agreeable surroundings:

> Whatever sense or nonsense may have mingled with the deliberations of the recent Congress, taste has assuredly been evinced in fixing its assemblage in this most fair city of Verona, gracious in its aspect in all points. Its noble palaces are doubly, trebly, numerous enough to lodge not merely all the sovereigns and ministers, and all their secretaries and dependent suites, but also to have given fitting accommodation to those mighty co-equals of the high allied powers, the quid-nunc purveyors to the Newspaper press [...] Be the Austrian government censured for what else it may, it shewed tact in selecting Verona, as a man of various estates and mansions might do when entertaining his choicest circle of friends. It is a scene of ingratiating beauty.[10]

The main reasons for Austria's tight control over Verona were both military and strategic. In 1837, the Scottish tourist J.D. Sinclair explained the situation.

> Being the headquarters of the Austrian troops in Italy, a very strong garrison is maintained in Verona. A better point could not be selected as a central depot, as it is equidistant from Milan and Venice, and near the high road to Vienna, which is always kept in the best state of repair, to enable the Emperor to reinforce his Italian army at the shortest notice, by either of the two great passes of the Alps situated in his own dominions.[11]

There were advantages for travellers in all this: 'The roads around Verona are excellent: that circumstance may be attributed to the value of the city as a military station to the Austrians.'[12]

The number of troops stationed there was substantial, particularly in the middle years of the nineteenth century, following popular uprisings in various parts of Italy, including Milan and Venice in 1848. Soldiers were employed to improve the fortifications, and to strengthen the principal forts; in 1854, the Austrians rebuilt Castel San Pietro, destroyed by the French in 1801, a substantial building that still stands today. The scale of the military presence had been noted by Lieutenant General Taylor in 1835:

> I arrived on a Sunday in Verona, and although I had seen troops in abundance throughout Lombardy, I was particularly struck by the numbers I there met in the streets and market place, the soldiers in their best clothes

in about twenty different uniforms, and looking uncommonly well. I was told that the next morning I might see 10,000 of these men (the garrison altogether consisting of 20,000) at work at the fortifications. The sight was indeed worth seeing, the repairs and extension of the works quite stupendous, and of course, with so many men employed in them, getting on most rapidly.[13]

As early as 1814, however, the Englishman Baring had observed that the Austrian presence was not at all popular with the local Veronesi: 'Several detachments of Austrian troops passed me here, going towards Milan. The Hulans, a sort of lancers on horseback, were much disliked by the inhabitants, as they stole wherever they could.'[14] This was an understandable local reaction to military occupation, given the disturbed state of the country. However, the dislike of the British for the perceived autocratic rule of the Austrian Empire was made evident in the many negative remarks made by travellers to Verona throughout the nineteenth century, up to the formation of the Kingdom of Italy in the 1860s. Mrs Jameson's visit to the Arena in 1821 was spoilt when she

> [...] ascended to the top and looked down into the Piazza d'arme, where several battalions of Austrian soldiers were exercising; their arms glittering splendidly in the morning sun. As I have now been long enough in Italy to sympathize in the national hatred of the Austrians, I turned from the sight, resolved not to be pleased.[15]

In the same year, 17-year-old Robert Marsden described as a 'repulsive spectacle' the fact that their troops and sentinels were generally stationed along one side of every square in the city.[16] By 1861, just five years before the Austrians left the city for good, Kate Crichton noted their continuing unpopularity, observing that

> [...] the number of white coats [as worn by the Austrian infantry] moving about enlivened the scene, but dark glances of hatred flashed from the expressive eyes of the civilians upon their wearers, as they sauntered down the streets, clanking their swords along the pavement.[17]

The bureaucratic way in which Austrian rule was administered was frequently commented on, due principally to the absolute necessity to have the correct paperwork. The Scottish peer Henry Cockburn described the problems that he and his party encountered in 1823.

> We were again tortured here about our cursed passports, after going & being authorized to go, thro' a dozen of Austrian towns, it was discovered at the police that they had not been signed by the Austrian ambassador in London & that therefore we could go no further – at one time I really believed that our journey was done – but this notable objection was at last got over by Mr Martinelli the banker to whom we had a letter from Coutts, & who behaved very kindly, signing a paper certifying that we were honest men & that he would be responsible for us. And in two days we discovered that they had actually been signed by the Austrian ambassador.[18]

Murray's *Hand-book* of 1842 was adamant about the importance of strict adherence to Austrian regulations, and had little sympathy with tourists who failed to obtain what was necessary before they set off. British travellers should get their passports from the Foreign Office; they could, if they chose, also obtain visas in London from the countries through which they intended to travel. The alternative for the visas was to obtain them en route; so far as entering Austrian dominions in northern Italy, 'no person can, under any pretence, cross the frontier without a passport signed by an Austrian minister'.[19]

Another Scotsman, The Reverend James Wylie, who arrived in the city in 1851, had a novel way of dealing with officialdom while also expressing his dislike of Austrian rule. The old balance of power between the major European nations was breaking down following the wave of rebellions in the 1840s, with the British foreign secretary, Lord Palmerston, actively supporting the Italian rebellion of 1848, an attitude that naturally made him unpopular with the Austrians, but well regarded by the locals.

> At its gates we were met, of course, by the Austrian gendarmerie. To have the affair of the passport finished and over as quickly as possible, I unfolded the sheet, and carelessly hung it over the window of the carriage. The corner of the paper, which bore, in tall, bold characters, the name of her Majesty's Foreign Secretary, caught the eye of a passenger. 'Palmerston!' 'Palmerston!' he shouted aloud. Instantly there was a general rush at the document; and fearing that it should be torn in pieces, which would have been an awkward affair for me, seeing without it, it would be impossible to get forward, and nearly as impossible to get back, I surrendered it to the first speaker, that it might be passed round, and all might gratify their curiosity or idolatry with the sight of a name which abroad is but a synonym for 'England'. After making the tour of the diligence, the passport was handed out to the gendarme, who, feeling no such intense desire as did the passengers to see the famous characters, had waited good-naturedly all the while. The man surveyed with grim complacency a name which was

then in no pleasant odour with the statesmen and functionaries of Austria. In return he gave me a paper containing 'permission to sojourn for a few hours in Verona,' with its co-relative 'permission to depart.' I felt proud of my country, which could as effectually protect me at the gates of Verona as on the shores of the Forth.[20]

Over the years, there were occasional visitors – including John Ruskin's wife Effie – who expressed more positive views about their Austrian hosts. In 1849, the couple stayed as usual at Due Torri, the favourite hotel of English travellers, with a room overlooking Piazza Sant'Anastasia. John, immersed as ever in his work on the architecture of the city, was quite happy for Effie and her female companion to be taken about during the day by dashing young Austrian officers. Some years later she recalled her time spent with them:

> I could not be better placed for seeing Austrian Society and I really admire them, so easily amused, so kind and good tempered & so eminently wellbred. I never am with them that I don't feel myself brusque and awkward and they are so different from the French who are so heartless with their politeness.[21]

On another visit in 1852 Effie was very excited when the famous Austrian General Radetzky arrived at the hotel to visit a Russian princess, and longed to be introduced to him. She got her wish when the Ruskins were invited to a ball held at the General's official residence, where she was 'presented to Radetzky who looked very glad to see me, and taking my hand instantly turned round and presented me to the Arch Duke Charles Ferdinand, which I believe was a very distinguished honour'.[22] Thereafter she danced the night away, while her husband John was happy to find a library where he could sit and read instead of 'having to stand with my back to the wall in a hot room'.[23]

The Prussian historian Friedrich von Raumer had expressed a cynical view of one aspect of Austrian domination a few years earlier:

> Unluckily I have found in Verona another confirmation of the oft-repeated complaint that the Austrian government attends only to material interests, but neglects, or even undermines, those of a higher nature. In my walks for hours through streets, great and small, I have not seen a single beggar; not a creature asked charity of me, though it was easy to perceive that I was a traveller. What does this prove, unless that the Austrian attends to such utterly trifling matters as the employment of the healthy and the relief of the necessitous, while it deprives its subjects of all that is most noble, namely, the opportunity of exercising the Christian virtues in the streets? The other

> governments of Italy, in the profundity of their wisdom, pursue a contrary course, and their subjects, equally sagacious and docile, profit by the lesson, and take care that from year's end to year's end there shall be no lack in the streets of sick, loathsome, and impudent beggars, in order that no Christian may ever want opportunity for the exercise of the Christian Virtues![24]

No doubt the various tourists who were wont to complain about beggars on other Italian city streets were happy not to be asked to exercise their Christian charity in Verona.

The de Goncourt brothers, in their *L'Italie d'hier* published in 1894, provided a description of the behaviour of Austrian soldiers manning the railway station in Verona – opened in 1849 – in the years up to the mid-1860s.

> How strange they look, those Italian station restaurants. Tubs of camellias round the tables, walls covered with unframed smoky canvases, and on the stove, a plaster statuette of Napoleon. Inside, Austrian officers drink, smoke and chatter quietly with airs of restrained seriousness, dazzling smiles and modest manners, quite exceptional for military in the presence of mere civilians. Some even sit alone, huddled in nooks to read volumes of poetry. Indeed, no doubt about it, these Austrian officers have all the advantages of men of the upper classes, well versed in art and letters, a cut above our French officers.[25]

These complimentary remarks about Austrian behaviour made by Frenchmen contrasted with the less flattering ones routinely made by English travellers.

Another feature of Austrian rule that had exercised the English for many years was the army's occupation of historic buildings within the city. As early as 1822 the Countess of Blessington had deplored the misuse of the Giusti palace, which

> [...] is converted into a barrack for the Austrian soldiers; and in its gallery, on the walls of which once glowed some of the finest pictures in Italy, may now be seen the rude cyphers, and still more rude sketches in charcoal of the soldiers; and on its floor, where walked dainty dames and admiring connoisseurs, now pace the rough-shod Austrians and their helpmates.[26]

Later on, Ruskin agreed that 'there is much grievous harm done to works of art by the occupation of the country by so large an army; but for the mode in which that army is quartered, the Italian municipalities are answerable, not the Austrians'.[27]

Ruskin was always careful to try and be even-handed about Austrian rule. He felt he should express his 'astonishment and regret at the facility with which the English allow themselves to be misled by any representations, however openly groundless or ridiculous, proceeding from the Italian Liberal party, respecting the present administration of the Austrian Government'. He had been unable to find any liberal Italian who could find 'a single *definite* ground of complaint against the Government', and had little patience with English lady visitors who 'on their first arrival invariably began the conversation with the same remark: "What a dreadful thing it was to be ground under the iron heel of despotism!"'.[28] He would certainly have had little time for a Scottish member of the Minto family who wrote in her journal in 1853 that 'Within the last two months the state of Austrian Italy has become most deplorable – on the one side nothing but tyranny of the most cruel description – on the other ruin & misery and burning for revenge.'[29] The notion of an Austrian autocracy that deprived the Italians of their right to a freedom enjoyed by the British was clearly deeply rooted, whatever Ruskin might have to say.

The correspondent of the *Edinburgh Evening Courant*, writing about Verona in the early 1860s, shared Ruskin's view that not everything was bad about Austrian rule:

> The German element evidently bears a larger proportion to the whole population here than at Venice, and the presence of so large a force, with the necessary strict police regulations of a fortified town, in a country full of disaffection, must make Verona on the whole an uncomfortable place of residence. It is said that the strictness about passports has increased within the last few days in consequence of the news of Garibaldi having entered Naples. All I experienced of this strictness was that my passport being taken from me on entering the gate, and a receipt handed me for it, which occasioned me a two-minutes' walk next morning to the Police Office, where a very polite employee, without a moment's delay, returned it to me.[30]

Other travellers were, however, less forgiving. The Reverend Henry Alford, dean of Canterbury, was understandably not happy with what he found in 1864; he accused the Austrians of committing acts of barbarism such as the turning of

> […] churches and cloisters into barracks, without the slightest regard to the precious works of art contained in them. During one day at Verona, as before at Venice, several instances occurred of our being unable to see frescoes described as being very beautiful, because the buildings containing

them had become military quarters or storehouses. I was naturally anxious to see an ancient church, dedicated to St. Thomas of Canterbury: thinking I might find there some representation, legendary or imaginative, of the murder perpetrated in my own cathedral. But I was told that I could not see the church, because it had been taken as a store of hay for the Austrian cavalry![31]

It was not just the misuse of Verona's historic buildings that caused upset; exception was also taken to the Austrians' attitude to the local populace. In the city in 1852, The Reverend David Drummond observed

[...] an exhibition of Austrian violence towards the people of the country. A poor fellow, with a cart, was run against by the driver of my fiacre, and instantly the Austrian on duty rushed out, and without waiting for an explanation, gave him a violent blow on the chest – refused to hear a word in his defence – obliged him to draw up his horse and cart to one side, and from what I heard afterwards, I rather fear, gave him a night's imprisonment! I cannot say that I witnessed many such instances of oppression; but, alas! It makes one's heart bleed to think of a country where such an act can ever be perpetrated with impunity.[32]

The English traveller George Sala, whose dislike of the Austrians knew no bounds, was one of the last travellers to describe Verona just before it became part of the new Kingdom of Italy.

We reached the fine old city, now converted into a frowning fortress, garrisoned by thirty thousand men, at midnight. It is a long drive from the Porta Vescovo to the city gates, and when we reached them they were closed for the night. Only after infinite trouble, and the thrice-performed rite of exhibiting our passports – first to a gendarme, whose lantern went out; next to a German who was drunk, and was for leaving us out in the cold; and last to a Croat sergeant, who could speak neither German nor Italian – were we allowed to make our way to a most infamous hostelry [...]

He was no happier once he began to explore a city he already knew well.

There is nothing new, nothing tidy here but barracks and fortifications [...] To anyone who has known Verona in its good days – to anyone who has turned over the pages of the sumptuous edition of Rogers's *Italy*, with its exquisite illustrations by Turner – the actual aspect of this historical and artistic place is most miserable. You can scarcely believe that you are in Italy. From one end of the town to the other there is the smell of the Austrian cavalry stable, and the guttural jabbering of the Austrian guard-room, and the white-coated Croats swarm like a plague of lice.[33]

All this was soon to change.

In 1796, the French had occupied the city, to be replaced by the Austrians in 1814 after Napoleon's overthrow. Now, about 50 years later, Verona was entering yet another stage of its turbulent history. After Austria's military defeat by the Italians' Prussian allies and some complicated manoeuvring among the Great Powers of Europe, the city and Venetia became part of the Kingdom of Italy in 1866, under the rule of Victor Emanuel II of the House of Savoy. This followed a plebiscite allowing the local population to decide whether or not to come under the rule of the House of Savoy. Various other territories across the Italian peninsula such as Lombardy, Tuscany and the Kingdom of Naples had already been incorporated into the new state; it was not until 1870 that the Papal States, the final piece of the jigsaw, were also annexed. So Verona was now part of Italy, with a fine equestrian statue of their new ruler Victor Emanuel II later erected in Piazza Bra. It would clearly be some time before it would undergo a transformation into something less of a military fortress and more of a truly civilian city playing its part in the newly united Kingdom of Italy.

CHAPTER 10

Shakespeare, Romeo and Juliet

> There is no world without Verona's walls,
> But purgatory, torture, hell itself.
> Hence banished is banish'd from the world,
> And world's exile is death
>
> *William Shakespeare,* Romeo and Juliet, *Act III, Scene 3, Romeo*

VERONA HAS ALWAYS been intimately associated with Shakespeare's tragedy of the lovers Romeo and Juliet, and English-speaking visitors almost invariably found their way to Juliet's so-called house and tomb. Some pondered the vexed question of whether Shakespeare had based his play on fact or fiction. In Verona in 1720, John Breval, travelling tutor and travel writer, heard of the discovery of a tomb that 'appear'd to contain the Bodies of a young Couple which had come by their Death in a very Tragical manner about three Centuries before'. Of course, for him this 'immediately call'd to my mind the celebrated Story of Romeo and Juliet, which is the Subject of one of the finest Pieces of Shakespear', although he could now find no trace of this alleged tomb.[1] A century later, the Irish author Anna Jameson had read two differing accounts of the lovers' story. One was Girolamo Dalla Corte's *Dell'istorie della città di Verona* of 1744, stating that the Montagu and Capulet story was fact; the second was by Louis da Porta who,

> [...] in his beautiful novel, la Giulietta [published in 1530], expressly asserts that he has written it down from tradition. If Shakespeare, as it is said, never saw the novel of Da Porta, how came he by the names of Romeo and Juliet, the Montagus and the Capulets: if he did meet with it, how came he to depart so essentially from the story, particularly in the catastrophe?[2]

She could not answer this conundrum.

Others in a romantic mood, like the American lawyer George Hillard in 1847, were happy just to accept that over Verona 'the spirit of Shakespeare broods. He is its spiritual lord. His immortal lovers have touched its towers with light, and mingled the breath of passion with its breezes.' He believed there were no authentic memorials to the lovers in the city, even if others were more credulous; for him, the tragedy of Romeo and Juliet was enough. 'The tomb which Shakespeare has built will outlast the amphitheatre, and endure as long as love and grief twine the rose and the cypress in the garland of life.'[3] About the same time, Catharine Taylor, in a letter to a younger sister, declared that 'Shakspere's characters live in our hearts, and we want not palpable objects to strengthen our conviction of the truth of their existence.' She also felt quite sure that Shakespeare had been to Italy:

> The more we see of Italy, and the towns which Shakspere has chosen as the scenes of his dramas, the more do I feel it difficult to believe that he never visited this lovely land; the descriptions, the whole atmosphere in which he places his characters, are truly Italian.[4]

Unfortunately for most tourists, a visit to the so-called 'house of the Capulets' inevitably ended in disillusion. In 1845, Charles Dickens found it to have 'degenerated into a most miserable little inn' with a yard 'ankle-deep in dirt, with a brood of splashed & bespattered geese'. There was also a 'grim-visaged dog [...] who would certainly have had Romeo by the leg, the moment he put it over the wall'.[5] In 1889, the American Theodore Child described the exterior of the house in Via Capello, with its advertisements for a bakery, for stabling and for horses to hire. Over the archway was a marble slab inscribed:

Queste furono le case dei Capuletti	(These were the houses
d'onde uscì la Giulietta	Of the Capulets
per cui tanto piansero i cuori gentili	Whence sprang Juliet
e i poeti cantarono.	For whom
	So many noble hearts have wept
	And poets have sung.)[6]

Child's description of the courtyard within paints a vivid picture.

> Beneath the archway the passage slopes up, and you enter a vast courtyard, the four sides of which are occupied by miserable buildings terraced

with rough wooden balconies, on which linen is spread to dry and to absorb the perfumes of this most foul-smelling spot. On each balcony is built a wooden shed on which is written the word 'Cessi' which means water-closet; the staircases are black holes thick with dirt; the courtyard is crowded with carts and vehicles of all kinds and redolent of ammoniacal smells; and next to the stables is a 'Caffe Trattoria,' a cafe and a restaurant where you can be lodged for the night. Over this filthy and stinking courtyard, enthroned in a flourishing vine plant, an image of the Virgin presides at one end, while at the other end, on the back facade of Juliet's house, are carved in low relief the speaking arms of the Capulets or Capelletti, namely, a hat, or 'Capello.' And it was here that Juliet had her garden; here that Romeo climbed her balcony; here that the two lovers poured out their souls, until they were surprised by the song of the lark, and the dawn warned them that they must part. This is the house; there can be no doubt about it; and we can imagine the Capulets and their retainers swaggering out of this vast courtyard and down under the archway to the street, ready to fall foul of those hated Montagues. But where was Juliet's balcony?[7]

Arnold Bennett, on his visit to Juliet's house in 1929, reflected a much more cynical twentieth-century standpoint. He went there

[...] to vent my rage at being shown Juliet's house, a picturesque and untidy tenement with balconies certainly too high for love, unless Juliet was a trapeze acrobat, accustomed to hanging head downwards by her toes.
This was not Juliet's house for the sufficient reason that as far as authentic history knows, there was never any Juliet [...] There not having been any Juliet, there could not have been any Juliet's house. Hence to label the building as Juliet's house, and to draw the special attention of simple-minded tourists to it as such, was an act of unscrupulous fraud, which the city authorities ought to have firmly and publically disowned.[8]

His so-called 'simple-minded tourists' in the twenty-first century still flock to the house in their hundreds, many writing their messages on the walls of adjacent houses – to the fury of their long-suffering owners – in the hope of securing the partner of their dreams.

The other place of pilgrimage was Juliet's so-called tomb outside the city walls, situated in a garden claimed to have belonged variously to a nunnery, a Franciscan monastery or a foundling hospital, and was later in the care of a family that charged an entry fee. The tourists who came to see the stone coffin made of red Veronese marble described it variously as a horse-trough, a fountain basin, a sarcophagus, a receptacle for washing vegetables, a water cistern or even – in 1859 by Captain J.W. Clayton, lately of the 13th Light Dragoons – as 'now a washing tub for the lusty nymphs of Verona'.[9] In 1826, the American journalist Nathaniel Carter was one of many visitors to notice that the coffin that allegedly held Juliet's body was provided with 'a stone pillow for the head, a socket in the bottom to hold the taper, and an aperture in the side to admit fresh air'.[10] Other than that, there was little to see. In about 1817, James Wilson's *cicerone* told him that the coffin had once had a lid with engraving on it, but it had been blown off by an explosion of gunpowder during the French occupation.[11]

Tourists' reactions varied. Some recognized this as a means for the custodian to make money, others felt disillusioned by the pretence that this could be Juliet's tomb, and yet others were carried away purely by the romance of the situation. The American journalist Junius Browne, visiting in 1870, declared that, although

> [...] the tomb is a deception for a mercenary purpose, it is well to have even a cenotaph to which sentimental pilgrims may go and indulge in the luxury of romantic sensibility. 'Gentle Juliet, she died for love,' I said experimentally, in Italian, to the uneducated girl who had admitted me. Her face changed in a moment; her eye moistened as she answered, '*Si, Signore, Giulietta infelice.*'[12]

Tourists from the United States were often easy targets. Theodore Child witnessed satisfaction on the part of both the custodian and some such victims in 1887.

> Just as we arrived at this classic spot the old woman finished a good stroke of business: she concluded a transfer of twenty-two photographs of the tomb to the twenty-two members of a 'personally conducted' party from Chicago and thereabouts, who were doing Verona in twenty-four hours under the command of a scraggy German boy who directed their movements by the shrill blasts of a pea-whistle. These worthy people, men, women, and children, seemed to appreciate Juliet's tomb, and I heard some of them express satisfaction at its bigness.[13]

In 1868, Latrobe, another American, had observed something similar at the tomb. 'Some remnants of old sculpture had been placed around, and photographs were for sale, representing a lady in black, in a most sentimental and lugubrious pose gazing mournfully upon the spectacle before her.'[14]

The Reverend Daniel Clarke Eddy of Boston, Massachusetts, acknowledged how disillusioned he felt on his 1851 visit.

> We had read Shakespeare, and wished to see the tomb of Juliet, which is here. Our romantic ideas had a fall; and what a fall! We entered a narrow passage, in which a man was washing the dirty wheels of a carriage, and where were several horses, which nearly trampled us as we passed on, and knocked at a rude door, which was opened by a woman with a child in her arms. She was an Italian woman, with dark skin, coal black eyes, piercing and glistening, and a form as graceful as a sibyl. Giving her babe to another, she conducted us through a stable into a garden. We passed along under a heavy overhanging grape vine, well hung with unripe fruit, to a little chapel, once used for devotional purposes, and in which a tolerable fresco of the crucifixion still remains. Here, in this chapel, which is now used for dovecot and hencoop, a stone tub was pointed out to us as the veritable coffin of Juliet.[15]

On his arrival in 1822, the great Shakespearean actor, William Charles Macready, whose first major role had been as Romeo in 1810, ordered his guide to take him directly to Juliet's tomb, despite the late hour.

> An old woman answered to our knocking, and led us by the light of 'a lanthorn burning' through her miserable habitation, our steps ringing on the hollow floor, into the garden or vineyard beyond. The splendour of the moon, that shone bright in heaven, penetrated the interstices of the vine leaves [...] The roaring of the Adige alone broke the silence of the night [...] I believed that I saw before me the sepulchre of her whom Shakespeare has taught us to picture as one of the fairest and the best, the gentlest and truest, of her sex [...] As I stood in the broad moonlight, looking on the bright planet in full pure glory above me, I thought that so she must have looked when the love-sick boy invoked her beams [...] I would rather have missed ten galleries of pictures than this one hour of dreamy, idle musing.[16]

Some tourists behaved in mildly eccentric ways, with Galiffe recording one such occasion in 1816.

> An English lady, who shall be nameless, and who had paid her devotions at this shrine some weeks before us, had taken it into her head to lay herself

at full length in this tomb, like a monumental figure, with her hands piously crossed on her bosom. But it is dangerous to tempt the devil, and especially in a monastery. The romantic visitor had no sooner clasped her hands on her breast, than a sudden gust of wind so disarranged her undefended garments, as to cause no slight confusion to herself, and some scandal to half a dozen male and female friends who accompanied her.[17]

Sometimes it was the guides who provided the amusement. In 1886, a group of young Americans went to the tomb with a guide who 'spoke the drollest broken English', and even gave them a rendition of parts of *Romeo and Juliet* that caused them to laugh 'until the tears ran down our cheeks'.[18]

It was common for tourists to try and take home a piece of Juliet's coffin as a souvenir. Visiting in 1826, Carter mentioned how fragments had formerly been carried away as relics; however, the 'present guardian watches with the eyes of an Argus, and will suffer no fingers to pilfer'.[19] The Wesleyan minister Wilbur Fisk noted ten years later that the Italians believed the English to be the main culprits in this respect, but that a custodian had now been appointed and 'further fractures forbidden'.[20] However, this vandalism was not confined to the English. Guidebook writer Pasquin had been there in about 1826, and asserted that a 'great princess (the Archduchess Maria Louisa of Parma) has had a necklace and bracelets made of the reddish stone of which it is composed; some illustrious foreigners and handsome ladies of Verona wear a small coffin of this same stone'.[21] When, in about 1851, The Reverend Daniel Eddy and his party wanted their marble souvenir,

> [...] our pretty gypsy guide would allow of no such thing. Dr. M. was bent on success, but the woman was immovable. He offered her money, but she indignantly replied, –
> 'No possible – no possible!'
> He then tried to coax her a little, and with fair compliments secure a piece of the marble; but though her reply to his persuasions was less indignant than before, it was no less firmly given: –
> 'No possible – no possible!'[22]

Others were content to leave their calling cards or bouquets of flowers on the edge of the tomb, or even in it. Child noticed that

> [...] the bottom of the sarcophagus is strewn with a thickness of several inches of visiting-cards; on the wall also are pinned up visiting-cards, mostly bearing Anglo-Saxon names; and on the wall over the sarcophagus is hung

a faded wreath with a card pinned on to it. This card bears the name of an English gentleman, Mr. Talbot Shakspeare, who is less famous than his homonym William.[23]

William Devereux, there in 1883, felt all this was excessive. 'I think it was carrying sentiment a little too far to leave visiting-cards and photographs in a desolate and deserted tomb, which we have no positive proof ever contained the remains of La Giulietta, as the Veronese call her.'[24]

Perhaps the last word should be left with the Baltimore lawyer John Latrobe who, although sceptical about the historical accuracy of the Romeo and Juliet story, concluded that 'the pilgrimages that have since been made to Juliet's tomb are in truth so many oblations upon Shakespeare's shrine'.[25]

CHAPTER 11

Scipione Maffei

Few towns have had a better share of historians than Verona: Saraina is still esteemed; Maffei owes his glory to his *Verona illustrata*; and Count Persico, by his excellent *Description of Verona and its province,* has shown himself a worthy successor of these national annalists.[1]

Antoine Claude Pasquin, 1839

THE ITALIAN RESIDENT best known to eighteenth-century visitors to Verona was the scholar and antiquarian, Francesco Scipione, marquis of Maffei (1675–1755). Those of a classical turn of mind were particularly interested in his collection of antiquities, on public display in a museum purpose-built by him and completed in 1745. Maffei took the unusual decision to exhibit these Etruscan, Greek and Roman statuary, altars and inscriptions out of doors, under a peristyle extending from the Teatro Filarmonico; although his museum has undergone various alterations over the years, it can still be visited today through an entrance just off Piazza Bra.

In 1750, the Englishman Thomas Broderick observed that this museum gave Verona an advantage

> [...] in which no city in Italy excels it; the collection of antique inscriptions. These are ranged in an elegant order round the walls of their great court, before the academy; and if we except only the Arundel marbles, are the greatest collection in Europe. They have been procured at a vast expence, from every place where the Venetians had power, and have been methodized by count Scipio Maffei, who has executed his part so well, as to do a lasting honour to his country, confer an obligation of the first importance on the literati of all parts of the world, and immortalize his own name.[2]

The German tourist August von Kotzebue described the extent of the collection. Visiting this museum in 1805, he noted that 'A few hours may be passed here very agreeably; for the number of the most interesting inscriptions amounts to about six hundred, and a residence of several months would be required entirely to exhaust this source of pleasure.'³

Maffei was passionate about all things classical, and particularly about any remains found in or around Verona, publishing his researches in his thoroughgoing folio volume of 1732 entitled *Verona illustrata*. This book was well known to foreign visitors, notably the English, as a consequence of Maffei's visit to England in 1736 where he met the likes of Lord Burlington and the Earl of Oxford. Whilst there, he was also made a member of the Royal Society of Antiquaries and received an honorary doctorate from the University of Oxford. However, this last involved an occasion not entirely to his liking:

> After putting on the heavy red doctoral gown with great ceremony, Maffei then had to endure an interminable oration in Latin in his honour; he said later that he had only managed to listen without blushing because he found the Latin as pronounced by an Englishman, as incomprehensible as any Indian language.⁴

The Scottish architect James Adam noted a purchase he made in 1761: 'List of books added to my collection in Italy – folios [...] Antiquities of Verona.'⁵ This folio volume was very likely to have been a copy of Maffei's book. In 1785 Hester Piozzi praised both the city and Maffei: 'How beautiful the entrance is of this charming city, how grand the gate, how handsome the drive forward [...] may all be read here in a printed book called *Verona illustrata* [...].'⁶

The size of this work, however, proved awkward for tourists to use as a guidebook. Thus in 1795 a scaled-down version called *Compendio della Verona illustrata* was produced, with the frontispiece declaring it to be principally for the use of foreigners. Sundry visitors with some knowledge of Italian did apparently use this smaller edition. Kotzebue, for instance, stated that on his 1805 visit he had 'inspected the museum with Maffei in my hand [...]'. For practical reasons, this was probably the smaller *Compendio*.⁷ That it was advisable to do so was clear to d'Uklanski in 1807:

> The keeper of the museum christens the busts and heads at pleasure, appropriating one to Livia, another to Tantalus, a third to Aeneas, easily misleading him who is a dilettante, but no connoisseur. To avoid groping in the dark, it is best to provide one's self with Maffei's description of the lapidarium, which is a key to the whole.⁸

The Reverend John Eustace, well-known as an antiquary, also advocated the use of this work even though he was later to publish – in English – his own very successful and comprehensive *A tour through Italy* in 1813.

While a visit to the *lapidarium* was essential to those in search of the antique, its contents were by no means sacrosanct to the French troops under Napoleon who invaded Verona in 1796. D'Uklanski observed:

> Some excellent specimens have been taken out of the cement by the French, and sent to Paris [...] An eminent specimen was the will of Epicteta, a Spartan lady, engraved on large flags, which the French removed from the wall. The same fate befell a Diomedes of bronze.[9]

It seems that many of these antiquities were not amongst the art works returned to Verona after the fall of Napoleon in 1815.

As well as for his provision of this public museum, Maffei was well known for his hospitality to visitors. In 1749, the Earl of Chesterfield advised his son Philip Stanhope, about to commence his Grand Tour, that 'Verona has a pure and clear air, and, as I am informed, a great deal of good company. Marquis Maffei, alone, would be worth going there for.'[10] Stanhope did indeed visit the city, accompanied by his tutor, Mr Harte, but it is not known whether he made contact with Maffei.

Another such aristocratic visitor was Lady Mary Wortley Montagu, who received a personal welcome from Maffei. In a letter of 1754 to her daughter, the Countess of Bute, Lady Mary gave a detailed description of how Maffei liked to pass his time:

> After having made the tour of Europe in search of antiquities, he fixed his residence in his native town of Verona, where he erected himself a little empire, from the general esteem, and a Conversazione – so they call an assembly – which he established in his palace, which is one of the largest in that place, and so luckily situated that it is between the theatre and the ancient amphitheatre.
>
> He made piazzas leading to each of them, filled with shops, where were sold coffee, tea, chocolate, all sorts of sweetmeats, and in the midst, a court well kept, and sanded for the use of those young gentlemen who would exercise their managed horses, or shew their mistresses their skill in riding.
>
> His gallery was open every evening at five o'clock, where he had a fine collection of antiquities, and two large cabinets of medals, intaglios, and cameos, arranged in exact order. His library joined to it; and on the other side, a suite of fine rooms, the first of which was destined to dancing, the second to cards – but all games of hazard proscribed, – and the others – where he himself presided in an easy chair – sacred to conversation, which always turned upon some point of learning, either historical or poetical:

controversy and politics being utterly prohibited. He generally proposed the subject, and took great delight in instructing the young people, who were obliged to seek the medal, or explain the description, that illustrated any fact they discoursed of.

Those who chose the diversion of the public walks, or the theatre, went thither, but never failed returning to give an account of the drama, which produced a critical dissertation on that subject. The walkers contributed to the entertainment by an account of some herb or flower, which led the way to a botanical conversation; or, if they were such inaccurate observers as to have nothing of that kind to offer, they repeated some pastoral description.

One day in the week was set apart for music, vocal or instrumental, but no mercenaries were admitted to the concert.

Thus at very little expense (his fortune not admitting a large one), he had the happiness of giving his countrymen a taste of polite pleasure, and showing the youth how to pass their time without debauchery.[11]

James Silk Buckingham, quoting the above letter in his account of his own travels a century later, added:

A young English nobleman doing like this in every county in England – and there are at least a dozen country gentlemen in every county town, whose fortunes would enable them to do this without feeling the expense – would effect more public good in correcting and refining the general taste, and giving an intellectual tone to both male and female society, than all the hunts, races, balls, and dinners, that are given in each through the season.[12]

This kind of more serious social gathering might well not, however, have been to the taste of gentlemen squires in many an English county town.

The young Joseph Spence, travelling companion of Charles Sackville, later 2nd duke of Dorset, gave rather a different account of an evening with Maffei in a letter to his mother from Verona, dated November 1731:

Here (you must know) lives the famous Scipio Maffei. He is by title a Marquis, and for learning one of the most eminent men now in Italy. He is an old bachelor, and talks as if the ladies had played him some scurvy tricks in his youth. Among other things he introduced us to a ball (where I was most horribly afraid of being asked to dance) and you cannot conceive how busy and officious the good old gentleman was among all the ladies, from the eldest to the youngest. He'd whisper each so soon as ever she stood still, and was sometimes so entangled in the ranks that he'd put the whole dance into confusion. However, everybody is fond of him, for he is a mighty good man, and has just built an opera house for them in Verona, which is a very pretty one. Round it are separate rooms for dancing, conversation, concerts etc, all contrived and carried on by this good gentleman, who into the bargain in his time has himself written operas and one of the best tragedies that was ever written in their language. So that, you see, he is a great scholar, a nobleman, a poet, and a spoiler of dances, all at one and the same time.[13]

The tone of the letter was clearly appropriate for Spence's mother, directed towards her son's social activities rather than his visits to Roman antiquities, for instance.

Spence, himself later professor of poetry at Oxford, met Maffei on another occasion, which provided yet a further example of the Italian's talents. Maffei was the author of several plays, including *La fida ninfa* which was in rehearsal during the Englishman's stay in Verona; despite a personal invitation from the great man and the lure of the play's music being by Vivaldi, Spence and his companion did not stay for the opening performance early in 1732 (Plate 8b). Another of Maffei's plays was *Merope*, a classical tragedy completed in 1712, which was sufficiently well known for Alexander Pope to be translating it into English at the time of the Italian's visit to Oxford in 1736.[14]

Lady Mary Wortley Montagu supplied further evidence of Maffei's love of both theatre and music. He tried unsuccessfully to persuade her to join a party of Veronese nobles who, according to him, enjoyed an annual excursion into the countryside that combined pleasure and music:

In the Autumn (which is here the pleasantest season of the year) a Band of about Thirty join their hunting Equipages, and carrying with them a Portable Theatre and a set of music, make a progress in the neighbouring Provinces where they hunt every morning, perform an Opera every Sunday and other plays the rest of the Week, to the Entertainment of all the Neighbourhood.[15]

How splendid it must have been to be witness to such a performance.

Maffei seemed to enjoy almost universal approbation from foreigners visiting Verona, but Horace Mann, that indefatigable gossip and correspondent of Horace Walpole, declared in a 1741 letter that 'Maffei constantly quarrels with everyone that contradicts him and declares them fools *ipso facto*.'[16] It may indeed be that the Marquis was used to getting his own way, but he undoubtedly had the interests of Verona at heart; not only did he provide cultural facilities for the upper-class residents of the city, but he was also aware of the needs of traders and businessmen. Englishman James Wilson, visiting in about 1817, noted that 'La Fiera is the spot where the two annual fairs are held, a convenience given to the city by that same great benefactor, the M Maffei.'[17]

Another traveller admired Maffei for being capable of changing his mind when he found himself in the wrong. The German John Keysler remarked thus:

> He is a very polite gentleman and most agreeable in conversation. Formerly he entertained no great esteem for the Germans; but now he is thoroughly cured of that prejudice; and, when he mentions the Leipsic academy, he knows not how to praise it sufficiently.[18]

Maffei also displayed a level of modesty over the naming of his museum of antiquities. According to the Frenchman Pasquin, writing in 1839, his friends resolved to call it the Maffeian,

> [...] though he had named it the Verona museum. The erudition of this good man was so lively, devoted, and persevering, that it may almost be called patriotism. Over the door of the theatre may at last be seen the bust voted to him by the Academy as well as the inscription to his honour, which he constantly refused while living, and even had it effaced when his fellow-citizens had put it up in his absence, a rare instance of the sincerity of this kind of modesty.[19]

Maffei's legacy continues to be a source of pride to today's citizens, with his imposing Palazzo Maffei in Piazza Erbe still standing as one of the few Baroque buildings in Verona. He is remembered principally for his authorship, his donation of antiquarian books to the Biblioteca Capitolare and his collection of antiquities in the *lapidarium*. Many of his contemporaries also recalled his generosity in providing a public space for the city's two annual fairs, so important for the trade upon which Verona depended.

CHAPTER 12

Verona's Many Churches

The churches of Verona
are numerous, magnificent, and replete with reminiscences.[1]

Antoine Claude Pasquin, 1839

TOURISTS SEEM RARELY to have visited more than four or five of Verona's principal churches. An exception was the Frenchman Antoine Pasquin, one of the most thorough explorers of the city, who detailed all the churches and their treasures in his *Travels in Italy*. Few visitors were as dismissive as The Reverend William Berrian from New York who, there in 1818, stated baldly: 'The churches of Verona are generally built in bad taste.'[2] In 1854, by contrast, the Gothic revival architect George Edmund Street devoted many pages to describing these historic buildings, enthusing in particular about San Zeno Maggiore, Sant'Anastasia and San Fermo Maggiore.[3] The Duomo or cathedral, San Zeno and San Fermo all dated back at least in part to the twelfth century, in a style known as Romanesque; other city churches included the fifteenth-century Sant'Anastasia, and the sixteenth-century Santa Maria in Organo and San Giorgio in Braida, both designed to some extent by Michele Sanmicheli.

Often the first church – and sometimes the only one – to be visited was the twelfth-century Duomo. Montaigne and his companion were early visitors there, recording their impressions in 1580.

> We went to see the cathedral, where M. de Montaigne was extremely surprised at the manner in which, upon such a day, and at high mass, the persons present conducted themselves; they were standing about in groups, even in the choir, talking to one another in no very under tones, with their caps on, and their backs turned to the altar, and, indeed, appearing to take

no heed of the service, except just at the elevation. There was an organ and some violins, which accompanied the service of the mass.[4]

In 1816, well over 200 years later, the architect Joseph Woods observed the same sort of behaviour, including the permitting of visits by tourists during services:

> It does not seem to be considered any sort of intrusion to go about these churches, even during the performance of the religious ceremonies. One frequently sees the Italians doing so themselves, and in the larger churches, the attendants, who hope to make something of your curiosity, take you about to all parts, and talk as loudly as if there were not a soul present. In general, however, they are very careful to bend one knee on passing opposite the high altar, and frequently make a similar obeisance at some of the side altars.[5]

The first comments visitors made about the structure of the Duomo were often directed at its ornate portico on the west front. In 1815, Dr Herman Friedländer, a convert from Judaism to Christianity, noted:

> The exterior of the cathedral is more attractive by the peculiarity than by the beauty of its ornaments. Its covered porch is supported by two spiral pillars, resting upon griffins; and a second porch, likewise on pillars, is erected above it. Two gigantic figures, in basso relievo, representing the famous palatines, Roland and Olivier, keep the watch near this porch [...][6]

Elizabeth Gibbes, travelling with her parents, had already heard in 1789 of the response of one visitor to these carvings. 'At the cathedral the ciceroni showed us the statue of Orlando, & that of Olivero (?) on the outside of the Church & told us of the enthusiasm with which an Englishman had kissed Orlando's toe.'[7] Lady Blessington later added, 'These personages have twisted mustachios, wear armour, and carry drawn swords; which formidable appendages give them a very grim and fierce appearance.'[8] The representation of two legendary warriors – albeit Christian – at the entrance to a place of worship was unusual, and likely to cause some comment.

The Duomo's architectural feature of columns supported on the backs of recumbent lions or griffins at the entrance to churches was common in Verona, something that the American priest Henry Field noted in 1858.

> To complete the strange effect, the columns in front rest their solid feet upon the backs of lions so that it requires but little imagination to animate

the whole structure; to imagine it a huge zebra or a cameleopard, couchant, but, if startled, ready to spring up and run away. Yet, strange to say, the effect of such a building here with all its Italian surroundings, is not unpleasing.[9]

Inside the cathedral, travellers were not particularly impressed. Aubrey de la Mottraye, a Frenchman who lived in England for many years and had seen Milan's Duomo beforehand, was rather dismissive in 1697, with the observation that 'the Cathedral is but small'. But he added for some reason that 'its Canons are Persons of the best Rank in Italy'.[10] The painting of the *Assumption of the Virgin* by Titian usually gave rise to some comment, except of course during its sojourn in France on Napoleon's orders; it was finally returned about 1816. The Prussian John Bramsen admitted, 'Our time permitted us merely to view the cathedral, and to admire the noble picture of the Assumption, from the pencil of Titian, which is its greatest ornament.'[11] It is understandable that he was in a hurry since, in a two-year tour with the eldest son of Sir John Maxwell, Bart, the pair managed to travel as far afield as Egypt and Greece.

The only other item of interest thought worthy of much comment was the tomb of Pope Lucius III who, having been driven out of Rome by local opposition, had been granted asylum in Verona and died there in 1185. Pasquin noted in about 1839 a curious feature of this tomb: 'A quaint antique quatrain, followed by a characteristic inscription, recounts the pontiff's adventures.'[12] Buckingham, who visited a few years later, noted that although he found the interior of the Duomo imposing, 'everything was dirty and neglected. We saw many pictures – originally no doubt of merit but now much decayed [...].'[13]

George Street was more impressed in the 1850s: 'The Duomo is a really fine church [...] with its lofty red marble columns [...]. The whole interior is really very solemn, and specially beautiful on this bright September day, with almost all the light excluded by thick curtains [...].' He decided he would stay on for a service.

> There was a great throng of people, and we had some difficulty in finding even standing room among them; we were not at all sorry, however, to have gone, for we came in for a sermon most energetically preached, and enforcing in very powerful language the necessity of repentance.[14]

The Biblioteca Capitolare, situated near the Duomo and founded in the fifth century, is one of the oldest libraries in Europe, housing many important ecclesiastical and secular texts. It is possible that Dante studied there;

Petrarch certainly did, unearthing some previously unknown letters of Cicero. Maffei also took an active interest in the library, donating a number of manuscripts in the early 1700s. There in 1820, Da Persico noted that the French had seized codices, manuscripts and rare printed books in 1797; only about two-thirds of these were later returned. Twenty years later, Pasquin calculated that the Biblioteca still held 1,600 manuscripts in Greek and Latin, dating from the fourth to the twelfth centuries; on her 1840 visit, Lady Blessington agreed with his assessment. William Chambers, there in 1862, found 'several palimpsests of great rarity', something which must have pleased him, as he had described Verona itself as 'very dull'. He added, 'The only thing we cared much about seeing were these literary curiosities.'[15]

San Zeno has been described as the finest Romanesque church in North Italy, and so is worthy of its own chapter, which follows on from this one. San Fermo Maggiore is an outstanding Gothic church with a Romanesque crypt; it also has a very fine wooden 'ship's-keel' coffered ceiling; Murray's 1842 *Hand-book* noted that 'such roofs are rare in Italy, and are peculiar architectural features of ancient Verona'.[16] As ever, Pasquin visited, giving his usual thorough description of San Fermo's content and pointing out that some of the 1510 bronzes on the Della Torre tomb by one Andrea Briosco, also known as Riccio, had been removed to Paris by Napoleon.[17] 'J.W.' also mentioned this Della Torre family tomb in 1862, together with a curious piece of information. 'In this church is also a monument to Antonio Pelacani (or "skin the dogs") and his wife Mabilia Pelavicini (or "skin the neighbours.")'[18]

The early fifteenth-century Dominican church of Sant'Anastasia received mostly favourable comments, despite the facade being largely unfinished, with only the portal decorated in different coloured local marbles. The architect Joseph Woods thought that, if the front had been completed, the church would probably be 'the most perfect specimen in existence of the style of architecture to which it belongs'.[19] It had been built to a design from the earlier period of the Scaliger dynasty; Pasquin considered that 'with its sculptured doors, majestic columns, lofty nave, cupola, and choir, [it] is a monument of the magnificence of those princes as well as of the epoch'.[20] The French historian Taine, there in 1864, had mixed feelings, describing Sant'Anastasia's art as from 'a primitive period' with

> [...] figures of the fifteenth century, occasionally a little clumsy, stiff and too real, but so expressive that the perfection of the masters appears languid alongside of their animated deformity. The chapel Pellegrini, wainscoted entirely with terra-cotta, is a large sculptured picture in compartments, where evangelical subjects unite and separate with admirable richness and originality of imagination.[21]

Occasionally, visitors noticed the two holy water stoups supported by hunchbacks just inside the church, one of which was the work of Paulo Veronese's father. Keysler, there in the 1730s, expressed his distaste: 'I could not but take notice here of a very great impropriety, namely, the holy water vessels at the entrance of the church are supported by two grotesque figures, representing harlequins or buffoons.'[22] On his visit in about 1846, Buckingham merely noted, 'The two fonts for holy water are supported by crouching figures, in marble, the size of life, most grotesque in their appearance […].' He made one further dismissive comment to the effect that 'the frescoes and paintings had nothing very beautiful in them, although we saw them all'.[23] It is perhaps surprising that rarely were observations made about the Pisanello fresco of St George for which this church is now widely famous: Pasquin did note their existence but made no further comment.

The church of Santa Maria in Organo featured large in travellers' accounts, more because of a wooden statue it possessed than because of its many undoubted architectural and artistic merits. One of the first people to mention this statue was the Protestant Francis Misson, visiting the city in the 1680s. He described how a French merchant had told him that the donkey on which Jesus rode into Jerusalem had left Palestine and crossed the sea, which had become as smooth as glass to assist its passage. After a long journey, the donkey finally took up residence in Verona; on its death, local monks had a wooden effigy made of it in which to store reliquaries or even the bones of the dead donkey. Subsequently, the effigy was carried through the streets of Verona at religious festivals.[24]

Many travellers repeated this story. De Blainville, who particularly disliked and distrusted Misson's book, went to Santa Maria in Organo in 1707 in order to see for himself.

> It was entirely upon the credit of this traveller, that we asked for a sight of these fine relicks; but the religious, to whom we addressed ourselves for that purpose, fell into a passion, and treated us as so many visionaries and hereticks, and we were afraid that they would even turn us out of their church as such by the shoulders. Being mortified with this smart rebuff, we made the best of our way out […][25]

Clearly, the clergy of the church were angry at the idea that heretics were visiting merely to view this relic and then fall to mocking it.

Fortunately, some were able to recognize the real artistic merits of Santa Maria in Organo. The main part dates back to the fifteenth century; its sixteenth-century front was designed by Michele Sanmicheli but unfortunately was never completed. One of the church's glories is the intarsia work on the choir stalls depicting architectural scenes, created by Fra' Giovanni da Verona in the 1490s. In his book of 1839, Pasquin admired the workmanship, but had his reservations.

> A wooden chandelier, in the chapel of the Holy Sacrament, the carvings on the wainscot of the choir, and especially the sacristy, by Frà Giovanni, an Olivetan monk of Verona, are perfect. I observed among these last the Coliseum, the tomb of Augustus, and other Roman antiquities which did not seem quite suitable subjects for a sacristy; they are another instance of the freedom of the arts in Italy before the council of Trent. This sacristy was mentioned by Vasari as the finest in Italy [...][26]

The church of San Giorgio in Braida situated in Veronetta across Ponte Pietra received many visitors, but mainly for its collection of pictures. It was said to be of ancient foundation, although the existing building with its impressive dome dated from the sixteenth century. Pasquin, there in 1839, was unable to name the architect conclusively: 'some attribute it to San Micheli, others to Sansovino, and it is worthy of both: but what belongs to San Micheli is the skilful daring with which the sides are supported in order to lay the cupola on the cross-aisle of the nave'.[27] The *campanile*, however, was certainly by Sanmicheli. Even the *Compendio* of 1795 written specially for tourists had little to say about the church itself, but a great deal to say about its pictures. These included Veronese's altarpiece of the *Martyrdom of St George*. Elizabeth Gibbes went there with her family and 'saw the Picture of St George by Paul Veronese – at St Giorgio'.[28] However, she was not impressed by it. Friedländer called the church 'rich in paintings, although that which crowns them all, the martyrdom of St George, by P. Veronese, is not yet returned from Paris'.[29] (This was returned after Napoleon's fall.)

San Bernardino, lying a little way from the centre of Verona, is a large and rather austere Gothic building. Pasquin was as thorough as ever in his description of its frescoes and altarpieces, but most tourists only noted the Pellegrini chapel. In 1816 Joseph Woods

> [...] visited the church of San Bernardino, where is a beautiful little circular chapel of the Pellegrini family, built by Michele Sanmicheli, who ranks among the best architects of this part of Italy; probably inferior only to Palladio [...] it is perhaps too high in proportion to its size. It has spirally fluted columns, and many other defects might be pointed out in the details; but though Sanmicheli furnished the designs, it was not finished under his

direction; and he is said, indeed, to have been very much dissatisfied with the execution.[30]

About 20 years later The Reverend G.W.D. Evans declared that the chapel's fault was 'like that of so many other churches and chapels in Italy [...] excess of ornament'.[31] Cadell, however, had had no adverse criticism to make in 1817, describing it as 'a round chapel highly finished, with a cupola, the whole interior formed of polished marble of a dull white, and of that particular kind called bronzino marble, from the neighbourhood of Verona, most accurately joined, and skilfully carved'.[32] His noticing of the use of local marble was fairly unusual among travellers, despite the extensive use of marble throughout the city, much of it coming from nearby quarries.

In 1839, Pasquin was one of the very few to comment on the church of Santi Nazaro e Celso, situated in Veronetta well away from the centre of the city.

> The oldest Christian antiquity of Verona, and even of all the Venetian provinces, is perhaps the church of Saint Nazarius and Saint Celsus, for it may possibly be of the sixth century. The grottoes adjacent served for retreats to the first Christians, and may be called the catacombs of Verona. The monastery is partly demolished and is occupied by a soap-boiler; this manufacturer is a friend of the arts, and has had the paintings of the seventh century which are still visible drawn and engraved [...][33]

Augustus Hare was able to find further details in the area in the 1870s:

> Behind this church (SS Nazaro e Celso) is a private garden (which once belonged to the monastery) backed by abrupt cliffs, in which is a most interesting caverned Chapel of the earliest Christian Art in the north, adorned with rude frescoes much like those in the Roman catacombs. From the outer cave, a roughly-hewn passage leads into this tiny sanctuary; both retain their ancient mosaic pavements. Over the centre of the vault is the Saviour in benediction: over the altar, S. Michael between SS. Nazaro and Celso; on the left is a tomb which has never been opened. The proprietor kindly allows the chapel to be visited on application at the house adjoining the church.[34]

One other out-of-the-way church rarely mentioned was the sanctuary of the Madonna di Campagna, situated on a hilltop just outside the city. Montaigne noted in 1580 that:

> As we were leaving Verona, we saw the church of Our Lady of Miracles, celebrated for a number of strange things that have taken place in it, in consequence of which the town entirely rebuilt the edifice, in a well-planned circular form.[35]

Lord Cranborne, son of Robert Cecil, earl of Salisbury, visited Verona on his Grand Tour in 1610–11, taking in the Arena and the Giusti Gardens as well as this sanctuary, which he described as 'done in the round', with its architecture being 'rather pretty'. Six months earlier another Englishman had visited, describing the building as being 'like the Cockepitt in Whitehall' and praising it as 'the best contrived peace of woorke in the worlde'.[36] It was designed by Michele Sanmicheli, but completed some years later by Bernardino Brugnoli. Later travellers seem rarely to have visited this church, other than the indefatigable Pasquin who described it as 'charming'.[37] By 1842, however, it was mentioned in Murray's *Hand-book*, making visits by tourists more likely.[38]

Pasquin's very full coverage of the churches of Verona and the art within them, in his *Historical, literary and artistical travels...* of 1839, included also (using his spelling) Saint Helena, Saint Euphemia, Saint Sebastian, Santa Maria della Scala, Saint Thomas *Cantuariense* and Saint Stephen. His was a guide which was as full as any visiting tourist could reasonably hope for; yet even he failed to mention the ancient and beautiful church of San Lorenzo just off the city's main Corso, and of great architectural interest.

Some tourists inevitably expressed their weariness after visiting endless churches. 'J.W.' in the 1860s said of San Fermo: 'There were many good pictures in this church, but really we were beginning to be heartily sick of seeing pictures, and therefore did not pay much attention to them.'[39] A little later, the American Latrobe summed up the question of church visits after restricting himself to the Duomo, San Zeno and Sant'Anastasia.

> There are more churches in Verona than those here mentioned, but, after the traveler has passed through as many cities as had already been visited by the party, he feels, unless he has a special vocation in that direction, that specimens are what he wants, rather than the entire collection; and if these specimens are peculiar and characteristic, so much the better.[40]

Many of those trying to fit in a visit to Verona's numerous churches would surely have concurred with Latrobe's opinions.

CHAPTER 13

San Zeno Maggiore

But it is, I think, the church of San Zenone,
with its detached campanile of alternate lines of brick and marble,
that strikes as it were the keynote of this city of antiquity and romance.[1]

Edward Hutton, Italy and the Italians, *1903*

EDWARD HUTTON, ITALOPHILE, travel writer and art historian, thought the church of San Zeno Maggiore, also known as San Zenone, 'by far the most interesting church in Verona, and [...] one of the finest Romanesque buildings in Italy'.[2] There was a church on the site in the ninth century, but the present building dates mostly from the twelfth century and was finally completed in about 1390. Not everyone viewed it as enthusiastically as Hutton; it was not really until John Ruskin championed it as an outstanding example of medieval Romanesque architecture that the merits of San Zeno became more widely recognized. Earlier travellers tended to comment on specific features such as the church's ancient bronze doors or the enormous porphyry basin that now stands near the west end, rather than remarking on the architectural character of the building itself.

In 1816 Joseph Woods, an architect by training, was one of the first to consider San Zeno within its historical context. 'The most interesting example at Verona to the antiquary, as a specimen of the architecture of the depth of the middle ages, is the church of S. Zeno. It is a most curious edifice, both externally and internally.'[3] About 20 years later, Hume Weatherhead was less impressed, saying that as a Gothic building San Zeno

> [...] affords samples of rudeness of sculpture not often to be met with. The visitor has only to observe that which was meant to adorn each side of the front portal, to see from what barbarous beginnings an art of so much sublime beauty may regenerate.[4]

Some time later, in 1854, the architect George Edmund Street set out to visit the church and, although finding it thoroughly neglected, found much to praise.

> A longish walk through squalid suburbs leads us to the open space in front of the noble basilica of San Zenone; it is a desolate waste-looking space, and the poor, old, uncared-for church looks now as though its day was well-nigh past; as if neglect and apathy were all that men could give now where once they were wont to lavish so much of their treasure, and love, and art.

He also found the cloister 'in a very sad state of filth, neglected and unused, and will, I fear, ere long become ruinous'. Despite all this, San Zeno's

> [...] proportions are so very grand, and its detail generally so perfect, that I think it may certainly be regarded as on the whole a noble example of its class; indeed, except the very best Gothic work of the best period, I doubt whether any work of the Middle Ages so much commands respect and admiration as this Lombard work.[5]

It is evident that architecturally well-informed visitors like Street used the terms Gothic or Lombard variously to describe this particular church.

In 1929, Arnold Bennett had obviously already had his fill of Italian churches, but still declared:

> One church, San Zeno Maggiore, in a squalid suburb, had to be inspected, no matter how serious your surfeit of churches. It has the reputation of being the finest Romanesque church in North Italy, with the oldest bronze doors, and it possesses a celebrated and large Mantegna picture, the Madonna Enthroned. Impossible to keep out of this renowned church, which was begun in the eleventh century – and too conscientiously restored in the late nineteenth.[6]

A tour of San Zeno reveals features that received particular comment over the years. In 1687, Misson was very negative about the relief carvings on the facade, mostly depicting scenes from Biblical stories: 'It must be confess'd, the Sculpters of that Age were miserable Artists. Never were there such wretched Figures as these in the Front of this Church.'[7] The panels attracting his attention were those depicting Theodoric the Ostrogoth on horseback pursuing a stag with dogs, with a contemporary inscription describing how the devil had sent the stag to lure Theodoric to hell. Buckingham, there in about 1846, commented that these particular panels

[…] are injured by holes made by the boys, who play about here at all hours of the day – some were spinning tops on our arrival. They pretend that they smell sulphur when these holes are made, and suppose this to be the mode in which the Evil One expresses his satisfaction.[8]

To the right and left of the front porch are red porphyry lions – 'of a genus not yet described', as Dudley Costello put it, in 1861 – bearing columns on their backs.[9]

The massive wooden doors forming the original entrance are now closed off to protect them from the weather; they are decorated with bronze panels depicting Biblical scenes from the Old and New Testaments, and are thought to date in part back to the ninth century. The early English traveller Coryat described these doors in 1608 as 'decked with many pretty little peeces of brasse, wherein many notable histories of the bible are passing curiously described'.[10] Joseph Woods called the 48 bronze panels 'curious, as early specimens of art, but not pretending to any beauty',[11] while a few years later, in 1826, Pasquin thought they provided 'grotesque emblems […] of curious workmanship'.[12] However, John Ruskin, who championed San Zeno and its Romanesque architecture whenever he could, called the doors 'the most wonderful I have seen in Italy […] wonderfully archaic, and the faces usually most barbarous, but in the telling of the story […] it would be difficult to match them'.[13] Most visitors today would probably be in agreement with Ruskin.

Visiting in 1864, however, the Frenchman Hippolyte Taine did not mince his words on the subject.

> We take a cab and drive to the end of the town, to San Zenone, the most curious of these churches […] some portions, as, for instance, the sculptures of a door, belong to the more ancient times; except at Pisa I have seen none so barbarous. The Christ at the pillar looks like a bear mounting a tree; the judges, the executioners and the personages belonging to other biblical stories resemble the gross caricatures of clumsy Germans in their overcoats. In another place Christ on his throne has no skull, the entire face being absorbed by the chin; the wondering, projecting eyes are those of a frog, while around him the angels with their wings are bats with human heads. The heads throughout are enormous, disproportionate and pitiful; below badly jointed limbs toss about floating bellies. These figures all swim through the air on different planes in the most insensate manner, as if the sculptor or founder aimed to excite a laugh.[14]

Clearly, nothing would have convinced Taine of the merits of these doors, whether championed by Ruskin or anyone else.

Some expressed curiosity about the large circular window above the main entrance, often described as a Wheel of Fortune because of the positioning of the emblematic figures carved around it. Hester Piozzi noticed the 'six figures curiously disposed [...] two mounting, two sitting and two tumbling'.[15] Buckingham gave a more detailed account.

> On the top of this western front of the Church, is a circular window – said to be the type of all subsequent ones of this shape, which form so great an ornament in the finest Gothic edifices of France, Germany, and England. It has here, however, a specific meaning. It is called the Wheel of Fortune, and represents, on the top, the figure of a king erect, in full enjoyment of sovereign power. The wheel is supposed to turn, and behold, on the right-hand side, the figure of the once prosperous monarch falling head foremost into adversity; another revolution brings him to the bottom, where he lies prostrate at the antipodes of the point from which he was first moved. But another revolution causes the wheel to ascend, and behold, he begins to resume a more favourable position; till a last revolution brings him back again to his original place.[16]

There was some dispute about whether this window was in its original position. Our architect Woods called it 'a wheel window, which interrupts the lines of the rest of the architecture; but from the simplicity of its ornaments, I am inclined to believe it part of the original structure'.[17] Pasquin, however, felt that the window had been re-sited.

> The great wheel of Fortune, by Briotolo, a Veronese sculptor of the eleventh century – a precious piece of workmanship suggested by the rapid rise and fall of the princes of that epoch – is now converted into a window in the front, and is not very well seen in its lofty position.[18]

Once inside the church, the visitor found plenty to interest him. San Zeno himself was the eighth bishop of Verona, dying in 380 (or possibly 371). In 1608, Coryat remarked on the saint's statue seated on a throne of Verona marble in the church: 'He is pourtrayed laughing and looking very pleasantly, in his left hand he held a reeden rod [...] at the ende hanged a counterfeited Trowte, in token that hee was much delighted in taking of Trowtes, as a Benedictine Monke tolde me.'[19]

In 1730, the antiquary John Keysler translated an inscription he found on a stone in the oratory chapel, which continued the fishing theme:

> Oft on this stone which lay upon the strand
> the Venerable Zeno took his stand;
> a patient fisher, with his trembling reed,
> intent to captivate the scaly breed.[20]

In the 1850s, the Congregational minister John Stoughton pointed out that the statue depicted the saint as an African 'and fond of fishing, one would think, from the manner of representation. Shrewd and merry looks this ancient worthy, an Isaac Walton of the fourth century.'[21] The American David F. Dorr, who described himself as 'a coloured man' and was, in fact, a runaway slave, was also at pains during his 1852 visit to emphasize that San Zeno was black, but for some reason thought 'his face is the picture of gloom, whilst his brow is stern and commanding',[22] in contrast to the view of Pasquin, who in 1826 had described the saint – far more accurately – as being 'in a roar of laughter'.[23]

The saint is buried in the crypt beneath the upper church, where, according to novelist Henry James, 'you wander among primitive columns whose variously grotesque capitals rise hardly higher than your head'.[24] Here, in Hutton's description of 1903, 'San Zeno lies buried in a stone sarcophagus, mounted in bronze, that, curiously enough, the setting sun, even in so underground a place, sometimes reaches.'[25] An anonymous Scotsman, visiting in 1864, had described San Zeno as 'by far the finest church in Verona, and a magnificent example of Lombard Gothic', but then added curiously, if patriotically, 'the crypt being the finest I have seen next to that of Glasgow Cathedral'.[26]

One other feature that called forth a host of different stories was the massive porphyry basin now standing in the north aisle of the church near the west door. Coryat had it situated inside San Zeno in 1608, but by 1663 Philip Skippon declared it to be 'before the church'; given the size and weight of the basin, moving it would have required considerable effort.[27] Woods, in 1816, said it was

> [...] from a single stone, the external diameter of which is 13 feet 4 inches, the internal 8 feet 8 inches; and the pedestal is formed out of another block of the same material. This stood originally on the outside of the church, and Maffei supposed it to have been intended for washing the feet of pilgrims, before entering the sacred edifice. If so, it would hardly have been elevated on a pedestal.[28]

In the same year, John Hayward declared in his diary that the basin was in fragments; people 'told me it was one of the acts of violence committed by the French soldiers' during their occupation of the city.[29]

De Blainville, after seeing this basin in 1707, undoubtedly gave the most vivid account of its arrival in Verona, while at the same time displaying his innate suspicion of myths held to be true by some Catholics.

> In a cell near that of St Zeno is to be seen a great basin of red marble, pretty much resembling porphyry; this basin is of a prodigious largeness and weight. We are told here, as an indisputable truth, that the devil Asmodeus being quite mad, that St Zeno, Bishop of Verona, said Mass every day in this church, with so much devotion that he converted even the most abandoned, took it into his head one day to go and take up this great basin, which served as a receiver to a fountain in the gardens of the Royal Palace at Lisbon, and without any manner of respect for the presence of Jesus Christ, which the holy Bishop was then elevating in the Sacrament, he threw this enormous vessel into the middle of the church with an amazing noise. It is not very clear whether it came in thro' the door, or broke the roof; but however that be, this accident interrupted the devotion of the good souls who were assisting at Mass, and gave such offence to St Zeno, that after having smartly reprimanded this most impudent devil, he ordered him immediately to carry the vessel to the place from whence he had taken it, under the pain of having a double strapade in Hell. The poor devil, quite stunned with this alternative, threw himself at the feet of the saint, asked pardon for his insolence, begging him to consider the monstrous weight of the basin, and that he was quite out of breath with having already carried it so far. The good bishop, touched by the reasoning and humility of the devil, commanded him only, by way of penance, to take up the basin, and place it at the outer side of the church-door, where it is yet to be seen, with the prints of his claws upon it. This merry story is believed here by the common people as an article of faith.[30]

San Zeno is known today as an outstanding example of Lombard Gothic architecture, visited every year by thousands of tourists. One particular attraction is the altarpiece by Andrea Mantegna of the Madonna and child with saints, dating from the 1450s. However, most early travellers often failed to mention it at all. In 1820, The Reverend Thomas Pennington observed without comment, 'Here also is an old picture of the Madonna by Mantegna (brought back from Paris four years ago)', after its temporary removal by the French.[31] Ruskin thoroughly disliked the painting, despite his admiration for some of Mantegna's work. For Henry James, however, 'The nobly serious character of San Zenone is deepened by its single picture – a masterpiece of the most serious of painters, the severe and exquisite Mantegna.'[32]

Not all visits to San Zeno were happy occasions. On his second visit there in 1864, the dean of Canterbury, Henry Alford, found a nasty surprise awaiting him in the form of a much over-decorated church.

> At Verona, I had prepared our party for being delighted with the magnificent old church of San Zenone, which was vividly in my own remembrance after an absence of eighteen years. What was my disgust, on entering it with them, to find it all packed up in crimson silk lined with white, swathed round the noble pillars, and extending across the raised chancel so as entirely to hide the eastern apse! Besides this, lines of outrageous stage-properties formed avenues up the middle aisle, and were fixed against the pillars: and moveable altars were erected here and there in the space, decked in a taste which would have disgraced a dancing booth at a country fair. To do the sacristan justice, he protested loudly against all this: it was *'brutto, bruttissimo:'* it was to remain only three days longer, and then *'la bella chiesa'* would be seen as usual in all its splendour.[33]

A number of visitors recorded their comments on the lofty bell tower or *campanile* of San Zeno, completed in the twelfth century. It consists of alternating horizontal courses of red and white, a feature common to many church buildings of this date. Architectural historian Robert Willis did leave his opinion in 1835, asserting that 'A practice more destructive of architectural grandeur can scarcely be conceived […].'[34] By contrast, Dudley Costello observed, in 1861, that 'the campanile of San Zenone is one of the most beautiful of its kind in the north of Italy'.[35] Today there can be few visitors standing in the piazza who would fail to see exceptional beauty in both the church and its bell tower, and to describe them as among the outstanding features of the city of Verona.

 CHAPTER 14

Religion through Tourists' Eyes

A gross Bigotry & Superstition [is] universally prevailing, amongst all Ranks of People.[1]

The Honourable William Fitzwilliam, 1769

BEFORE THE REFORMATION, a steady stream of English pilgrims and scholars made their way to Italy. The pilgrims were intent on visiting Rome, centre of the Universal Church and seat of St Peter's successor. The scholars, on the other hand, went to study at Italian universities such as Bologna or Padua; the latter was one of the oldest in Italy and was well known for its faculties of medicine and law. The Catholic scholar John Caius, later founder of a Cambridge college, studied there for five years from 1539 to 1544, while the Protestant traveller and writer Fynes Moryson was also there in the later 1500s. Even after the Reformation, it was still possible for English Protestants to be admitted to Italian universities, particularly to those under the rule of the more tolerant Republic of Venice, provided they behaved discreetly.

It was inevitable, however, that, from the second half of the sixteenth century onwards, the issue of religion would make the visiting of Italy by Englishmen problematic. This was both because of the perceived dangers of Protestants being exposed to Catholic influence, and because of the physical risks English 'heretics' might now run. In February 1596, Edward Smyth, travelling as tutor to Francis Davison, son of Queen Elizabeth's secretary of state, denounced the whole of Italy as a place 'where God is so dishonoured, true religion abolished, piety contemned, and all horrible and monstrous sins publicly maintained'.[2] So worried were the English authorities about these dangers that a licence had to be granted for travel to Europe, something that the Earl of Essex managed to obtain for Smyth and Davison.

Two years later Lord Burghley wrote: 'Suffer not thy sonnes to pass the Alps, for they shall learn nothing there but pride, blasphemy, and atheism.'[3] By 1619, the authorities in England were so nervous of popish influence that there was an outright ban on the English visiting Rome.[4] Some Protestant visitors managed by particular means to avoid any personal threat to themselves as so-called heretics; for instance, the Protestant Fynes Moryson used his considerable language skills to adjust his nationality or religion as the occasion demanded. Thus he posed as Dutch or German in the more dangerous parts of Italy, or as a Frenchman when visiting the Jesuit College in Rome.[5] This particular line of defence cannot have been open to many travellers.

From the point of view of any Protestant tourist in Italy, there was so much evidence of Catholicism 'on view', from the number of churches to the endless depictions of religious art, that there were bound to be many comments – mostly negative – on the subject of religion. One historian of the Grand Tour has noted that, in the mind of the eighteenth-century traveller, 'Catholicism was equated with autocracy, drew on credulity and superstition, and led to misery, poverty, clerical rule and oppression.'[6] This was a fairly standard attitude, but an occasional traveller did manage a less biased approach. For instance, de Blainville in 1707 merely provided factual information about the organization and practice of religion in Verona.

> Verona is the capital of the Veronese, and Suffragan to the Patriarch of Aquilea. It boasts of having had thirty seven bishops canonized, among whom is honest St. Zeno, who was so good-natured as to pardon the devil Asmodeus, for insolently interrupting him in Divine Service.[7]

Visitors over the centuries often made mention of San Zeno himself, the eighth bishop of Verona, who lived in the fourth century and was recorded as being a miracle worker and author of sermons, about 90 of which still survive. He is still the city's well-respected patron saint, with his feast day celebrated every year in April.

Many tourists, however, were forthright in their attacks on the Catholic religion and its practices as recorded in their travel accounts. On a visit to Santa Maria in Organo in the early 1720s, the artist and traveller Edward Wright saw the statue of the ass that allegedly carried Jesus into Jerusalem. He retold the legend, but with additional comments for the benefit of readers in England, which revealed his innate religious bias against Catholicism:

> It is related by some that the remains of the ass that carried our Saviour are pretended to be within the body of the ass [...] How ridiculous soever such

stories may be, I think 'tis of use to mention them, that the English readers who have not been abroad may see by what gross means the people are imposed upon.[8]

The German John Keysler, visiting Verona in the 1730s, was exercised about the difficulties experienced by a Protestant in writing about the religion of another country, particularly a Catholic one.

I have often considered with myself whether it be not practicable for a protestant to write an account of his travels through Italy, in such a manner as not to discover what religion he be of; as it is a qualification requisite in an impartial historian, not to be in favour of any country or religion, so far as the latter implies the external difference of churches or communions.[9]

He felt himself unable to be impartial while in Italy, however, for various reasons, including the presence of exactly the same purported relics of saints in many different churches across the country. His measured reasoning was a rare response to the issue of religious bias. Joseph Spence did not show such a thoughtful attitude in a letter to his mother in 1731. 'We are to go to Rome [...] I own I should long to see it more than a[ny] place in the world, if it were not so full of your Papishes.'[10]

In the early part of the eighteenth century, the political threat to Britain from the Catholic Old and Young Pretenders, exiled descendants of the Stuart kings, was seen as very real. Both James and Charles spent time living in Italy, often in Rome, and were the focus of attention from those Catholic English families who had chosen to live abroad so as to practice their religion freely. The government in England inevitably viewed Rome as a breeding ground for plots to restore the Stuarts to the throne, an issue that became somewhat less contentious after the defeat of Bonnie Prince Charlie at the battle of Culloden in 1745. The political situation in Europe also became somewhat more settled and less threatening to the British state, now presided over by the Hanoverians.

Although there might have been less national concern about the political threat, attitudes towards 'Papists' generally did not alter, with anti-Catholic views still in evidence well into the nineteenth century, even if often expressed rather differently. The Scotsman Adam Hay used a mocking commentary to give voice to his views while travelling from Mantova to Milan in 1825.

Had part of the way a friar for my travelling companion. He was very ignorant – Didn't know where Scotland was! Had never been beyond his little place or his parish more than to Cremona &c. He asked about the

Protestant belief – and was much interested when I told him about our clergy &c. Thought we could not go to Heaven. Laughed at our Priests marrying – What? They don't go to the theatre – but they have wives. Want of words prevented me from reasoning with him. But even if I could have conversed freely he was so bigoted to his opinions that nothing but a miracle could have convinced him.[11]

During his visit to Verona in the 1830s, the tourist Thomas Barlow was equally outspoken, observing that he was now

[...] in a country, whose inhabitants are, for the most part, either under foreign yoke, or quailing under the reign of priestly tyranny, headed by the self-styled successor to the Apostles, the Holy Father, who, having the fabulous keys, locks up in ignorance the minds of his besotted subjects.[12]

Ruskin found a particular reason for criticizing some local Catholics in Verona who failed to show proper respect for their own cathedral.

I have seen with my own eyes, an Austrian Catholic Huzzar tether his horse to a pillar of the cloister of the Duomo of Verona, and a Veronese Catholic washerwoman at the same moment (day at least, to be accurate) tie her clothesline to the nose of the griffin who sustains the northern pillar of its porch. I watched presently a priest come out of the cloister, and under the line, apathetic apparently to both phenomena, for which in reality *he* was answerable, and neither the huzzar nor washerwoman.[13]

He felt this was not just disrespectful to the building; the priest had failed in his responsibility to admonish those who used the cathedral's precincts in such a way.

The Scottish physician Dr George Hume Weatherhead, in the city in 1833, chose a lengthy parody of the story about the statue of the ass in Santa Maria in Organo to drive home his point about the cult of relics.

As many towns have striven with pious and laudable industry to obtain possession of some relic or other of value, Verona is not behind the other places in Italy so blessed; for it can, or at least could, boast of possessing the carcass of the identical ass on which our Saviour rode when he entered into Jerusalem; and the story [...] which the good people of Verona tell, is as follows: – The ass, it seems, when given 'the keys of the field,' that he might pass the remainder of his days as he wist, wearying, it would appear, of rambling about Palestine, took it into his head to travel [...] he must

> needs see foreign parts, and, by way of novelty, Neddy preferred going by sea. But how to accomplish this was the crux, for the reader must know that there were no steamers in those days; when, all of a sudden, and without any hyperborean assistance, the waves flattened as if by a smoothing iron, and the liquid element became hard as crystal. So Neddy walked forth on his travels [...] he at length arrived, dryshod, at Verona, and there abided. After living in great credit for several years, Neddy at last went the way of all flesh – he died one day; an event announced by a lamentable and universal braying over the whole land: never before was there a more melancholy melody heard at the funeral of any ass like unto this, not even in Arcadia. Divine honours were paid to his relics, which were religiously preserved in the belly of an artificial donkey, to the long and great joy and edification of all good souls. This sacred bijou is, or was, kept in the church of Our Lady of the Organs; and the holy statue, with its still more holy entrails, used formerly to be carried in procession by monks in full pontificals on the lamentable anniversary of poor Neddy's death – a ceremony which, I regret to say, the lukewarm piety of the age has caused to be discontinued.[14]

Some travellers attended services in local churches. The American Nathaniel Carter, for instance, left a measured account of a service in Sant'Anastasia in 1826, although still betraying a certain distaste for Catholic practices, or perhaps merely a feeling of uncertainty about something that seemed so foreign to him.

> In the early part of the evening, I strolled to the chapel of St. Anastasia, a stupendous fabric. On entering the door, I heard the voice of one crying in the wilderness of columns and chapels; but it was too dark to distinguish whence the words of the preacher came. In a few minutes the brilliant shrines were all lighted up, flashing a flood of splendour through the long Gothic aisles. A numerous audience, chiefly of females, sitting in chairs and wearing white veils, as also the speaker himself mounted in a pulpit, came into view. The remnant of a popular harangue cost me a sous for a seat, and another sous for the hat, which was kept rattling about my ears, till the collector was appeased. After the sermon, an organ struck up, and a full chorus of voices produced a fine effect. A ceremony followed, which was new to me. A priest touched the heads of throngs of people, who pressed to the altar, with a small silver crucifix, and then held it to their lips to be kissed. The rite occupied an hour or more.[15]

An anonymous Scotsman's visit to Verona in 1830 coincided with a religious festival that he clearly enjoyed, although he was uneasy about what he saw as idolatry:

The morning's walk through Verona turned out highly amusing – It was a 'gran festa' – The whole population, male and female, turned out in their gayest attire to visit as many of the 40 churches this city contains, as their devotion – i.e. the devotions of the women, I never vouch for that of the men – extended to. [...] Now as it was near the birthday of the Virgin all her shrines were decorated with wreaths of fresh flowers and the lamps in front of them trimmed and lighted. The chapel of the Virgin divinity in the cathedral displayed her image of silver, with innumerable tapers burning before it – a purple light was admitted through a fan light above the shrine, so as to produce a very pretty effect. The faces of the congregation were devoutly turned towards the altar of the Goddess, kneeling, praying, counting beads in honour of her. What the deuce! is idolatry in these days of unbounded liberality?[16]

Captain Clayton, who called his 1862 book *Il Pellegrino* or *The Pilgrim*, was clearly anti-Catholic, judging by the tone of his remarks. Having been in Verona in 1859, he described his visit to

[...] the everlasting *duomo*, which to the traveller to all Italian towns, is an architectural black dose to be got over and done with as soon as possible. There was being celebrated within, at the time, a *festa* on account of the Virgin. The organ played one tune; the choristers sang another; and the people, who were sprawling in heaps all over the floor, playing a quiet sort of religious leapfrog, howled whatever air they could most conveniently pitch upon the moment. [...] The incense steamed; large bright eyes of damsels flashed through the flowing veils; the gaudy priest groaned the monotonous chant and went through the usual athletic exercises and gymnastic evolutions required by the service; and the whole terminated by a brilliant *morçeau* on the organ from Bellini's opera of 'I Puritani', and a grand display of squibs and Catherine wheels in the piazza outside, all of which must have been particularly gratifying to the soul of the Virgin.[17]

Some visitors were curious about any local orders of monks and nuns. In 1580, Montaigne visited

[...] a convent of monks here, who call themselves Jesuits of St. Jerome. They are not priests, nor do they perform mass or preach, and the great majority of them are mere ignoramuses; they make the most of their money by their excellence in distilling lemon-flower water, and similar preparations. Both here and elsewhere, these monks wear a white under-dress, with a robe of dark brown over it, and small white skull-caps; there are some very fine young men among them. Their church is handsomely fitted up, as is their refectory, which was laid out for supper when we went in.[18]

In 1608 Coryat had a more depressing encounter with a religious group on the way to a funeral.

> I observed a very mournfull shew performed by Monkes in Verona. For I saw eighteen couples of them accompany a corse of one of their Fraternity to Church, being attired with blacke buckram vailes, and marked with the signe of the starre on the left side of their breasts, girt with a black girdle, their heads covered with a blacke hood that came over all their shoulders and hid all their face. Before their eyes were made two holes to looke out: each of them carried a burning candle in his hand of virgin wax, and some of them three candles [...][19]

This kind of funeral procession was, however, quite normal in Italy, whether the deceased were monks or laymen. On another occasion in 1732, Skippon reported it in a different context.

> We saw a malefactor that was hang'd in the chief piazza, and was left on the gallows till the evening, when he was taken down by this procession, viz. first, some boys went before a cross and a black banner, then two black lanthorns with lighted candles; and after them came many men, habited in black, their faces covered with a black hood, and they singing a doleful tune.[20]

Edward Wright fared better in the early 1720s when he visited the church of San Giorgio and found there 'a Convent of Nuns, few in number, but mostly noble. We were told they were to be removed into other Convents, and to leave theirs to Friars, who were to succeed them in it.'[21] Seventy years later, Sarah Bentham 'visited the Convent of Santa Lucia where Three Nuns came to the Grate & chatted with us & with them came a very pretty Young Lady who was in her years of probation'.[22] All this was about to change; once Napoleon had assumed power across the former Venetian territories in the late 1790s, closed orders were abolished and many religious houses shut down. Murray's 1842 *Hand-book* stated that the Convent of San Giorgio was reputedly 'splendid' in the past, but had been sold off by the French 'for something less than the worth of the materials and is now almost wholly demolished'.[23]

Other visitors made enquiries about the presence of any Jesuits. In 1738–9, the French academic de Brosses went to a performance at the Arena and commented:

> I have never seen so many monks at any church ceremony as there were at this theatre, but there were no Jesuits, and I asked the reason for this. A priest near me said, in answer to my question, that, although more pharisaical than the others, they also occasionally came to the play.[24]

The Roman Catholic priest, Alban Butler, made a similar enquiry in 1745.

> At Verona, and other towns belonging to this state, when I enquired if any Jesuits were established amongst them, I was answered, as at Lucca, 'God be thanked, there are none,' a sentiment entirely opposite to that entertained by all the other towns of Italy.[25]

Why the particular towns of Verona and Lucca were so opposed to the Jesuits was not explained.

The treatment of the Jewish inhabitants of the city, restricted as they were to an area adjacent to Piazza Erbe, aroused several comments. In 1580, Montaigne's companion reported: 'We also went among the Jews, and M. de Montaigne visited their synagogue, and had a long conversation with some of the leading men, respecting their religious ceremonies.'[26] Coryat noted briefly in 1608 that 'There are some Jewes in this city, though not so many as in Venice or Padua, who are shut up from the Christians in their Ghetto by three gates.'[27] Visiting about 100 years later, de Blainville fleshed out these brief remarks, providing details of the regime the Jews lived under.

> Not far from the Exchange lies the Jews Street, which is a great deal larger and cleaner than that of their brethren at Frankfort, tho' not so long. Like that there are two gates one at each end of it, guarded by two soldiers, who are relieved from time to time; they lock the gates every night at seven o'clock, and carry the keys to the governour; so that the poor Israelites are as it were imprisoned in their own street every night, till two other soldiers come next morning at eight o'clock to open their gates.[28]

These restrictions on those of the Jewish faith were common in Italian cities and elsewhere in Europe.

Several travellers had views on Italian church music, but the remarks about *castrati* made by Dr Veryard of Devonshire, visiting in 1682, can only be described as bizarre in the extreme; no other visitor to the city has been found supporting such comments.

> I observ'd that their Vocal Musick in Churches is principally that of Eunuchs, and the Italians are wonderfully taken with their voices tho' Strangers rarely fancy them. Poor People usually cause their Children to be castrated for that intent, drying their testicles and carefully preserving them; for otherwise they are incapacitated to take Priests' Orders. They ordain none that are maim'd or imperfect; but provided they have them in their pocket, they are well enough qualified. Eunuchs are known by their Complexion, and therefore when such of them as are in Orders come to say Mass in a place where they are not known, they must produce their dried Materials (which they purposely carry with them in a Box) before they are permitted.[29]

An anonymous Scot expressed strong views about the shortcomings of church music in Verona in 1864:

> Our inspection of the Duomo was sadly interrupted and our enjoyment marred by the intolerable and most unmusical nasal din created by a host of priests who, if they were praying or chanting, must have had a peculiar idea of the music acceptable in Heaven – I recollect Mr McFarlane the Minister of Anochar (?) narrating that the music the angels danced to is the Scotch Bagpipes and certainly they are heavenly music compared to the infernal din we listened to today in the Duomo of Verona![30]

Not every one would be happy to find bagpipe music in heaven.

So the remarks made by post-Reformation travellers to Verona were often negative, not only those made by the British, but also by those from other parts of Europe. Catholicism was regarded as something foreign and even threatening to those from countries whose history had been deeply affected by Protestantism; Italy displayed its religion so evidently that it is perhaps not surprising that so many expressed their active hostility. Perhaps the last word can be left to Eustace, whose *A classical tour through Italy* of 1815 was one of the most widely used guides, and who was himself a Catholic: he advised the traveller not to take an intolerant attitude to the Catholic Church, but to adopt 'the compassionate indulgence of a mild and humble Christian'.[31] These admirable traits were not much in evidence in many of the accounts left by travellers.

 CHAPTER 15

The Scaligeri Monuments

The tombs of the Scaligers, once sovereign lords of Verona, which stand in a small enclosure in one of the public streets, form a highly picturesque object. They are six in number, each bearing the scaling ladder (scala) and eagle, the remarkable device of the family.¹

The Reverend Charles Williams, 1854

THE SCALIGER OR Scaligeri family ruled Verona from 1259 until about 1387. Like other North Italian towns and cities, Verona had been an autonomous commune from the beginning of the twelfth century; later it came under its own ruling family. This family, also known by the name della Scala from their heraldic emblem of a ladder, once ruled extensive territories, including the cities of Vicenza, Padua and Mantua. Can Grande (or Big Dog) was the most powerful of the Scaligeri, ruling between about 1311 and 1330; he is remembered particularly for giving shelter to Dante during the poet's exile from Florence. In the never-ending struggles for control in an Italy divided into so many small states, rulers tended to side with either the Ghibelline or Holy Roman Imperial power, or the Guelf party and the papacy in Rome. Because of the city's geographical position, Verona's rulers found it to their advantage to be on good terms with the Imperial power which controlled territory to the north, up the valley of the River Adige.

The Scaligeri were responsible for many buildings, including the Castelvecchio palace – now used as the city's museum – and its battlemented brick bridge across the Adige, but their most remarkable legacy must be the group of family monuments which stands to this day in the heart of Verona, just off Piazza Dante – or dei Signori – and next to the tiny church of Santa Maria Antica. Many travellers admired these tombs for their unique architectural form, while others had their reservations about the Gothic style in which they were built.

One of the first Englishmen to comment was the adventurous traveller from Somerset, Thomas Coryat, in 1608; his description is worth quoting at length for his sense of amazement at the strange spectacle:

> I saw the monuments of two of the noble Scaligers of Verona in a little Churchyard, adjoyning to the Church called Maria Antiqua, but a little way distant from that Palace where they lived in former times [...] The fairest whereof is that of Mastinus Scaliger, standing at one corner of the Churchyard, which is such an exceedingly sumptuous Mausoleum that I saw not the like in Italy [...] Upon the toppe of all, even upon a little pinnacle standeth the statue of Mastinus Scaliger himselfe on horsebacke made of alabaster. It doth very neare represent the living shape of him. For it is said it was made in his life time [...] The other monument is of Canis Grandis, or Magnus Scaliger, which standeth in another corner of the same Churchyard right opposite unto this, the same being a very magnificent thing, adorned with many pillars and statues of marble, but something inferiour to this [...] Also there is a third monument of another Scaliger Prince, called Canis Signoris; which is erected directly over the Church dore, the Epitaph whereof I could not perfectly reade.[2]

Alban Butler, Roman Catholic priest and hagiographer, accompanied the Earl of Shrewsbury and his sons on their Grand Tour, visiting Verona in 1745: 'The lofty Monuments of the Scaligers, lords of Verona, are very curious, and their engravings, odd fancies, and inscriptions, are not a little diverting.'[3] Forty years on, though, Thomas Martyn, priest and distinguished botanist, described these mausolea of the Scaligeri as 'curious old monuments, in a bad taste'.[4] In the late 1780s, Hester Piozzi wrote about her visit to 'some fine old black-looking monuments [...] to the memories of the Scaligers'. At this time, the architecture of the Middle Ages – and hence the Scaliger tombs – was described as 'gothic', a term that was in origin derogatory because of its association with the destructive Goth tribes. For Piozzi, the Goths had been guilty of 'tyranny and gloomy suspicion' as well as 'gross superstition, indulgence of brutal appetite, and diabolical revenge'.[5] Hence, by association, she did not care for the tombs.

Such attitudes reflected a period when medieval architecture in Italy was little admired or understood because it did not resemble northern European architecture, and because the Middle Ages were regarded as primitive and barbaric, just like the Goth tribes. It was not really until the nineteenth century that opinions about Gothic architecture and art would change fundamentally, with people such as John Ruskin championing Italian medieval buildings, and in particular the Scaligeri tombs. There was, however, an eighteenth-century visitor who indicated a shift of opinion regarding the Gothic. Thomas Broderick, in Verona in 1750, wrote thus to a friend.

> One's sentiments, in regard to what is beautiful, change very often in the course of a few observations [...] You saw me just now in love with the Doric arch to such a degree as to condemn myself for having been pleased with any thing in the Gothic style: I am now in humour again with that rude exuberant taste. I have seen the tomb of C. Scaliger, lord of Verona [...][6]

Scotsman Joseph Forsyth also admired these monuments, while marvelling at their survival. Visiting in 1803, he described them as 'models of the most elegant Gothic, light, open, spiry, full of statues caged in their fretted niches; yet slender as they seem, these tombs have stood entire for five hundred years in a public street, the frequent theatre of sedition [...]'.[7] On the other hand, William Rose, translator of Italian poets, admitted when writing home in August 1817 that he shared the general prejudice against any Gothic buildings because 'all notions of ideal beauty were lost at the time of their construction'. He did concede, however, that these particular tombs had ' an odd sort of poetry' because they provided 'an image of the life and death of the man whom they commemorate'. He also thought – rather perceptively – that Gothic architecture presented a different character in Italy than in more northerly countries, 'everything Gothic having caught something of a new colouring from this southern clime'.[8]

Heinrich Heine expressed his enthusiasm in 1826, while wishing the tombs could be seen more clearly.

> They are as wonderfully beautiful as the proud race itself, and it is a pity that they are crowded together in a narrow corner in order to take up as little space as possible, and where there is hardly remaining room for the spectator to study them conveniently [...] this corner is crammed full of stirring deeds, of high-wrought sentiments, and of lordly magnificence.[9]

Unfortunately, his criticism of this lack of space is even more relevant for today's crowds of tourists. An anonymous Scot visiting about the same time admired the monuments, too: 'The mixture of gothic and roman ornament in these picturesque structures is delightful, and sets all known and established rules of taste at defiance. Tant mieux – people are a great deal too positive in these matters.'[10] His remarks demonstrate clearly how important 'rules of taste' with regard to art were thought to be; he, however, was prepared to make up his own mind.

Ruskin loved Verona's mediaeval architecture. In a letter to his father in 1852, he wrote: 'I think the Gothic of Verona more and more superb every time I examine it – and it is curious how many new things I find out every time.'[11] He had a particular passion for the Scaligeri tombs, praising them in his *Stones of Venice*, 1851–3. (He had intended to write a *Stones of Verona*, but was never able to do so.) He was particularly fond of Can Grande's monument, 'the consummate form of the Gothic tomb'. Above the king's recumbent form is an arched *baldacchino*, topped by a statue of Can Grande on horseback, with

> [...] his helmet, dragon-winged and crested with the dog's head, tossed back behind his shoulders, and the broad and blazoned drapery floating back from his horse's breast, – so truly drawn by the old workman from the life, that it seems to wave in the wind, and the knight's spear to shake, and his marble horse to be ever more quickening its pace [...]

He admired the tomb of Mastino II, the next chronologically, as 'altogether exquisite as a work of art [...]', while that of Can Signorio he thought was 'the stateliest and most sumptuous of the three', but was 'coarser', being of a slightly later date.[12] Like many others, Ruskin admired the delicate ironwork curtain of linked sections that helped to protect the monuments, but did not prevent people from seeing them. To this day, this ironwork curtain with its ladder emblems is still in almost perfect condition, while the statue of Can Grande, replaced by a facsimile on the actual tomb, can now be found under its protective roof at the Castelvecchio museum.

Ruskin sketched these Scaligeri monuments frequently over the course of his many visits to the city between 1835 and 1888. He felt very deeply that the city authorities were guilty of a lack of care towards the tombs, or, when work was carried out, he criticized it for not being done to a high enough standard. He was not, however, above taking advantage of previous restoration work. He wrote to his mother that he

> [...] got at the stone-mason who long ago restored the pieces of the tomb of Can Signorio, and got from him one of the original little shafts of the niches [...] It is only about a yard high, and I shall carry it home myself like a barometer, wrapt in paper.[13]

On James Silk Buckingham's visit in about 1846, the tombs were indeed under repair.

> They stand in the open streets, but though they have been exposed for five hundred years, to all the vicissitudes of weather and popular tumults, they have not suffered any material injury from either, and are still among the most perfectly well-preserved monuments of the city.[14]

On the other hand, by the 1870s the American Junius Henri Browne was expressing regret that part of one monument was 'a fine specimen of the Gothic, but has grown so dingy and has crumbled so much in the several centuries it has stood there that a large part of its beauty is lost'.[15] This was exactly the kind of disrepair that Ruskin deplored.

Henry James admitted in 1873 that he was not fully able to appreciate the tombs' architecture, but admired them all the same.

> The tombs of the Scaligers, with their soaring pinnacles, their high-poised canopies, their exquisite refinement and concentration of the Gothic idea, I can't profess, even after much worshipful gazing, to have fully comprehended and enjoyed [...] But even to the hurried and pre-occupied traveller the solemn little chapel-yard in the city's centre, in which they stand girdled by their great swaying curtain of linked and twisted iron, is one of the most impressive spots in Italy. Nowhere else is such a wealth of artistic achievement crowded into so narrow a space; nowhere else are the daily comings and goings of men blessed by the presence of *manlier* art.[16]

It is perhaps curious to use the word 'manlier' to describe such elaborate and airy structures, unless James was referring to the martial way in which the deceased are represented.

In 1926, art critic Robert Byron likened Can Grande's equestrian statue to a fourteenth-century fresco, calling it

> [...] an exceptional work of art that can only be compared with the equestrian fresco in the Palazzo Publico, at Siena, by Simone Martini. The horses in both are draped to the fetlock; and there is something unusual, and at the same time satisfying, in the implied movement of an animal beneath the conventional but now unfamiliar folds of formal drapery. [...] The court yard is enclosed by a low wall, on top of which is stretched a kind of gigantic

wrought-iron chain mail, introducing into its design the family badge, the ladder. Although dating from the fourteenth century, it is still as flexible as a gold purse.[17]

These unique Scaligeri tombs are still there for all to see, protected by their chain-mail fencing; very occasionally, tourists are allowed to pass through into the enclosure to get a closer look. One of the family's palaces across from the monuments is now used as local government offices, while most of its frescoes and interior decorations for which it was noted have long since disappeared over the years. The little church of Santa Maria Antica still stands near the tombs and is said to contain the final resting place of that well-known Veronese benefactor, Scipione Maffei. Lady Blessington paid a visit there in 1822 on the insistence of her *cicerone*; she could not resist the chance of seeing the tomb of one 'whose works have afforded me too much instruction and pleasure, not to make me desirous of visiting his last earthly resting place'.[18] Maffei himself and his place in the city's history have their own chapter.

CHAPTER 16

Piazza delle Erbe

Communicating with the *Piazza dei Signori* on the one side of the Scaligieri palace, and overlooked by the great Campanile, is the *Piazza delle Erbe*, the great market place, surrounded by structures of the most varied and truly Italian architecture.¹

Murray (pub.), Hand-book for travellers in Northern Italy, *1842*

PIAZZA DELLE ERBE, often known just as Piazza Erbe, was based on the site of the old Roman Forum and seems always to have been a fruit and vegetable market. In 1608, Coryat described it as 'The Principall market place of the City' where he saw

[…] a marvailous pleasant fountaine, adorned with a very ancient marble image, wearing a crowne upon her head; that is said to be a representation of Verona […] Besides, at the higher end of this market place there is erected a very stately marble pillar with the winged Lyon advanced.²

The presence of this and the other images of lions symbolized the dominion of the Venetians over the city from 1405 onwards.

Despite the importance of this market place to the city, few seventeenth-century travellers made particular comments about it. Philip Skippon, there in 1663, did make a note of how large the herb and fish market was, 'where at one end is erected a great marble pillar […] A fountain here, and the pavement is divided into small areolæ of brick.'³ Much more expansive comments were provided by local resident Scipione Maffei in 1732, when he invited 'il forestiere' – the stranger – to visit the piazza in the early morning. There he would see a display of produce that could not be found elsewhere: the famous 'Fiorentini' peaches, figs, melons, pears, asparagus, artichokes of extraordinary size, grapes, including the sweet black 'marzemina' variety, and quantities of lemons and oranges.⁴

Goethe must have included a visit to Piazza delle Erbe as he wandered round the city in the late 1780s, given his real interest in the everyday lives of local people.

> The squares are very full on market days; there are fruit and vegetables without number, and garlic and onions to the heart's desire. Then again throughout the day there is a ceaseless screaming, bantering, singing, squalling, huzza-ing, and laughing. The mildness of the air, and the cheapness of the food, makes subsistence easy.[5]

When the poet Heinrich Heine was there in about 1826, he showed more interest in the women than the produce, noting that 'where the vegetable market is held, moved a crowd of picturesque figures, women & maidens, faces with languishing great eyes, graceful, supple limbs, of a lovely yellow colour, naively dirty, created rather for the night than for the day'.[6]

Pasquin, however, was more taken up in his guide of 1839 with the history of the square, while also making reference to the French occupation and the destruction wrought:

> On the Piazza delle Erbe is a column, erected in 1524, and formerly, according to a decree of the grand council, a debtor had only to touch this column, to find shelter from the pursuit of his creditors; a singular expedient, proving that it was already felt necessary to prevent the rigours of imprisonment for debt, so terrible in free states, which our improved legislation is attempting to correct. The Venetian lion, an excellent work which surmounted this column, was broken in 1797. The statue of Verona (Madonna Verona) in the same square, formerly had a sceptre and a crown to show that this city was once an imperial and royal residence, but these were broken off in 1797, and it is now covered with an *arena* that gives it altogether the air of a statue of Cybele, an emblem of the fecundity of the earth, which does not seem ill placed in the centre of a market.[7]

This statue later recovered its crown, but the lion was not replaced on its column until 1886, well after Verona had become part of the Kingdom of Italy.[8] One other change had been made some 50 years earlier when, in 1834, a pavement of stone blocks had been laid across the square.

An anonymous Scottish visitor clearly had an interesting range of experiences there. At the beginning of his visit in 1841, he got 'up early to look at the market, it was a busy scene and one to tempt a lover of fruit like myself but the grapes were sour and the plums and peaches hard as stones'. However, the next day proved more rewarding. His companion, a doctor, came rushing in early to exhort him to come and see the fish on the market.

> It was the fast day and truly a fine supply of fish there were for the catholic population of Verona. There were Tunny and lots of nameless fish from Venice, chub tench carp eels [...] from the Lago di Garda, every fish from the Adige, but the pride of the market were a couple of trout about six pound each and perfect in shape, colour and everything; the doctor was standing in ecstasy before them when I arrived exclaiming 'Oh aren't they noble fish and to see them among such ugly brutes!!' [...] We bought a slice of our trout at 8d a pound and found him excellent, red fleshed and firm, in fact one has to study the shape of the head before the difference between this and a salmon is evident.[9]

Louisa Costello felt carried away by both the produce and the piazza's architecture, just a few years later:

> Shops of all sorts are round, chiefly jewellers and bakers, oddly mixed. the former are not very splendid, and the latter are filled with singular-shaped loaves [...] Two fountains occupy the centre of the market place, or Mercato Vecchio, one Gothic and one in the form of a Roman temple. The whole space is occupied by stalls, at which the vendors sit under large fixed umbrellas, with their luxuriant stores of fruit and vegetables, and baskets of all kinds of graceful forms scattered here and there; pyramids of loaves piled on tables, and pyramids of glasses for iced water crowned with a bouquet of lilies are placed in different quarters. A fine carved and painted hall of justice raises its beautiful facade above these groups: rich arcades and delicate porticoes are jammed in with low mean houses and shops, and countless balconies and bright-coloured awnings come out richly against the dim dingy buildings they adorn. A high Campanile crowns the whole, peering over the confused scene, like an inquisitive spirit, ghastly long and thin, and belonging to an age gone by.[10]

Louisa did note there could be drawbacks for an artistically inclined tourist.

> We went several times into the Piazza del Erbi, with a hope of being able to sketch some of the groups and buildings with which this curious spot is crowded, but were so persecuted by inquisitive neighbours of all kinds,

most of them extremely filthy, that we were soon constrained to give up the attempt.[11]

Occasionally, it was the behaviour of an Englishman who inadvertently found himself the centre of attention. John Ruskin, staying as usual in the hotel Due Torri next to the church of Sant'Anastasia, made a spectacle of himself as he walked down towards the piazza in 1876, his mind perhaps being on higher things. He recounted how

> [...] in a frosty morning in Verona I put on my dressing-gown (which is of bright Indian shawl stuff) by mistake for my great-coat; and walked through the full market place, and half way down the principal street, in that costume, proceeding in perfect tranquillity until the repeated glances of unusual admiration bestowed on me by the passengers led me to investigation of the possible cause.[12]

In 1854, architect George Edmund Street found himself fascinated by the umbrellas, still a major feature of the square today.

> We soon found ourselves at the end of the Piazza dell'Erbe, the most picturesque square of the city, and at an early hour of the morning quite a sight to be seen. The whole open space was as full as it could be of dealers in vegetables and fruits, all of them protecting themselves and their stalls from the intense glare of the sun under the shade of prodigious umbrellas, at least five times as large as any of ordinary size, and certainly five times as bright in their colours, the prevailing colour being a very bright red. Altogether it was a thoroughly foreign scene [...] An hour or two later in the day when we passed, the people, the umbrellas, and the fruit were all gone, and somewhat of the charm of the place was gone with them.[13]

Most travellers described the umbrellas as red. However, William Smith, there in 1880, declared them to be white.[14] By 1913, the artist Walter Tyndale was emphatic that 'in the whole of Italy I have never seen the Piazza delle Erbe equalled'. His umbrellas were, though, undoubtedly red. 'Nothing but sun and weather could have made the crude cochineal dye of these umbrellas take every shade of red that ever left a Titian's palette.'[15] In 1927, Eric Vincent, professor of Italian at Cambridge, did not specify a colour, but did add an extra dimension to the activities of some tourists.

> Verona has a market-place full of umbrellas under whose shade a number of old ladies are prepared to sell vegetables on a sliding scale of prices.

English travellers have a habit of painting pictures of this market-place and hanging them on their spare-room walls when they get home.[16]

There is a description of Piazza delle Erbe in *L'Italie d'hier*, by the French de Goncourt brothers, published in 1894, that deserves quoting in full for its details about scavenging dogs and the sale of woodpeckers as food. The pallid and frail women they mentioned have very little resemblance to those 'created for the night', as described by Heine in the 1820s.

In the Market Square:
Near a pink marble pillar touched by sunlight rising with the time of day as on a Maypole, a huge house front, completely frescoed over, depicting figures like Anteus and Encelades, clambering up to the heavens amid awesome whirling colossi; frescoes, not unlike a Michelangelo painting, showing gigantic wrestlers in arenas, pockmarked in the fabric of the wall, by windows with heads peering out.

Down below, under huge awnings of white canvas, where the light shines through, there are bursts of rainbow colours, the shawls and bonnets of market women selling their vegetables and cornflowers and poppies against a backdrop of greenery, lettuce, leeks and cabbage spread out at their feet.

Some are swarthy market women, hair piled high above their foreheads in waves like those of Ionian capitals on pillars, some are fuzzily fair-haired and their unkempt curls frame their oval faces like glowing sunbeams.

Many of these tradesfolk are old country women; they wear tiny straw hats from which stray locks of hair escape, entangled with enormous golden ear-rings dangling from their ears. Greying whorls brush against their golden statuesque profiles, almost as if carved from boxwood.

In the midst of this vegetable medley, blood red haunches of beef are displayed on the flights of steps of ruinous palaces, alongside offal, round which pale bristling dogs lap up animal sweetbreads; spread out on counters are green woodpeckers, yellow red-polled birds, a local delicacy. Nearby, little posies are on sale set on long stalks, items of all kinds and colours, and little donkeys weave their way through, loaded with firewood, hidden under their twiggy burdens.

All the morning long, little Verona housewives potter about rubbing shoulders with elderly pink-nosed Italians; they carry their purchases in straw baskets concealed under their cloaks. Their movements are languid, white lace veils over their heads, rounded foreheads, close-set eyes, mouths tensed anxiously – frail women these, evincing all the charm and pallid gentleness of a Botticelli or a Gozzoli, and in this Italian north they could be the living models of primitive art.[17]

Piazza delle Erbe today is one of the few remaining parts of Verona where some buildings still have on their walls the painted figures and designs described by the de Goncourt brothers. In earlier times there were many such frescoes across the city, sometimes commented on by travellers, but unfortunately most of these have now disappeared. The Gothic Revival architect, William White, described the piazza thus in 1895:

> These houses are now but poorly inhabited, and no regard whatever is paid to their preservation; the frescoes are consequently in a state of rapid decay [...] It is to be feared that these last remnants of this important characteristic of Veronese domestic architecture will in a few years be completely lost.[18]

Today the market continues to occupy the entire square, with throngs of tourists browsing through the stalls, or enjoying a coffee or a glass of wine in one of the adjoining cafes before moving on to explore other parts of the city.

 CHAPTER 17

The Giusti Gardens

And it is perhaps here in these gardens that the very atmosphere of antique Italy, Italy of the sixteenth and seventeenth centuries at the least, is to be found.[1]

Edward Hutton, Italy and the Italians, *1903*

THE GIUSTI FAMILY'S famous garden in Verona seems to have been an ongoing attraction to visitors and tourists over the centuries. It was – and still is – situated in the Veronetta district, behind the family's large palazzo, and extends up the hill behind as far as the remains of Castel San Pietro. This garden can still be visited nowadays, with access through the entrance gate to the palazzo, which is not itself currently open to the public. The statues, hedges and cypress trees described by early visitors are as impressive as ever; it is, however, surprising that none of them made specific mention of the sixteenth-century *mascherone* or huge grotesque stone mask that looms over the garden from the hillside.

The first Englishman to leave a description of the Giardino Giusti was Thomas Coryat, there in 1608.

> Also the Italian [Count Augustinus Justus] shewed me his garden, which is a second Paradise, and a passing delectable place of solace, beautified with many curious knots, fruites of divers sorts and two rowes of lofty Cypresse trees, three and thirty in a ranke. Besides his walkes at the toppe of the garden a little under St Peters Castle, are as pleasant as the heart of man can wish; being decked with excellent fruites, as Figges, Oranges, Apricockes, and with Cypresse trees. In one of these walkes is a delicate litle refectory: at one side whereof there is a curious artificall rocke, adorned with many fine devices, as scolop shels, and great variety of other prety shels of fishes brought from Cyprus: and mosse groweth upon the same as if it were a naturall rocke. This place certainly is contrived with as admirable

curiosity as ever I saw, and moystened with delicate springs and fountaines conveighed into the same by leaden pipes.

As ever, Coryat's prose is very evocative of the places he visited.[2]

This description precedes one written by a Veronese doctor, philosopher and poet, Francesco Pona, in 1620. Pona saw the garden at the height of its glory, a house and garden 'so important that it became known by the name of that branch of the family'.[3] He described the many statues of ancient deities and heroes, the magnificent cypress trees, the lawns, the citrus trees, the flowers and hedges. There were also huge mirrors to trick the spectator into believing figures were approaching him, when these were in fact only his own reflections. In the grotto there were artificial representations of shells, coral and mother-of-pearl; elsewhere there were mosaics, fountains and other water features. As Pona climbed to the Loggia on the hill behind, he described the wonderful view over the city, the River Adige and the surrounding country as far as the town of Mantua.[4]

It seems that Pona saw the Giusti palace and its gardens at the peak of their splendour. Later, the garden was made smaller and was no longer as well maintained; like everything else in Verona, it was badly affected by the 1630 plague that reduced the population of the city by two-thirds within a few months.[5] However, tourists continued visiting, with John Evelyn there in 1646.

> In the evening we saw the garden of Count Giusti's villa, where are walks cut out of the main rock from whence we had the pleasant prospect of Mantua and Parma, though at great distance. At the entrance to this garden, grows the goodliest cypress, I fancy, in Europe, cut in a pyramid; it is a prodigious tree both for breadth and height, entirely covered, and thick to the base.[6]

Ten years later, Sir John Reresby commented that, in Verona,

> The palaces are many; the gardens extraordinary, especially that of Signor Augusto Justo, for not only a great variety of plants, flowers, and greens, but for volories of birds, grottoes, fountains, from whence water throws itself by the turning of keys, in the shape of birds and beasts.[7]

Philip Skippon, there in 1663, remarked on the cypresses, as well as 'a pretty grotto cut out of the rock, and a cage of birds'. Further up the hill he found a little chapel to Our Lady, and finally 'a place like a steeple' which led into another garden with two summer houses, a well and 'a fair prospect of the city and country'. He also noted one novelty: 'One quarter of the lower garden is a little island, with a narrow mote for swans, very handsomely adorn'd with statues and marble walls.'[8]

Joseph Addison, essayist and poet, was less impressed when he visited in 1701–2, making no specific reference to the exact site.

> I have not yet seen any Gardens in Italy worth taking notice of. The Italians fall as far short of the French in this Particular, as they excel 'em in their Palaces [...] I went to see the Terrace-Garden of Verona that Travellers generally mention.[9]

Later eighteenth-century tourists were more enthusiastic. William Freman wrote in Italian in his 1728 diary:

> Count Giusti's garden is very pleasant, enjoying a beautiful view of the city and the countryside. There is a grotto so designed that, if four people stand one in each corner, those standing opposite can hear each other clearly even if they speak quietly, whereas the other two cannot hear anything and nor can anyone standing in the centre.[10]

It was still the cypress trees that particularly caught the eye; according to John Keysler in about 1730, the garden held 'a very grand walk of cypress-trees, some of which exceed a hundred feet in height and are above two hundred years old'.[11]

Charles de Brosses, visiting in 1739, also admired the cypresses, which 'give a most striking look to the spot, worthy of one in which the magicians of old held their Sabbaths'. However, he also had an alarming experience; 'I got lost in a maze, and I was an hour, wandering round under a blazing sun, and would have been there still had I not been taken out by one of the people of the place.'[12] Hester Piozzi was rather vague about her visit in about 1785, saying she was shown 'an agreeable garden belonging to some man of fashion', but did not provide his name; nor, sadly, did she name an Englishman who was said to have hired the Giusti palace for a season. She felt that 'the grotto disappointed me', despite it being cut into the living rock, because more advantage could have been taken of its situation. On the other hand, 'I never saw cypress trees of such a growth as in this spot.'[13] A few years later Elizabeth Wynne observed a statue there which 'is of stone but which resounds when struck with another stone like bronze',[14] a feature apparently unnoticed by other visitors.

The garden continued to be a tourist attraction into the nineteenth century. The American Nathaniel Carter was there in 1826, shortly after the Congress of Verona, but not in ideal conditions.

> Crossing the Ponte di Navi, so called from its being the rendezvous of boats, and the point of embarkation on the Adige, we visited the Giuste Garden, celebrated by Addison and other travellers. It has acquired new fame by the sittings of the late Congress of Verona. The grounds are situated on a steep acclivity, embellished with pyramids of cypress and other ornamental trees [...] We commenced an ascent; but the rain came down with such violence, and the alleys were so flooded, as to compel us to retreat.[15]

Ten years later, Lady Murray observed many of the features mentioned by earlier travellers, but the form of the clipped box was novel:

> The lovely garden of Count Giusti with its lofty cypresses, forms one of the most striking features of Verona, which abounds in beautiful and varied subjects for painting [...] There is a small chapel, an aviary, and a flat parterre, reaching from the foot of the hill to the palazzo of Count Giusti. Box clipped into the form of sofas, and abundance of flowers, a labyrinth, and some very Dutch-looking statues complete the catalogue of objects the garden possesses.[16]

Pasquin provided some additional information in 1839, after harking back to Pona's book.

> The great Giusti palace, finished about the close of the sixteenth century, was described, as well as its garden, by that indefatigable writer and physician, Francesco Pona, of Verona, in a scarce little book oddly entitled *Il Sileno*, Verona, 1626, in-8vo. This palace has become a military lodgment, occupied by the Austrian commander and his troop. Its beautiful gallery which was enriched by the principal remnants of the Molino Museum of Venice, was sold by the government about 1825. The garden is still frequented; its prospect, grotto, echo, and labyrinth, are in repute at Verona; but it is melancholy; its continually recurring steps, formerly used for drying cloth, recall the time when the woollen manufacture was followed by nobles, and not thought derogatory.[17]

Augustus Hare took his mother there in 1868 at sunset. 'Mother was able to climb up to the summer-house at the height, and the gardener gave us pinks and roses.'[18] Another Englishman, Edward Hutton, later reminisced that 'Here best of all I have found my desire, and recalled in my heart the Italy that is my fatherland.'[19] For him, the garden seen in the evening was

> [...] finer even than those of Hadrian's garden, near Tivoli [...] The majestic and melancholy cypresses, that yet in their cheerful enthusiasm for heaven are beautiful, like ideal monks with hands pointed in prayer, or like solemn tapers ecstatically burning for the glory of our God, seem to invest the scene with a new kind of beauty, that leads us at last to the contemplation of the beauty of holiness. And, on the eve almost of leaving Italy, it is some such emotion of her ideal self that we would carry away. All the panoramic life of Venice; the melancholy splendour of Rome, with its worldly ambitions, its modern vulgarity and degradation; the hideous brutality and ignorance and noise of Naples, seem now to fade into just nothing at all before the quiet beauty and calmness of Verona as seen from these gardens [...][20]

CHAPTER 18

Local Artists and Aristocratic 'Collections'

What I have seen of pictures I will but briefly touch upon […]
S. Georgio is a gallery of good pictures,
all altar pieces, and all remarkable, if not of equal value.
But what subjects were the hapless artists obliged to paint? And for whom?[1]

Johann von Goethe, Goethe's travels in Italy, *1885*

VERONA WAS ABLE TO BOAST many home-grown artists. Probably the best known of all, certainly so far as tourists were concerned, was the native-born Paolo Caliari, known as Veronese, who in reality spent most of his working life elsewhere in the Veneto, particularly in Venice. As Mme Octavia Walton Le Vert, the American socialite from Georgia, put it while seeking out his work in the city in about 1854: 'Verona is the birthplace of Paolo Veronese, the admirable painter, but we saw very few of his paintings there; they embellish the galleries of princes in other cities. However, the inhabitants have the glory of calling him compatriot.'[2]

Although the churches of Verona were full of works by lesser-known native artists, it is difficult to find many visitors who went beyond commenting on paintings by famous names, such as Titian and Veronese, to be found in the major churches that included the Duomo, San Giorgio Maggiore and San Zeno.

The second edition of Giorgio Vasari's seminal *Le vite de' più eccellenti Pittori, Scultori e Architettori* (Lives of the Most Eminent Painters, Sculptors and Architects), published in 1568 did include biographies of lesser-known Veronesi artists such as Fra' Giocondo, Liberale, Caroto and Girolamo dai Libri. Although there was no complete English edition of Vasari before 1847, any early traveller able to read Italian would have benefited from consulting the Lives. In fact, there were eighteenth-century travellers who took the trouble to find and admire local works. Edward Wright, visiting in the early 1720s with Lord Parker, mentioned an altarpiece in San Giorgio by Paolo Farinati, 'a very good Picture', as well another by Domenico Brusasorzi.[3] Keysler in the 1730s also noticed these two works, as well as one by Girolamo dai Libri of the Virgin: 'the carpet on which the Virgin stands is justly admired'.[4]

Some 30 years later, the French astronomer Jérôme de Lalande admired the work of the Brusasorzi brothers, Farinati and Antonio Balestra, and particularly praised Giambettino Cignaroli, whom he regarded as one of the best painters in Italy at the time. He also claimed that Cignaroli had been much in demand by 'the rich Englishmen who throw their money about in Italy'.[5] Indeed, an anonymous Scotsman did visit this painter in July 1770 and reported thus in a letter: 'I forgot to mention yesterday that we had seen Sig Cignaroli at Verona, one of the most eminent modern painters, and that we had bargained for a picture of Susanna & the elders for which he asked 130 sequins.'[6] Unfortunately, he did not report the outcome of his bargaining, and it seems that nothing is now known of this painting.

Nineteenth-century travellers could have become aware of local artists if they consulted the *Compendio della Verona illustrata*, the pocket-sized 1795 guidebook in Italian aimed specifically at foreigners. (In 1815, The Reverend John Eustace was still recommending this as the best local guide, despite the availability of his own *A classical tour through Italy*.) It may be that Pasquin, for example, did use the *Compendio*, with its detailed description of the contents of Verona's churches, given the thoroughness of references to works by local artists in his own guidebook. The *Descrizione di Verona e della sua provincia* of 1820 by the Veronese Giovanni Battista Da Persico also promoted local artworks, including the little-known frescoes – still in excellent condition and well worth a visit – in the library of San Bernadino, but made no mention of its Veronese artists, Francesco and Domenico Morone.[7] Surprisingly, perhaps, this particular information was later supplied by the very British Murray's *Hand-book* of 1842.

During the middle years of the nineteenth century, John Ruskin was an enthusiastic champion of Verona's art:

> For example, if I were asked to lay my finger, in a map of the world, on the spot of the world's surface which contained at this moment the most singular concentration of art-teaching and art treasure, I should lay it on the name of the town of Verona. Other cities, indeed, contain more works of carriageable art, but none contain so much of the glorious local art, and of the springs and sources of art [...][8]

His particular passion, however, was for Gothic art and architecture, which showed itself in his many sketches and paintings of buildings from the Middle Ages. So it is not surprising, perhaps, that Ruskin seems to have had little time for local artists from later periods. One expert has described matters thus: 'With the only exception of Veronese, he seemed indifferent – or almost so – to the work of the city's artists; of Liberale, Girolamo dai Libri, Domenico or Francesco Morone, Farinati or others of the fifteenth and sixteenth centuries, he said nothing.'[9]

Some visitors found themselves agreeably surprised by the local Veronese art. The Countess of Blessington admitted freely in 1840:

> Until I visited Verona, I was not fully aware of the merit of the school of painting to which it gives its name. Many of the pictures are excellent, and would not lose by a comparison with those by more celebrated masters.[10]

In 1876, Augustus Hare also felt that these local painters deserved wider recognition: 'The pictures in the Churches and Gallery would not, with a few exceptions, be of any great importance outside Verona, but are exceedingly interesting here, being almost entirely by native artists.'[11]

Most nineteenth-century tourists were, however, less likely to concern themselves with such minutiae. For the most part, they continued to follow a more predictable and well-trodden route round the city's major churches in pursuit of works by Titian, Paolo Veronese or possibly even Andrea Mantegna, rather than trying to come to terms with painters with unfamiliar names like Giolfino, Brusasorzi or Farinati. This was despite the efforts of various English guidebooks, such as Murray's 1842 *Hand-book*, to widen visitors' horizons. This even counselled a traveller not to use his usual artistic judgement when in northern Italy, but instead to make a judgement based on local circumstances and considerations:

> [...] without in the least deadening his sense of beauty, or slighting any excellence, he should learn to value the objects presented to him, as illustrations of the annals, manners, morals and opinions of the country [...] In this point of view, artistical merit is a secondary consideration.[12]

It followed through this advice by strongly recommending paintings of the Madonna and saints by two home-grown artists, Paolo Cavazzuola and Domenico Morone, in the church of San Bernardino: 'No lover of art should pass through Verona without seeing this picture.'[13]

Nearly all travellers mentioned visiting the church of San Giorgio in Braida on the far bank of the Adige, where a work by Paolo Veronese was to be found. An early reference to his *Martyrdom of St George* – then in the monastery of San Giorgio – was made by the Englishman John Clenche in 1675, when he described it as 'so much esteemed, that a lord-marshal of England could not buy it for 2000 pistoles'.[14] Edward Wright was rather more specific in the 1720s, giving his opinion on a work in which 'an old Priest of Apollo' was compelling the saint 'to worship a Brazen Statue of the Idol. There are several other Figures in the Picture which is a very gay one and painted with a great Freedom.'[15]

In 1773, the Scotsman Patrick Home

> [...] strolled out in the forenoon to St George's church where there are two good pictures of Paul Veronese – St John [actually St George] led to sacrifice to idols and refusing, not without faults, but great fire and expression. St Barnabas reading the Gospel upon sick peoples heads – all the magnificence of decoration in Architecture [...] that distinguish his pictures – Above the door St John baptizing our Saviour by Tintoretto [...] has fine expression – another large picture with a Crowd of figures.[16]

The artist Joseph Wright of Derby, however, was less impressed with the St George in 1774; the work is 'in good condition, but slightly painted, & in other respects nothing extraordinary'.[17]

Fifteen years later, Elizabeth Gibbes voiced her personal view of the Veronese: 'The meek & resign'd attitude of St George very fine; my sister admired the High Priest, I did not like him.'[18] This was another work of art later removed by the French and not returned till after 1815, a fact noted by visitors including William Wilson in 1837.

> This noble picture was carried off to Paris, where it excited much admiration; and during its stay there it underwent the process of repairing and cleaning, which, though it has removed dirt, has also injured many of the tints, and impaired the general harmony of the piece.[19]

There were other paintings by Paolo Veronese in the city, but not many visitors bothered to look for them. Herman Friedländer, travelling with the German Romantic artist Philipp Veit, was an exception when he tracked down a Madonna by Paolo Veronese in San Paolo, another Veronetta church: 'It is a brilliant composition; everything in it is treated with the ease, freedom and grace [...] of high life.'[20]

The most frequently visited city church was probably the Duomo, where travellers went particularly to see Titian's *Assumption of the Virgin*. Some merely registered the fact that they had seen it, while others did express an opinion. De Blainville, visiting in 1707, saw 'a great many excellent Pictures' in the Duomo, among them the Titian.[21] De Lalande thought, in 1766, that Titian had made the Virgin excessively bright and had placed her too high up on the canvas, although he liked the depiction of the apostles.[22] In 1820, the artist Marianne Colston pronounced the work as 'considerably inferior' to Titian's version of the same subject in Venice.[23]

On into the nineteenth century tourists continued their pilgrimage to the Duomo, still often without any real comment. Upon seeing the work in the late 1820s, Pasquin did have something to add:

> Titian's Assumption, brought back from Paris, is interesting, if it be true that he has painted San Micheli [the famous Veronese architect] under the features of the apostle in the centre, with his face turned towards heaven, and one hand on the sepulchre.[24]

Ruskin, writing in his diary in disdainful mood, declared that the painting was 'disappointing from its extreme quietness and faded look'.[25] Few visitors were as direct in their opinions about the Duomo's art as an anonymous Scotsman in 1830, as he went

> [...] into the Cathedral to take my leave of a sublime 'Assumption' by Titian, and to make another attempt to relish the Twelve Apostles painted round the choir by Giulio Romano in fresco. But it won't do – never saw such pumpkin-headed loons in my life – gaping and staring, too like the wax heads in Mr Truefit's in Burlington Arcade.[26]

This was a somewhat unexpected comparison.

An altarpiece that is now one of the most admired in Verona received very little attention until well into the nineteenth century, and even then the tourists' remarks were not always favourable. This is the Madonna and child with saints in the church of San Zeno by Andrea Mantegna, placed there in 1459 and still in its original frame. Giorgio Vasari, in the 1550 edition of his life and work of Italian artists, had described the work as 'most beautiful', even though admitting that Mantegna's 'manner is seen to be somewhat hard and sometimes suggesting stone rather than living flesh'.[27] By 1795, the *Compendio* merely stated that the altarpiece in San Zeno was the work of Mantegna, without any comment, whereas Da Persico, in his 1820 guidebook, asserted that this artist's name was worthy of great praise. The principal section of the altarpiece was back in place by this time, after its enforced absence in Paris, but without its three original predella panels, which are to this day in French museums. Da Persico saw the substitute copies, roundly condemning the French looting of the originals.

The indefatigable Pasquin was in San Zeno about 1826 and, as well as the altarpiece, he found another work 'by Mantegna, who has likewise painted in the cloister a very fine fresco of the Infant Jesus standing and blessing the universe, a touching and noble picture that nothing but the genius of Christianity could have inspired'.[28] It seems that nothing is now known of this fresco. Ruskin, whose dislike of much Renaissance art was deeply ingrained, condemned Mantegna's altarpiece out of hand – it 'is utterly vapid & contemptible: the most painfully wooden, mechanical, lifeless piece of automaton grimace I ever approached'; he particularly disliked the Virgin's face and found the garland of fruits 'coarse & glaring'.[29] When someone as respected as Ruskin expressed such strongly negative views, this could well have influenced opinions of this masterpiece late into the nineteenth century.

The more enthusiastic travellers did visit churches like Santa Maria in Organo, San Fermo, SS Nazaro e Celso, San Bernardino and Sant'Anastasia. This last contains the fresco by Pisanello of the legend of St George, now very well known but then rarely mentioned, except by Pasquin who described Pisanello as 'a celebrated Veronese master of the first epoch of the Venetian school'.[30] Given Ruskin's passion for medieval art, it is surprising that he did not enthuse about these frescoes, particularly as he always stayed in the Due Torri hotel adjacent to the church in Piazza Sant'Anastasia. Edward Hutton, there in about 1910, found the fresco of St George was not visible at all. He believed, improbably, that it had been moved to the sacristy in about 1901, but found that the priest in charge claimed to know nothing, merely shrugging his shoulders. 'This, of old, I have learnt to be a sign that knowledge is not to be imparted, rather than that your shrugger is himself ignorant.'[31] There is another work by Pisanello in the city, a fresco of the Annunciation on the Brenzoni wall tomb in San Fermo Maggiore, but again rarely mentioned except by the tireless Pasquin. By 1842, details of this work had found their way into Murray's *Hand-book*, which might have encouraged some tourists to seek out the fresco.

It was also possible to visit private palaces such as that of the Bevilacqua family to view their collections of art and sculptures, with guidebooks providing a long list of the family's treasures. About 1740, Keysler, for instance, saw 'a fine set of paintings; the principal [among these] are a representation of Paradise by Tintoretto, and a Venus half naked viewing herself in a looking glass held by an Amorino or Cupid, by Paolo Veronese'.[32] This famous collection had, however, been sold by 1815, the proprietor being bankrupt, according to a Scotsman believed to be called Seaforth.[33] William Wilson gave more details after his 1836 visit:

> The greater part of the collection of antiques, for which this palace once was celebrated is now dispersed. In order to prevent their being carried off by the French, when they entered Verona, the finest of the statues were concealed in some of the cellars; and they were afterwards purchased by the then crown prince, now king of Bavaria, who has since added them to the other treasures of plastic art which adorn the Glyptotheca at Munich.[34]

The artist Marianne Colston had paid a visit instead to the Palazzo Albarelli in 1820 where 'we saw a small, but remarkably fine, collection of paintings, by Paolo Veronese, Titian, Bellini, Giorgione, etc. I was particularly charmed by one painting of the last master, representing Abelard and Eloisa.'[35]

This eighteenth-century fashion for assembling 'collections' or 'cabinets' was certainly well established in Verona, with many travellers applying to view them. These might contain not just paintings, but miscellaneous articles as described by de Blainville on a visit to the collection of Count Moscardo in 1707. It consisted of

> Books, Pictures, precious Stones, Metals, Chrystals, Plants, Petrifactions, Medals, Monies, little Statues, Instruments used by the Pagans in their sacrifices [...] Vases, Arms, Head-dresses, and Shoes of different Nations, Clocks of all Kinds, Shells, Fossils, Mirrors of mixt Metals, Coral Trees, Amianthus Stones, monstrous productions of Whims of Nature; in short, every Thing that can be imagined, curious, rare, or extraordinary.

That was not all. The Count, who conducted the party round personally, had one final item to display. This was a chastity belt or 'a Padlock to keep the Ladies chaste, upon which the good Count, who is both a Canon and a Priest, was very merry and witty'. De Blainville was having none of this. 'I took the liberty to tell him that no other than a jealous-pated Fool could be capable of inventing such a machine [...] since the Ladies were too cunning to be thus imposed upon by their Husbands.' The Count agreed, but said that Italian husbands believed that 'this little Precaution is an excellent Preservative against the Growth of Horns', or, in other words, it would prevent them from becoming cuckolds through the infidelity of their wives.[36]

Thomas Nugent, the Anglo-Irish antiquary, saw this collection in the 1740s and mentioned that there was a gallery and six other rooms 'all filled with antiquities and the greatest curiosities in art and nature'. In addition to the variety of things listed by de Blainville, he believed he had seen paintings by Raphael, Giulio Romano, 'Holben', Titian (several), 'old Bassano' and 'a vast many others, all by Paul Veronese'.[37]

There were more specialized collections, too. Hester Piozzi was particularly fascinated by the magnificent fossils from Bolca, a village on Monte Purga in Lessinia, not far from Verona and still very well worth a visit; these fossils had been well known since the sixteenth century and now form the core of the city's excellent *Museo di Storia Naturale*. In about 1785, she visited the fossil collection of 'Signor Vincenzo Bozza' and wrote: 'scarcely anything except the testimony of one's own eyes could convince one that flying fish, natives, and intending to remain inhabitants, of the Pacific Ocean, are daily dug out of the bowels of Monte Bolca near Verona'.[38]

The following year Hester wrote to her daughter, Hester Maria, saying:

> I shall really bring home some Specimens of great Value – the People are so excessively kind, they make me quite ashamed, and when I read *my Name* this Morning in ye Musaeum written up in Gold Letters:
> *Ornamento d'Inghilterra Grazia d'Italia: dei Tesori della Natura Interprete, Custode & Dispensatrice,* I was fairly overwhelmed, and could not say one Word.[39]

It would appear from this that Hester was being acknowledged for some particular contribution she had made to the museum.

Following Napoleon's campaign against closed religious orders in the city, a public art gallery was set up, with a collection of 'the spoils of suppressed religious houses in the city and neighbourhood', according to an anonymous Scotsman visiting in 1830. He was not impressed when he 'turned into the Town-Hall to see a collection of ragged old pictures stuck like posting bills upon the bare walls – some scaling off and in a state of rapid decay [...]'.[40] In about 1846, James Silk Buckingham was rather more enthusiastic on his visit to

> [...] the *Palazzo di Consiglie or Pinocatheca*, or collection of paintings from suppressed Convents and Churches. Among these only a few interested us. One of these was a grand assembly, in which the Senators of Verona were presenting the keys of their city to the Doge of Venice; this is said to be by Titian, and the drawing, grouping and colouring, were well worthy of his reputation. Besides this, the only ones that excited our admiration were the

raising of Lazarus, the Deposition from the Cross, by Paul Veronese, and two or three large historical paintings of battles and sieges.[41]

The French historian Taine found the Pinacoteca located in Palazzo Pompei by 1864, containing the works of Verona masters such as Falconetto, Turodi, Crivelli, Paolo Morando, Bonifazio and Veronese.[42]

Verona was known at one time as *la picta* because of the paintings on the outside of a number of its buildings. Charles de Brosses, there in 1739, reported:

> The houses, for the most part, were painted externally in fresco by Veronese or his pupils, but all of this is so faded that hardly a trace is now visible. The remains make one regret that the rest has perished.[43]

By the late 1820s, Pasquin observed:

> Painting in reality runs along the streets in Italy. Mantegna executed two frescos on the house of the painter Giolfino, his friend, with whom he had lived as a guest; a poetic and not uncommon manner with the artists of the fourteenth and fifteenth centuries, of acknowledging hospitality. Mantegna's frescos are now scarcely to be recognized: having first been barbarously whitewashed, an unskilful cleaning followed, and when I saw them they were again half covered by a large green Venetian blind.[44]

At the time of Lady Murray's visit in 1835 some frescoes were still visible.

> Many of the houses have paintings on them. The Last Supper, after Leonardo da Vinci, was extremely well done. The signs over the doors were minutely and really well finished; and at night I observed many with pictures, painted entirely for strong effect, and lighted by a lamp.[45]

Because these frescoes were not maintained, inevitably they deteriorated as time went by. Theodore Child was still able to see some work allegedly by Paolo Veronese and pupils of Mantegna in 1887, but nowadays few traces are left except for some examples on house fronts in Piazza Erbe.

Today, works of art may still be seen in the city's major churches as well as in less-visited ones, including Santa Maria in Organo, San Bernadino and SS Nazaro and Celso. The reputation of Verona's home-grown artists has grown, following the work of art historians and researchers over recent years; these artists are particularly well represented in SS Nazaro e Celso, which today's visitor should try hard not to miss, even though it is a little out of the way in Veronetta. Tastes, too, have moved on, with visitors now showing a keen interest in the Pisanello frescoes which received little attention in earlier times. There is also an extensive collection of early paintings, many by local artists, to be found in the Castevecchio museum, as well as others in the Gallery of Modern Art in Palazzo della Ragione, off Piazza dei Signori.

Perhaps in conclusion it is worth noting a small sample of foreign artists who undertook sketches, paintings and prints of the city. Mention has already been made of John Ruskin, William Brockenden, John Hayward and Louisa Costello, who are known from their own accounts to have been sketching in Verona. Another was the Frenchman Baron Charles Rivet, on a tour with the painter Richard Parkes Bonington in 1826. Rivet wrote to his mother as follows:

> This morning at 10 o'clock we were in Verona! I did not cease to move my crayon, until 5.30, so my hand is fatigued. Verona is a very picturesque city. If it were possible to do all the remarkable things one sees, it would take 8 days of assiduous work.[46]

Parkes Bonington himself sketched or painted views of Corso Sant'-Anastasia, Piazza Erbe and the Castelbarco tomb in Piazza Sant'Anastasia.

There were other artists known to have produced images of the city, although not all may actually have visited it. These included the Venetian Bernardo Bellotto, the Swiss-born Henry Fuseli, the French Mme Vigée Le Brun, the Englishmen William Henry Bartlett, William Callow, Edward William Cooke, Miles Birkett Foster, Albert Goodwin, Robert Goff, James Duffield Harding, Henry Gally Knight, Thomas Little, Samuel Prout, Henry Rushbury, William Clarkson Stanfield, J.M.W. Turner, Walter Tyndale, and the English women Lady Henrietta Fortescue and Marianne Colston. The traveller Leitch Ritchie was one of many who would have seen topographical engravings of Verona taken from original drawings; in 1832, he noted that 'A nearer view of Verona, taken by Mr. [William Clarkson] Stanfield from the heights, represents the city to the utmost possible advantage.'[47] All these people and more wished to take advantage of a city that seemed to demand that visitors try to reproduce some of its charms to take away as souvenirs or aids to memory.

CHAPTER 19

Music and Theatre

The theatre is far from good & the music & singing & dancing worse.[1]

Henry Bankes, 1779

FROM AN EARLY DATE Verona was well known for its societies that promoted music, theatre and learning, these subjects proving far more interesting to visitors than the sacred music to be heard in the city's many churches. No remarks by tourists specifically about *musica sacra* have yet been found, despite the fact that Verona had a distinguished history of religious music, with a college to train acolytes established as early as 1440.[2]

As Keysler noted, there was an Accademia dei Filarmonici in existence from 1543,[3] when 'the Philharmonic society established the laws of this academy, and devoted themselves to the muses', music being its principal activity.[4] The Accademia dei Filarmonici later instituted the study of literature, mathematics, philosophy and Greek as well.[5] In 1740, in the same building as this Academy, Keysler also found another, that of the Filotimi, 'instituted for the improvement of bodily exercises, as riding, fencing, dancing etc'.[6] This second society had been founded in 1565.[7] A particular feature of the city's musical life was the *ridotto* (or retreat) held in the private houses of noblemen; Count Mario Bevilacqua, for instance, employed a number of professional musicians to entertain his friends in the later years of the sixteenth century.[8] Such was the Count's musical reputation that many sets of madrigals were dedicated to him.

Less than 30 miles separate Verona from Mantua where the premiere of Monteverdi's *Orfeo* was performed before the Gonzaga court in 1607, with the increasingly famous castrato Giovanni Magli among the cast.[9] In Verona, a work with many of the characteristics of opera was performed in 1632 in honour of the visiting Venetian military captain Andrea Vendramin; it was entitled *Il guidizio di Paride* and involved musicians, singers and dancers.[10] In 1637, Venice opened its first public opera house, earlier performances having been private and restricted to the aristocracy.

Castrati did not reach the peak of fashionable popularity as opera singers until the following century, but John Raymond, visiting Verona in the 1640s, found that the locals 'are so addicted to Musick, especially that of the Voyce (which indisputably is the best,) that great Persons keep their Castrati viz. Eunuchs whose throates and complexions scandalize their breeches'.[11] It is certainly possible that such a 'great Person' in Verona might have employed a castrato to give private performances in his personal *ridotto*.

It should be borne in mind that, in the early years of the Grand Tour, music in Italy had the reputation of being lascivious and liable to corrupt young minds. Even as late as 1813, Eustace was still warning against it: 'It tends rather by its effeminacy to bring dangerous passions into action [...].' Youthful travellers should be cautioned against 'a taste that too often leads to low and dishonourable connexions'.[12] Enough visitors attended musical performances, however, to indicate that his strictures were generally ignored, and that visits to the theatre were commonplace. The Veronese Scipione Maffei took a particular interest in promoting both music and drama; he saw to the building of a public Teatro Filarmonico, which opened in 1732 with a performance of his own *La fida ninfa*, with music by Vivaldi[13] (see Plate 8b). Unfortunately, this theatre, designed by Francesco Galli-Bibiena, burnt down, but had been rebuilt by 1754. Maffei also encouraged the local nobility to take part in musical performances, usually in private venues.[14]

A few years later, the two academies and the theatre were all established in the same building, according to Keysler.

> In the hall, which is very large, are the portraits of the Patres, or presidents of this academy [dei Filarmonici], which are always four in number. In an apartment on the left-hand are kept the old musical instruments with which the nobility of Verona formerly amused themselves; and this gave rise to the present foundation.[15]

Other apartments were kept for the Filotimi and for public meetings where the nobility of Verona met several times a week to play cards, while the Teatro Filarmonico provided performances of music and theatre. In 1788, Charles Abbot noted in his diary that this theatre

[…] is very ill-shaped & poorly decorated but it is large – and the stage large – there are twenty boxes in each row & five rows. The singularity of the shape of the theatre is that instead of the boxes continuing on each side in a line up to the stage – stop short & have an angle between the last box in the body of the House & the stage box which stands upon the Proscenium. In this angle, which is very considerable, there is on each side of the House a statue.[16]

The idea of a central building devoted to the arts appealed to a number of visitors. In 1740, Thomas Martyn described how 'One of the apartments [in the Academy] serves as a rendezvous of good company of both sexes every evening; it is called *camera della Conversazione*, and is furnished at the public expense.'[17] In 1771, Lady Miller noted with approval this Italian custom of providing a central point where

[…] people of fashion of the town meet every evening […] It is a much more sociable plan than the receiving their acquaintance in their own houses, which occasions much trouble and some expence. I should think, that were this practised in some of the country towns in England, under proper regulations, it might be productive of more society and rational amusement, than the continual dining about with country neighbours, and the teasing importunity of visitors, not always in themselves agreeable.[18]

The Reverend Alban Butler, there in 1745, could see another advantage.

The Academy, or assembly of gentlemen who have formed a club for conferences on the belles lettres, contains halls and chambers well furnished with pictures, books, a chamber with instruments of musick, &c. How commendable are such academies of young gentlemen, compared to those clubs whose amusements consist in drinking or gaming![19]

The eighteenth century in particular saw several visitors recording aspects of the city's musical life. In 1765, Jérôme de Lalande attended a performance of *Antigone*, music by Giuseppe Sarti, in the theatre, with the female lead taken by a singer called Aguiari who had a 'voix surprenante', but was generally known as La Bastardina or La Bastardella because she was said to be one. She was paid 350 sequins or 4200 livres for about 15 appearances in one month, during which time both foreigners and local people came to enjoy her performances.[20] In 1770, Mozart and his father Leopold arrived in Verona for a concert in what is now the Sala Maffeiana in the Accademia Filarmonica, for which Mozart, then aged about 13, was paid ten gold *zecchini*; the plaque in the Sala recording this visit is still in place.

However, when Charles Burney, engaged in writing his *The Present State of Music in France and Italy*, published in 1771, arrived in the city the previous year, he observed that there was no opera, serious or comic, taking place. He did note though:

> The short space of time I staid at Verona was not sufficient for many musical enquiries; but I was afterwards informed by an English gentleman, who had resided several years in that city, that it contains, besides several able professors, a great number of dilettanti, who both perform and compose in a superior manner.[21]

Michael Kelly, the famous Irish tenor, arrived in Verona in 1780 with an introduction to the then Count Bevilacqua who asked him to perform privately at an 'elegant concert for the first people of Verona'. The Count later saw to a more public benefit concert for him, which was well attended, with Kelly earning 71 *zecchini* – about £30 'British' or £5000 in today's money – during the evening. He expressed himself impressed with musical life in the city. 'There was not a city in Italy of its size, at the time I visited it, which could boast of so many good musical amateurs, vocal and instrumental, as Verona.' He was even taken, much to his surprise, to the local gaol, where the gaoler and his family were between them able to play double bass, cello, violin and harpsichord, while two of the daughters sang. 'They were all enthusiasts and excellent performers [...] and I returned to my hotel [...] much gratified by the pleasant evening I had passed, *though it was in prison*.'[22]

August von Kotzebue visited the city on several occasions, finding the standard of music improving each time. In 1805 he observed:

> The theatre of Verona is, in every respect, one of the best that I have met with in Italy. When I passed through the town the first time, the opera buffa indeed was not above mediocrity, and none of the singers seemed to surpass the others [...]. At my second visit to Verona, I found the opera and ballet still further improved. The piece represented was *la Cappriciosa pentita*, with exquisite music by Fioravanti.[23] The prima donna, Ceccarelli, was by no means handsome; and the tenor, Campitelli, a very indifferent performer; but the two buffos, Guglielmini and Bartolucci, were of a superior order.

So far as the theatre was concerned, he described it as

> [...] large and handsome: in the curtain I counted fourteen or fifteen rents. Illusion is not particularly studied: when the scene changes, the decorations

are removed before it is finished, and during the representation the candle-snuffer walks about just where he pleases. French grenadiers kept guard, and the greatest part of the audience was likewise composed of this class.[24]

Henry Coxe (a pseudonym for J. Millard) noted in 1814 that performances in the Roman amphitheatre or Arena took place only in the summer. For the winter, there was a modern theatre

> [...] which is used only in the month of November for the serious opera, before the carnival begins in the other principal cities of Italy. It has five rows of boxes, 27 in each row. The entrance is through a noble portico, decorated by the Marchese Maffei with Etruscan marbles and inscriptions [...][25]

Two years later the Genevan historian Jacques Galiffe was carried away by a performance of *Tancredi*, composed by the youthful Rossini.

> His music is of the right school; unaffected, easy, elegant, and graceful. There are passages in Tancredi of great effect; particularly in the first finale, where the subject demands them [...] The composition is original, warm and brilliant; and peculiarly remarkable for that singleness and uniformity of style, which characterizes the works of the great masters, such as Cimarosa and Paesiello.

He also praised the performers: 'The whole was extremely well sung, especially by the two ladies and the tenor, who were excellent artists.'[26] Major Frye in 1818 described the theatre as 'exquisitely beautiful, and very tastefully fitted up'. He also claimed to have 'assisted at the representation of *La Gazza Ladra*, one of Rossini's best operas'.[27]

Galiffe, however, did have one reservation about a performance that commonly took place between acts:

> [...] there was a ballet, danced by what the Italians call Groteschi. I ought not, however, to say danced, because it was very unlike that graceful art: I should rather say, whirled and jumped; for it consisted entirely of such extravagant leaps and feats of agility, as to excite the most violent laughter, the first time we saw it. But it is not ridiculous to the Italians: they like it exceedingly, and applaud it with the same enthusiasm which we should bestow on a good comedy, or a ballet danced by first-rate Parisian artists.[28]

The artist John Hayward, visiting in 1817, was similarly unimpressed with the ballet section which he saw as part of an opera by Niccolò Piccinni:

> [...] 7 o'clock went to the Teatro Filarmonico – saw the opera buffa of Griselda [...] Singing mediocre – dancing in the ballet consisted principally in feats of strength – male & female – entirely devoid of grace – fatigued with seeing such unnatural and indelicate exertions left the theatre at 9 o'clock.[29]

The American Nathaniel Carter had a much more enjoyable experience in 1826.

> The evening was passed at the Opera. Among the performers was a Miss Barca, a Veronese girl, whose melody of voice infinitely surpassed any thing of the kind I have witnessed in Italy. Her person is not good, nor her face pretty, nor her action graceful; but her vocal powers are unrivalled. She warbles without effort, in all the sweetness and plaintive tenderness of the nightingale. The tones appear to drop spontaneously from her lips, breathing the very soul of music, and possessing an innate pathos, beyond the reach of art. She has been upon the stage but a few months, and her style of singing is natural, easy, and unaffected. In Paris, London, or New York, she would realize a fortune, in a few seasons. I went a second time to hear her in the same part, and my first impressions were fully confirmed.[30]

There were several other smaller theatres in the city; it is unclear which one was visited in 1818 by Henry Matthews, fellow of King's College Cambridge, whilst on his 'wild goose chase after health', as he believed. He was not enthusiastic about his experience.

> I went in the evening to the theatre; but the house was dull, dark, and dirty; and the audience seemed to come with any other object rather than to hear the play; for, they talked amongst themselves, as loud as the actors on the stage. When there is no sympathy between the actor and the audience, nothing can be more tiresome than a play. The reaction is wanting, to give it spirit; for when a play goes off well, it is, I believe, because the audience bring at least one half the entertainment along with them.[31]

This was by no means the first time a complaint was levelled by visiting tourists against Italian audiences, which were inclined to behave badly in concerts; they would listen to the main arias, but would otherwise talk, drink and eat throughout the performance.

Captain Clayton had a varied evening at another theatre in 1859:

> We [...] went to the Teatro Ristori, most elegantly fitted up, where we found two sisters who played wonderfully on the fiddle, a representation of

> Bonaparte's last days at St. Helena (the English being of course held up as everything that was most disgraceful in conduct and hideous in person), lots of beautiful women, and some very bad smells.[32]

Quite why the performers portrayed the English in such a bad light is not clear; perhaps the treatment meted out by the British to the exiled Napoleon was the cause, although in past years the Veronesi had had little occasion to sympathize with the French.

One or two visitors noticed how ordinary Italians showed their love of singing while at work or at play in the city. Goethe, in Verona in 1786, always enthused about the way Italians lived as much as possible in the open air.

> At night singing and all sorts of noises begin. The ballad of 'Marlbrook' is heard in every street; – then comes a dulcimer, then a violin. They try to imitate all the birds with a pipe. The strangest sounds are heard on every side.[33]

('Marlbrook' or *Marlbrook s'en va-t-en guerre* was a song, popular all over Europe, about the 1st Duke of Marlborough at the 1709 battle of Malplaquet.) In 1814, Samuel Rogers heard 'Young men, silk-weavers, in a workshop singing in parts a chorus in an opera familiar to my ear & in a style that there seemed delightful.'[34] Ruskin, too, observed this:

> The only really beautiful piece of song which I heard at Verona, during several months' stay there was the low chant of girls unwinding the cocoons of the silkworm, in the cottages among the olive-clad hills on the north of the city.[35]

Later, there was another style of music in Verona to welcome the visitor. In 1847, the American George Hillard heard the band of the Austrian garrison playing in the public square.

> It was difficult to believe that such delicious strains could proceed from figures so coarse and countenances so stolid [...] A blind man would have said of these Austrian bands that none but heroes and patriots could breathe such strains. Perhaps, however, these poor fellows were possible heroes and patriots. If lower than their music, they were higher than their faces. A German without a heart is not often to be found. The feeling which these coarse men put into their playing was the voice of the soul, striving to break out of its rude prison [...] They were thinking of the homes from which they had been torn; and the voices of their children mingled with the pathetic tones they drew from their instruments.[36]

In 1851, Ruskin, too, experienced a memorable musical event during Austrian rule. He was staying as usual at Due Torri, as was the Empress of Russia. The city's Austrian governor had ordered three military bands to perform some music for her outside the hotel. The bands arrived in Piazza Sant'Anastasia, preceded by soldiers bearing torches, and played the Emperor's hymn:

> [...] the burst of solemn and simple music from so many instruments, composed together the finest piece of mere *effect* I have ever seen in my life [...] it was but a parcel of Croats playing music to a middle-aged lady [...] but for intensity and completeness of stage effect, I never saw anything to beat it – or equal it.[37]

About the same time, the German historian Friedrich von Raumer witnessed a rather different event in a church, combining both a military band and a poetry reading.

> I heard the sounds of lively military music issuing from a church, and found that the city gymnasium was holding a poetical sitting, at which twenty-eight compositions in all metres were recited in honour of Scaliger. What powers of production! some admirers may exclaim ; what diversity in unity ! [...] There was no end to the shouting and clapping of hands. A troop of little happy urchins in particular clapped till their hands were quite red, and the trumpets drowned their fortissimo. You missed just the best, you may say; and I will not contradict this mild interpretation.[38]

So Verona has had a long history of musical performance, with visitors over the years coming to expect good music in its local theatres and concert halls. The best-known musical event in the city nowadays is the opera series that takes place in the Roman Arena during the summer. This practice began in 1913 with a performance of *Aida* to celebrate 100 years since the birth of Verdi, and has developed into the annual season that celebrated its 100th anniversary in 2013. (There were breaks during the war years 1915–18 and 1940–5.)

Today's visitors can also find musical events during the winter months at the Teatro Filarmonico, as well as free concerts in many of the city's churches and at Verona's music school, the Conservatorio de Musica 'E.F. Dall'Abaco' situated near Piazza Sant'Anastasia.

CHAPTER 20

Matters of Health

Its Situation is so pleasant, and the Air so pure and wholesome,
that several Roman Emperors have lived long here on that very account.[1]

Henri de Blainville, 1767

JUST NEAR VERONA is a small place called Caldiero (sometimes Caldero), which has been famous for the medicinal properties of its baths for centuries. Caution was evidently required, however. Vasari tells us of an artist, one Francesco Monsignori, who had kidney problems. He therefore 'with the leave of the Marquis and by the advice of the physicians went with his wife and many servants to the Baths of Caldero [...] to take the waters'. After drinking the water one day, he

> [...] allowed himself to be overcome by drowsiness, and slept a little, being indulged in this by his wife out of compassion; whereupon, a violent fever having come upon him in consequence of his sleeping, which is a deadly thing for one who has just taken that water, he finished the course of his life on the second day of July, 1519.[2]

In 1555, Sir Thomas Hoby of Bisham Abbey seems to have risked the plague to meet up with his brother there for whatever health cure they were expecting:

> After xxij dayes abodd at Caldero, to take the water, we departed thense in cumpanie with Mr. Wrothe and Mr. Cheeke, who were then cumm from Padoa, for that the plague, that was ceased before owr cumming from thense, begann again to encrease.[3]

One William Turner, an English herbalist with an Italian medical doctorate, gave a lengthy account of the medicinal properties of the 'Calderane bathes' in 1568, following a visit there eight years earlier. Amongst many other things, he believed they were good for 'all kinde of scabbes and itches, and for all spottes in anye parte of the bodye'; also for 'fretting, gnawing, wasting and creping sores'. Furthermore, they 'healeth the hitchcock or piskinge', could also cure infertility in both men and women and are 'good for women that are vexed with the whyte floures'. Turner cited the opinion of two Veronesi doctors, Alleardus Phisicion and Anthonius Fumanellus, as to the merits of the baths; the latter advised people 'to go down into the water or to drink it or have it poured upon a man or by provoking sweat by the vapours of it'.[4] In the late 1500s, Francesco Scoto also commented that the baths were 'helpful for the sterility of women'.[5]

Verona itself was often commended for its healthy air. In 1586, the dramatist Valerini asserted that people from Mantua, Ferrara, Vicenza, Brescia and Milan were advised by their 'medici prudenti' to go to Verona to escape the polluted air in their own cities.[6] Albanis Beaumont noted, two centuries later, that because the city was 'nearly at the foot of the Alps, the air is both serene and healthy',[7] while in 1817 Major William Frye approved its 'remarkably healthy climate'.[8]

One further instance of the city's wholesome reputation comes in a letter from Maria, duchess of Gloucester, to her father, Sir Edward Walpole, in June 1777. Her husband, the Duke of Gloucester, brother of George III, had been so unwell while in Venice that the family had decided to move on, with Maria 'hoping the air of Verona (which is as good as Italian air can be in the summer) would set him right again'.[9] However, by late June the Duke had been forced to leave the city at once. One of his attendants wrote to the British Resident in Venice that, although the Duke was very weak,

> [...] he cannot think of employing a foreign Physician. His constitution is most delicate. Mr Bryan, the Domestic Surgeon, has advised him going immediately, really to save his life [...] The Duchess, as you may easily believe, is full of care and trouble.[10]

There was one seventeenth-century traveller who felt that the act of travel itself was beneficial for one's physical and mental health. William Aglionby, who first published an English translation of a selection from Vasari's book on eminent Italian painters, was in Verona in November 1685, and wrote to a friend: 'we arrived hither, and are burrowed in a warm chamber by the fire'. He continued thus: 'It is pretty strange, that without any other prescription than hard jogging, and harder beds, foul linen, and coarse fare, I have not known such a thing as a pain [...].' He now believed 'laziness a great disease, or at least a fosterer of many', and he would 'make strong resolutions against it when I come again to England'.[11]

William Patoun, that much-travelled Scottish connoisseur, gave some good general advice to the unnamed eldest son of an English peer in the 1760s:

> Avoid eating Sallad with much Oil in Italy [...] relaxing food in a hot Country often occasions ruptures. A Medicine Chest is not Necessary for your Lordship, but I should think it prudent to carry with you a little Rhubarb and Scotch Pills, a little Friars Balsam some sticking Plaisters, some Nitre and Salt of tartar to make a saline draught upon occasion: or what is equivalent some Spirit of Hartshorn (scarce to be had in Italy) which with a little Vinegar makes the Spirit of Minderari so much used in fevers. A little good Jesuits Bark is likewise advisable. I hope in God your Lordship will have no occasion for the Above, but they are easily carried. Be not afraid of Ice in All Shapes during the hot Months. I never knew it hurt any body. Do not attempt to walk out on foot in the day time in the great heats. It often occasions Violent and fatal Fevers.[12]

There were, of course, varying opinions about the local climate and its effect on health. The most striking came in a book called *Climate of Italy in relation to pulmonary consumption*, 1852, by Thomas Burgess MD, who wrote thus about north Italian winters:

> Mr. B. Honan, an accurate observer, and a gentleman of authority, who has had many years' experience of the climate from residing in different parts of Italy, both north and south, writes from Verona, in the month of January, 1850, in the following unmistakable *ipsissima verba*, which are true, generally speaking, although somewhat vernacularly expressed: 'There are many humbugs in Italy, but there is none against which I more complain than its climate. I never spent so severe a winter as this, and I seek in vain any one corner where I can find shelter from the dry and piercing cold. In all northern climes the houses are prepared for the severity of the weather, and with good stoves, thick carpets, well-closing doors and windows, and our bright sea-coal fire, we defy the winter; but in Italy the cold is more intense within the house than without, as not a single window or door is air-proof, and a bright fire only increases the number and bitterness of the various currents which it inhales through every chink. At the moment whilst I write I am assailed in front, in flank, and rear,

and my palsied fingers can with difficulty hold the pen, though Nature has not made me one of the shivering race; but I cannot tolerate humbug in any shape, and above all, the humbug of an Italian climate.'[13] Writing from Rome in the middle of the following May, the same author observes: – 'The weather is still cold and disagreeable, and the humbug of an Italian climate applies as much to the spring at Rome as to the winter at Verona.'[14]

It was not just the cold winters: there were occasions when the plague could cause problems for travellers. Montaigne complained in 1580:

> If we had not been provided with certificates of health, which we procured at Trento, and had confirmed at Rovere, they would not have let us enter the town [Verona], and yet there was not the slightest rumour of the plague; but it is the custom here, which is probably kept up for the purpose of cheating travellers out of the fees which they exact for the health-certificates.[15]

The risk of plague was, however, something never to be trifled with; it is estimated that nearly two-thirds of Verona's population died in the 1630 epidemic, and outbreaks continued even into the nineteenth century.

Sometimes travellers had to spend time in quarantine in the local *lazaretto* if they came from an area known to have suffered an outbreak of plague. Verona's Lazzaretto di Porto San Pancrazio, to a design attributed to Sanmicheli, was begun in 1549 but not completed until 1628; it was situated well outside the city walls near the Adige, in an area then sparsely populated. In the early 1700s, Lord Lonsdale and Alexander Cunningham had occasion to be detained there, but were apparently satisfied with the conditions. 'They have been 14 days in the Lazaretto of Verona & are very contented with their treatment there.'[16] During the period of Austrian domination, the *lazaretto* was used as an ammunition store, and gradually fell into disrepair, so that little remains of it today; it seems, however, that a project to restore it has recently been agreed by the local authority.

Yellow fever could be another hazard, as Kotzebue found out in 1805:

> The yellow fever has rendered the tedious formality of Austrian police, if possible, still more tedious. There are stations on which you can scarcely proceed half an hour without being obliged to produce your passports and certificates of health. Many a valuable hour is in this manner lost by the traveller. I applaud the adoption of the most rigorous precautions against that dreadful disease; but where the multiplication of them is productive of no benefit whatever, I cannot help considering them as superfluous. He who deceives one post with his passport will probably find it an easy matter

to impose upon all the rest. A general in Tyrol has presented a proposal to government, to strip every person coming from Leghorn stark naked, to burn his clothes, and to supply him with new ones at the emperor's expense. I doubt whether this plan will be approved.[17]

There are records of various other health problems that beset travellers in the city. Henrietta Spencer, Lady Bessborough, was taken ill there in November 1792 with a severe cough and fever. 'At Verona I was quite confin'd & oblig'd to put on a blyster & be blooded.'[18] In the same year Lady Palmerston was most anxious about her husband:

> We sent for Doctor Farga, the most eminent physician of Verona. He found it to be a fever of the country; a kind of intermitting which in the autumn the inhabitants are extremely subject to [...] He gave him the bark [quinine] [...] It has agreed with him extremely.[19]

On occasion there could also be good news on the health front: in 1794, it was reported by Lady Webster that Lady Fitzgerald had given birth. 'At Verona we found Ld. & Ldy. Fitzgerald; she was suddenly brought to bed there.'[20]

Tourists had varying experiences when it came to their health. On a walking tour in the 1830s, George Hume Weatherhead arrived in Verona; unfortunately, on his very first night he had to leave the opera for his hotel because he felt so unwell. 'But I only shifted the scene of my ailment, not its action; for I had not been long there before I found myself in a high fever', which made him delirious. The next morning he 'got up about eleven, notwithstanding that I felt as if my brain were bound round with a cord, and crawled out to see the Tombs of the Scaliger Family'. Unfortunately, the same fever attacked him for four consecutive nights, after which he felt somewhat better, but then suffered 'a fit of the ague'. He decided it was now time to move on, so taking 'a little quinine and a whole bottle of wine [...] I shouldered my knapsack once more, and trudged on towards Milan'.[21] This somewhat unorthodox treatment appeared to work sufficiently for him; he was, in fact, a doctor of medicine. His undertaking of a tour on foot was unusual, with most visitors travelling either on horseback or by carriage.

So tourists over the years did what might have been expected of them. They brought some well-known remedies from home, such as Friars Balsam and Jesuits Bark or, when the problem needed more expert advice, they summoned a local doctor. One wonders how the non-Italian speakers managed to communicate their symptoms effectively, or to understand the advice given; perhaps hotels popular with tourists generally had access to someone with some degree of fluency in English.

 CHAPTER 21

Visitors' Views on Local Agriculture and Industry

Here are vines, mulberries, olives; of course, wine, silk, and oil: everything that can seduce, everything that ought to satisfy desiring man.[1]

Hester Piozzi, 1789

THE EVER-OBLIGING Franciscan preacher Barduzzi provided an enthusiastic description of agricultural production in and around Verona in 1489.

> Verona enjoys to the full a healthy climate and ample soil. She bears a rich annual harvest of grain like whitest ivory, choicest wine of every kind, and olive oil of the highest quality, and has abundance of all varieties of fruit, of indescribable sweetness [...]

He claimed the area was rich enough in 'grain, costly oil and wine and excellent cheese' to allow export to Germany and elsewhere. So far as the sheep industry was concerned, 'Verona has no rival [...] for the softness and whiteness of the fleeces from her flocks' which produced 12,000 bolts of cloth a year from 'her great workshops'. Barduzzi believed that the profit to Venice from taxes paid by Verona in the late 1400s was worth more than 100,000 gold pieces annually.[2]

Francesco Scoto, whose guide to Italy was published in about 1600, was concentrating on the excellence of local food production.

> This city abounds with all things necessary. Their fruits are all delicious, but the figs *Bardolini* exceed all others. It hath fish very sweet from the Lake Garda, good meat from the excellent pasture, exquisite wines from the hills, good corn from the vales, and good health from the ayr, although somewhat piercing.[3]

Eighty years later, John Keysler enthused particularly about the wide range of fruit and vegetables available. 'The country about Verona produces good peaches, melons, figs, strawberries, truffles, very large artichoaks, asparagus, chestnuts, apples, pears, plums, grapes, olives, and esculent herbs.'[4] He also visited one of the city's annual fairs, where he noted the extensive sale of the medicinal herbs or 'physical plants, which are gathered on Monte Baldo'.[5] He was not the only tourist to mention Monte Baldo, which lies to the east of Lake Garda, and was well known for its health-giving herbs. In 1786, Albanis Beaumont acknowledged the fertility of the area.

> Although the greatest part of this province is not only mountainous, but filled with romantic and extensive valleys; yet the soil is particularly rich, and well cultivated; for it amply furnishes the inhabitants with every luxury as well as necessary production.[6]

Many travellers were fascinated by the way that grapevines were trained to grow from tree to tree; these could be pollarded trees, or sometimes mulberry trees. In the 1790s, Sarah Bentham was travelling the road from Vicenza to Verona:

> [...] and at this Time The Road was Lined on each side with Vines hanging in Festoon-like Arches from Tree to Tree – Loaded with Grapes; the quantity incredible, and the Scenery Picturesque, for between the pollards which Supported the Vines the Land was Cultivated with wheat, maiz or Turky Corn.[7]

As the American George Rapelje approached the city from Brescia in 1821, he

> [...] went through several villages, mostly inhabited by the farmers, peasants, &c. This being the time of their vintage, the girls, women, boys, and men, were all employed gathering the grapes, and the road was crowded with ox carts or wagons, with large vats, or pipes, of an immense size, and all filled with grapes to be expressed; the presses belong in the villages.[8]

The abundance of mulberry trees grown mainly for the silkworm industry was the subject of much comment. It has already been noted that George Tappen, on his way from Verona to Milan in 1803, regretted the fact that the French had destroyed the livelihood of many peasants by hacking down these trees for fuel.[9] By 1830 the mulberry trees had recovered from the depredations of the French armies, with the American Rembrandt Peale observing: 'Along the whole road, men, women and children, were busy in collecting bags full of mulberry leaves to feed their silk worms, stripping the trees entirely naked, and afterwards trimming the branches.'[10]

A few years later, the Scottish antiquary William Rae Wilson felt this method of harvesting rather spoilt the appearance of the countryside:

> These trees are most carefully attended to, and return a great profit to their owners; yet so far from serving to enliven the landscape they rather make a desolate appearance, their leaves being nearly all stripped off, and little more than naked branches to be seen, so that they looked as if blighted; and the appearance was all the more singular because so little in unison with the season; although by a little stretch of fancy they might be represented as having divested themselves of their superfluous clothing on account of the heat, and therefore to have accommodated themselves well enough to the season.[11]

There is no doubt that the silk industry was of great importance to Verona's economy, as was made clear by Franceso Scoto. He declared that the trade in wool and silk was so extensive at Verona, that 'The merchandise of cloth and silk maintains above 20,000 handicraftsmen'.[12] By the end of the eighteenth century it has been calculated that there were 250 silk looms in operation in Verona, with buyers arriving from Munich, Vienna and Berlin; in fact, when Venice imposed new duties on the export and transit of silk in 1776, the outcry from Verona and the surrounding province was such that these taxes were withdrawn.[13] De Blainville had commented just a few years earlier on 'a vast number of silk-weavers' working within the city.[14]

Marianne Colston noticed one effect of the wealth created by this trade in 1820.

> We saw many handsome looking houses, or, as they are termed, palaces, which belong to silk merchants. This article constitutes the principal part of the trade of Verona. How great are the obligations of Italy to the insect which produces this beautiful substance! By it the inhabitants of her poorer villages are preserved from starvation, and those of several of her cities raised to opulence and luxury![15]

Some 15 years later (1835), Lady Murray observed that 'The great employment of the lower classes is winding silk, which is a great branch of their commerce.'[16] Thomas Barlow from Leeds managed to find his way into a silk mill in 1836, but was somewhat dismissive of the technology: 'Adjoining this warehouse is a silk mill [...] Some men were propelling a rude species of mill in a manner more like that practised in our treadmills, than in our manufactories.'[17] Here spoke an Englishman from a country already transformed by the Industrial Revolution.

One other industry that flourished in the city itself was the working of leather. In the 1780s, Reichard observed: 'The gloves and skins prepared at this place are in much request.'[18] In 1807, Baron d'Uklanski found that the 'shoemakers [...] and glovers work in the streets'; however, the result of their leather-working was 'the insufferable smell that pervades every quarter and affects the air'.[19] In 1821, Robert Marsden noticed the way that local shopkeepers advertised their wares.

> The tradesmen here follow the example of those in the other Italian towns, and perhaps to a greater extent: not satisfied with having their name and business printed in large letters, they prefer a more descriptive appendage: on the shutter of a shoemaker we see represented a man trying on a pair of shoes; on that of a glover, a lady fitting herself with gloves.[20]

Arthur Young, the well-known English agriculturalist, spent time in and around Verona in the late 1780s. He commented on the local soil: 'The territory of Verona is, in general, indifferent, and would not be of great value, were it not for water, and much industry.'[21] He also made detailed notes about local yields, crop rotation, as well as the cost of land and of water (this last being particularly important for the growing of rice). The Veronese habit of combining the training of grapes up trees with the cultivation of other crops beneath did not find favour with him, leading him to describe the local wheat yield thus: 'We have not, upon the poorest lands in England, so wretched a crop: to what are we to attribute it, if not to general bad management, united with the execrable system of incumbering their fields with pollards and vines.'[22] He did also comment on the depressed state of the wool industry and its decline over the years.

> Here is a woollen fabric that still maintains some little ground; though the declension it has suffered is very great. I was assured that 20,000 manufacturers were once found in a single street; this, I suppose, may be an exaggeration, but it at least marks that it was once very great; now there are not 1000 in the whole city; in the time of its prosperity they used chiefly their own wool, at present it is imported.[23]

Rice was another crop found growing locally; it has been suggested that it was introduced here as early as the late fourteenth century.[24] Pasquin noted the name and figure of Teodoro Trivulzio, former governor of Verona, sculpted on Porta Vescovo in the city; 'it was he that first introduced the culture of rice into the country of Verona in 1522', thus making himself a great benefactor to the local community.[25] Galignani's *Guide*, a reissue of Coxe's *Picture of Italy* published in 1815, also observed that the Italians 'grow rice in the vallies that are unfit for pasturage or corn'.[26]

One other crop came to the attention of the Scotsman William Cadell, who was surprised, two years later, by the widespread cultivation of Indian corn and its many uses, for instance for polenta, while the stalks became cattle food, and the discarded sheath

> [...] called foglia which envelopes the ear, [and] is generally used in Italy to stuff mattrasses, and is well suited for that purpose. The beds most common [...] consist of two tressels of wood or iron, on which boards or reeds are laid; on these a thick mattress of foglia, and over it the bed, without bedposts or curtains.[27]

Some years earlier, in the hotel Due Torri, Friedländer had also praised the benefits of a 'palliasse of maize-straw, which is shaken every morning'.[28]

On his way to Verona in 1823, another Scot, Henry Cockburn, made some curious observations about the habits of local peasants during harvest.

> The day is intensely hot, and the poor peasants have been cooling themselves along the road by eating gourds & melons under trees – these & other fruits being exposed everywhere for sale on the high way as freely as potatoes with us. But they are not half so good, & tho' it looks & sounds well to see or to say that an Italian ditcher rests on his long spade to eat a bunch of grapes, but no one who has ever tasted a good potato with moderate heat [would] envy him.[29]

The option of eating a potato – whether of moderate heat or not – would probably not have appealed to any Italian ditcher at the height of summer. Nor is it quite clear from this account what the peasants were harvesting, other than fruit. William Wilson, around 1835, met with one obvious way that the locals tried to keep cool during these hotter months:

> [...] the greater part of the peasantry we met [...] had so disencumbered themselves of their garments as to be, some of them, in a state more than

half-way approaching nudity, making a very liberal display of their skin, which was tanned many shades darker than buff.[30]

By 1826, William Thomson was declaring himself favourably impressed with the fertility of the land locally, but had his doubts about whether the local inhabitants made best use of it.

> The valley between the Adige and the Po is rendered very productive by alluvial deposits, which fertilize the soil. Most of the extensive plains in northern Italy are similarly enriched, but the same natural advantages are not always turned to equally good account. Whether this arises from ignorance or supineness on the part of the agriculturists it would be difficult to determine.

He went further, attributing various economic failings to war, climate and even to the influence of the Roman Catholic Church.

> The continual wars and change of masters have thrown back the Italians and arrested the march of the useful arts amazingly during latter times. Climate and education, doubtless, tincture the Italian character very strongly; and days, and sometimes weeks, of abstinence must be detrimental to the working classes, by prostrating both their physical and moral powers; and the continual church festivals, which are strictly observed, interfere greatly with their labours.[31]

Strangely, given the importance of the stone and marble quarrying industry around Verona, visitors to the area seldom gave it much attention, other than merely to acknowledge its existence. In 1766, de Lalande did note that the houses, bridges, pavements and other buildings in Verona were almost all of marble, because of the ready supply from the many local quarries; he quoted a certain Spada, who had listed as many as 35 different varieties to be found in the vicinity.[32] Twenty years later, Beaumont named two of these as 'Mischio di brentonico [e] lo Giallo di Torri'.[33] A certain Mr Seaforth, visiting Verona just after the defeat of the French in 1815, was much impressed by the way marble was used. 'In the streets the value of the durability of the marble is seen in almost every door – for in passing one is arrested constantly by most exquisitely chiselled work in the highest state of preservation.'[34]

Here is a passage by an Englishman, passionate about the varieties of marble to be found locally:

Verona 1846.
There is a marble with a clear yellow ground and clouds (not veins) of lilac and pale purple melted in it, that takes a very even and glossy polish, it is called Brentonico from the place where it is found in a mountain about 22 miles distant from Verona [...] & is so harmonious & delicate that I am inclined to assign it the first place among all the coloured marbles found in these northern parts of Italy. It was in great request for the decoration of altars in Verona, both in coloured panels and ballusters during [a] great part of the last century, so excellent specimens of it are to be seen in many of the Churches, and Maffei in his *Verona illustrata* where he commends/vaunts the beauties of the marbles produced in the district, mentions this the first, & the yellow of Torre (when of a full & deep orange dye) the second. It is fallen strangely into disuse, & the quarry from whence it was extracted is said to be so deep & so encumbered, that although it might still be had from thence in any quantity, it could only be procured (at least on the first reopening of the works) at a vast expense.[35]

These were the words of William John Bankes, written while conducting, from Italy, the refurbishment of his house in Dorset. This included an extensive use of Italian stone, with Bankes hoping to have two lions sculpted in the famous Veronese red marble still seen all over the city; he did, in fact, have a locally sculpted red marble well head shipped to Kingston Lacy.[36] Other items dispatched by ship from Venice included table legs made in *duro marmo bianco di Verona*, and a number of splendid Torre marble door surrounds still in situ in the Dorset house. Bankes described them thus in a letter to his sister:

[...] all the five door frames for the drawing room of the richest yellow marble sculptured & polished & above all two sort of pedestal pieces of furniture for lights to stand one on each of side of the great doors under the pictures of the King and Queen, sculptured in the same, & with tablets of real serpentine let into them.[37]

Bankes's extensive correspondence gives names of some of the Italian craftsmen he employed, with one Michelangelo Montresor from Verona submitting two bills in July and August 1846 for those marble door surrounds.[38] Another of his ideas was to get a local stonemason to produce a stone carving from nature in the manner of the famous English woodcarver Grinling Gibbons. This was attempted by a Veronese called Salesio Pegrassi, described by Bankes as 'really a great genius'. He wrote to his sister Anne that 'the success of the dead woodcock & dove suspended with masses of foliage has far exceeded my expectations, & in looseness & truth, & even delicacy are not much inferior to Gibbons' works'.[39] This panel in *marmo bianco di Verona* is also on display at Kingston Lacy, together with a second one depicting fish and aquatic plants. One Professor Luigi Gaiter, in the local *Foglio di Verona* of September 1849, noted Bankes' commissioning of so much work from local artists; he praised both the skill of Pegrassi and the fact that 'this liberal Englishman' was spending his money encouraging local craftsmen rather than 'impoverishing Italy' by removing its antique masterworks.[40]

So agricultural produce of various kinds, wool and silk for fabrics, and stone for the building trade were the principal items to attract the attention of travellers over the centuries. Arthur Young was the most thorough and knowledgeable observer, providing copious details of local land prices, different kinds of silkworm, and tithes and taxes on various agricultural products. Most visitors, however, were interested principally in the more striking and unusual aspects of local industry and agriculture: the growing of mulberry trees for silk production, or the cultivation of vines, pollarded trees and crops all together in the same piece of ground.

CHAPTER 22

The Dress of Local People

The women are very pretty, and wear white mantillas and rich gold earrings, chains, and crosses.¹

Lady Murray on the women of Verona in 1835

THE WAY LOCAL people dressed always seemed to interest visitors, many of whom were able to compare the clothes and appearance of the Veronesi men and women with those from other Italian towns. Comments by male travellers seem rather easier to come by than those by women, but then, of course, there were more of them to record their impressions.

As early as 1489, Bernardino Barduzzi, although a Franciscan friar, had noted 'the superb attire of the ladies of Verona, woven from gold thread and silk'.² For Montaigne in 1580, however, 'the women [of Verona] were very plain, and indifferently dressed'.³ A hundred and fifty years later, about 1730, John Keysler was more complimentary, noticing first the ladies themselves: 'The Veronese women are well shaped, and of a fresh complexion, for which unquestionably they are obliged to the goodness of the air.'⁴ He also found something particular to interest him:

> At Milan, as at Bologna and Verona, most curious artificial flowers are made of paper, wax, feathers, cotton, and sturgeons' skin, exactly resembling nature; and in this art the nuns particularly excel. These ornaments are never worn by the gentlemen, except at masquerades and in carnival time, nor by many ladies; but the altars in churches and genteel apartments are crowded with them, and also great quantities are exported.⁵

Were these the ornaments Hester Piozzi referred to in a letter of 1785? 'The Women of Fashion all over the North of Italy go without Caps old as well as young, & dress their Hair fantastically with Flowers &c. never thinking of Fashion, & studying only how best to set off their Charms.'[6]

Goethe, travelling in 1786, was clearly something of an expert on the details of women's clothing. As he walked around Verona, he looked out for the

> [...] women of the middle-ranks [...] The *Zendale* and the *Veste*, which serves this class in the place of an entire wardrobe, is a costume completely fitted for a people that does not care much for cleanliness, and yet always likes to appear in public, sometimes at church, sometimes on the promenade. The *Veste* is a gown of black taffeta, which is thrown over other gowns. If the lady has a clean white one beneath, she contrives to lift up the black one on one side. This is fastened on so as to cut the waist, and to cover the lappets of a corset, which may be of any colour. The *Zendale* is a large hood with long ears; the hood itself is kept high above the head by a wire-frame, while the ears are fastened round the body like a scarf, so that the ends fall down behind.[7]

No other traveller seems to have remarked on this curious 'hood with long ears'. It was men's headgear that attracted Adam Walker's attention in about 1787. 'The gentlemen dress as in France, only here, as in Germany, the hat is of an enormous size, and cocked so as to have the hind flap very wide, and the front quite perpendicular.'[8]

Walker, although supposedly more at home lecturing on Natural Philosophy, made several remarks, some rather uncomplimentary, about the Veronesi. For him,

> The people are horribly swarthy, have keen black eyes, and black hair, which the women plait into a long rope, and coil it round and round on the back of the head; all the rest of the head is uncovered. Some wear small straw hats, turned up all round at the edge. The genteeler women wear black veils, and ladies dress as they did in England a few years ago, when long waists were the fashion.[9]

In 1796, Elizabeth Wynne, who had the privilege of being invited to the homes of her Italian relatives, noted in her diary that the ladies she met there were 'true Italians, some pretty but have no grace and dress frightfully badly'.[10] She also had something scathing to say about one group of local men: 'our postillions from Verona had their necks bare with golden chains round them, rings in their ears, and on their fingers, with artificial flowers upon their hats – what a manly garb!'[11]

There was then the question as to what the male visitor to Italy should wear. In 1776, William Patoun provided some advice about the dress code for an English aristocrat.

> A Certain degree of dress is Necessary in Italy. The dress Cloaths are Gold Stuffs, and Embroidery for high Gala. Furnish yourself at Paris or Lyons. I shoud prefer Paris, as the Taylors are better and the expence much the same. A black Velvet Coat & Lyons Waistcoat is a most useful Change all the Winter. Laced Cloaths are not much Worn abroad, except for undress: and the English seldom wear any thing but plain Cloaths in travelling. The Cheapest Embroidery is to be had at Milan & Naples. Flowered Silks are very Cheap in Italy. A Suit at Florence does not cost above Eight Guineas: and the plain silks three or four only. A Demi-saison Velvet is a most useful genteel Coat, for Autumn and Spring.[12]

In the 1780s Goethe found the Veronese interest in clothing extended to what a foreigner was wearing:

> Although the people are careless enough with respect to their own wants and occupations, they have a keen eye for everything foreign. Thus in the very first days, I observed that everyone took notice of my boots, because here they are too expensive an article of dress to wear even in winter. Now I wear shoes and stockings nobody looks at me.[13]

How matters of dress were regarded by the upper classes of Verona could also affect foreign lady visitors to the city. In 1701, a local society, *La Compagnia della conversazione,* had been founded by a group of nobles with the objective of providing a place where they and their families could meet socially. In 1773, a scandal broke out after five ladies attended an evening event dressed in an unseemly fashion; they apparently wore crinolines of dimensions that revealed their figures, thereby causing much scandal. Respectable families – particularly those with daughters of eligible age – refused to attend further events until the matter was resolved. By a subsequent ruling only women dressed in a decorous fashion could be admitted; this rule was also extended to 'foreign' women or *forestiere* who could also attend so long as they adhered to the same dress code as respectable Veronesi matrons.[14]

A variety of clothing, both male and female, caught the eye of travellers as they approached Verona. This time, Adam Walker described a basic dress code in the countryside: 'The common men go almost naked; seldom any shoes or stockings, sometimes both sexes wear a piece of wood, hollowed into the shape of a foot, and a leather strap fastens it.'[15] On special occasions things were different. In 1816, John Cam Hobhouse noted: 'The country [between Verona and Montebello] on the day we passed seemed to have poured forth all its population into the roads. All classes, gaily or neatly dressed, were hurrying to the fair at Verona [...].'[16] The same year, Swiss Jacques Galiffe showed an intense interest in the ladies themselves:

> [...] on the road to Verona. I am persuaded that I saw a greater number of handsome women in that space, than I had seen in all Europe besides; and many of them were more exquisitely beautiful than any individuals I had ever met with. What peculiarly characterizes their style of beauty is the commanding nobleness of their countenance, mingled with a degree of mildness and candour. Our post-boys could not conceive, why we made them stop so frequently, or why we chose to be driven so slowly.[17]

Headdresses worn within the city were of particular interest. In 1846, Louisa Costello described how

> The women of Verona wear white veils instead of black, and carry their fans with the same graceful air as at Milan. In the market-place I observed many whose head-dress was a straw hat, and not a few, in Welsh fashion, with black beaver hats, men's shape, particularly inelegant and unsightly. I afterwards got accustomed to this unbecoming costume, which is common in the Tyrol, but can never be reconciled to its effect [...] I looked in vain amongst the townswomen and men for the beauty of Juliet or of the 'loving Proteus'. Nevertheless, at a distance, the girls with their large green fans and in their white muslin veils and dark dresses looked picturesque, and some of the commoner sort, wearing white muslin shawls elaborately embroidered and their heads covered with square handkerchiefs, were pleasing to the eye. If this white drapery were always fresh and clean, it would be very pretty, but as that is not the case, one cannot but regret that black is not more general.[18]

A Scotsman, in Verona in 1830, found that

> The female attire is very winning – a simple white veil thrown over the head. Their figures, it is true, have nothing of the Zephyr or of the fawn or of the gazelle; they are rather round and plump and substantive; yet are they peaceful & even elegant, with good feet and very pretty features. Attended high mass this morning, at the Cathedral, and vespers in the evening at the

same – looked about in vain for a representative of Juliet among the half-veiled kneeling beauties.[19]

William Gardiner also hoped to find women in the image of Juliet in 1846:

As the Veronese ladies glided past me – light as Psyche – I looked for a Juliet. Being without hat or cap, I might have felt the force of their eyes, but a veil of gauze thrown over their heads, and half covering their persons, baulked my curiosity.[20]

Some years earlier, Leitch Ritchie had noted a hair ornament worn to be seen beneath this veil:

Among the lower class of females, the pin, run through the knot of the hair behind, is either laid aside or much shortened; but, to make amends, the knob of silver, or mother-of-pearl, is increased from the size of a pigeon's sometimes to that of a goose's egg.[21]

There was clearly a difference of opinion on the veil versus the bonnet. Most of our tourists preferred the veil, but none was quite so eloquent on the subject as the American lawyer and author George Hillard, on tour in 1847:

I was in Verona on Sunday. The weather was fine, and the streets were filled with well-dressed persons of both sexes. Of the women, the majority wore veils, but a portion, apparently of the higher classes, were in bonnets. In the comparison, the former had greatly the advantage. A veil seems the natural covering of the female head, because in its flow and folds it resembles the waving and floating of the hair, and it crowns and shades the face in the same manner. Its lines blend with the rest of the dress gracefully, and without abrupt transitions; and it can be so disposed as to suit every style of face and head. We are accustomed to bonnets, and do not recognise their essential ugliness [...] but no one whose eye has rested for any time upon the beautiful head-dresses so common in Italy will ever be reconciled to the bold, staring front and incongruous ornaments of a bonnet. A veil is not only a beautiful piece of dress, but it is the most expressive and symbolical of all forms of costume. It is the representative of purity, gentleness, and modesty [...] Art, in all its forms, welcomes and adopts it; but, before a bonnet, the poet drops his pen, the sculptor his chisel, and the painter his brush.[22]

Never before can the veil have received such plaudits, nor the bonnet such condemnation.

By 1883, however, things had taken a turn for the worse so far as female headdress was concerned, according to William Devereux. 'I did not find much to praise in the beauty of the Veronese ladies, who, less wise than those of Padua, discarded the graceful and becoming head-attire of black lace, and adopted excruciating and deforming Parisian fashions.'[23]

The German August von Rochau compared the Veronesi with other Italians in 1850:

> In personal appearance the people are very much like the Milanese; fine stately men, and little women with mostly handsome faces, but clumsy figures and rather awkward deportment, who do not know how to conceal natural defects by any art of costume. Their children, however they dress really prettily, and I admired especially the golden circlet passing across the top of the head, by which the back hair of the young girls is confined.[24]

Naturally, at carnival and fair time, the locals would do as the Venetians did, and wear masks. Alban Butler had already noted this in 1745: 'At Verona we found every body masked in the streets, it being then one of their principal fairs. The mask is esteemed part of their dress in Venice and in its dependant towns.'[25]

The definitive judgement in the matter of local attire may perhaps be left with the artist Joseph Wright of Derby, writing in his journal of 1774–5:

> The women are in general handsome, they walk admirably, and have a gentility and ease about them peculiar to themselves. 'Tis not in the costliness of their habits that they outdo the English, but in the form and manner of wearing them.[26]

The same could be said of Italian – or Veronesi – women today, many of whom seem to manage an apparently effortless elegance. Verona itself is now full of expensive clothes shops, particularly in via Mazzini, where today's tourists can be seen indulging in window-shopping during the evening *passeggiata*.

CHAPTER 23

English Views of the Italians

> I had been taught the national prejudice,
> of supposing England the finest country in the world:
> when I travelled through France,
> I found no reason to change my sentiments,
> or to dispute the justice of those accounts to which I had owed them;
> but Italy gives me a new opinion.[1]
>
> *Thomas Broderick, travelling from Verona to Vicenza, in 1750*

THAT THE ATTITUDE of the English to Italy and the Italians changed substantially over the centuries is indisputable. In his book *The Scholemaster*, published posthumously in 1570, Roger Ascham, tutor to the Princess Elizabeth before she became Queen, clearly regarded the country as a den of robbers and papists, to be avoided by all true Englishmen. The religious divide between Protestant and Catholic from the time of the Reformation onwards could cause strong antagonism. All this did not, however, stop Englishmen from visiting the country in increasing numbers after 1700, either as Grand Tourists, scholars or simply as travellers. After the French revolutionary wars, the English (and Scottish) middle classes joined in, although now displaying less concern for the classical and much more interest in Italy's smaller towns and cities, with their varied art and architecture from different periods. It has been suggested that these nineteenth-century visitors were, on the one hand, more censorious and prejudiced than the Grand Tourists; they tended to look down on the Italians for their poverty and lack of economic development, coming as they did from a country of greater prosperity. On the other hand, these travellers also displayed an interest in wider aspects of Italian life and – at least some of them – in the Italians themselves.

On the whole, eighteenth-century Grand Tourists spent little time relating to any but upper-class Italians to whom they would have brought letters of introduction from well-connected individuals at home. Eustace maintained that 'Introduction to the higher class in Italy is not very difficult [...] A letter of introduction to any person of rank will enable the traveller to gain admission to evening parties.'[2] This had been true in 1769, too, when the Honourable William Fitzwilliam noted in his diary that travel in Italy was more agreeable if one spoke the language and came 'well Recommended to People of Fashion'.[3] As a member of the English aristocracy, he would have had no difficulty in obtaining introductions to members of the Italian nobility.

There was little incentive, however, to consort with Italians of lower rank, other than the innkeepers, postilions or *vetturini*, who were exactly the people that tourists complained most loudly about. William Fitzwilliam was aged 57 in 1769 when he undertook his travels, with no need of a tutor; he would have dealt himself with the innkeepers and others he met along the way. Some of these encounters must have been disagreeable, given the force of his remarks made on leaving Italy. He felt that his trip had certainly been worthwhile as the country afforded much 'both for Instruction as well as Amusement'. Nevertheless, while acknowledging that some Italians were 'worthy people', he felt that 'most appear in the most Disadvantageous Light'. He knew that 'Cunning, Lying, Dissimulation, Jealousy, Malice, Revenge, Cruelty and Cowardice' were universal traits, but felt that 'here they show themselves in a Superlative Degree'.[4]

Some Englishmen felt that consorting with one's own nationals while travelling abroad was not to be encouraged. As early as the 1590s, Francis Bacon had advised the Earl of Rutland both to profit by association with the best of the local people and in addition to 'restrain your affection and participation from your own countrymen of whatever condition'.[5] It appears, however, that this good advice tended to fall on deaf ears. In a letter of 1750 to her daughter, Lady Mary Wortley Montagu deplored 'the Custom of the English of herding together, avoiding the Conversation of the Italians'.[6] In the 1760s, William Patoun agreed:

> The Consequence in general of the English herding together are these, a great encrease of Expences: vying with each other in Equipage dress &c. Loss of time, temptation of gambling for want of other Amusement, with many other pursuits, which are Needless to mention.[7]

William Fitzwilliam positively advised 'my young Traveller' to travel alone, although he knew that in reality the English preferred to be with their compatriots. He felt, too, that with a companion, there was the danger of a divergence of opinion en route: 'Thus they go on, in a kind of Matrimonial State, and can't well get a Divorce, till they Return to their own Country.'[8]

Eustace, in his 1815 guidebook, was another strong advocate of making the most of one's time in Italy by associating with local people; he advised the English 'to converse with the natives of the country, to frequent public assemblies and courts, and, on the other hand, to take an occasional range through the humble walks of life [...]'.[9] Goethe would have agreed strongly with this advice; his account of his time in Verona in the 1780s is notable for his interest in the ordinary people he saw during his wanderings through the streets. Mrs Jameson's attitude was, unfortunately, quite different, displaying her strong prejudices. She stated quite bluntly, in her *Diary* of 1826, that 'I have not many opportunities of studying the national character; I have no dealings with the lower classes, little intercourse with the higher.' Nor did she care if the locals were 'what I hear them styled six times a day at least, – a dirty demoralized, degraded, unprincipled race', because her interest was only in 'all the treasures of art and nature which are poured forth around me'.[10]

There were one or two features of Italian life that aroused strong prejudices, other than the usual tourist complaints about overcharging by innkeepers, bad behaviour by postilions or arguments with customs officers. Dirt, either in public places or in the hotels, had always been an issue. Murray's *Hand-book* of 1842 agreed that 'no *Italian* inn is ever *neat,* if it is even clean', but felt that 'the male travellers (as to ladies, the case is hopeless) will, by exercising a certain degree of philosophy, be enabled to tolerate a portion of these annoyances'.[11] Dirty conditions were also an issue in England in the eighteenth and nineteenth centuries, particularly in urban areas: the Industrial Revolution had rapidly increased the gap between the living conditions of rich and poor and, from Hogarth to Dickens, there was no shortage of artistic or strongly worded literary comment on the more squalid conditions in London and elsewhere. As middle-class women joined the ranks of tourists, they were also very critical of the perceived lack of cleanliness to be found on the Continent. Sarah Bentham probably summed up the British attitude to the whole issue on her return to Harwich, remarking that, after breakfast, 'I went into a Warm Bath, and Rejoiced that I could change Dirt for Cleanliness, and My Dear Son did the same.'[12]

There was also one upper-class Italian habit that caused particular outrage among the British; this was the custom of cicisbeism, by which a married woman could take up with a man who acted, at least ostensibly, as merely her escort in public places. This was a result of parents marrying off their daughters very young; if the couple failed to get on, by custom the wife was allowed a *cicisbeo* or *cavalier servente*. In 1769, the Honourable William Fitzwilliam particularly condemned this: 'the Sacred Laws of Matrimony publicly Violated & Adultery Established by the most cogent of all Laws: the Law of Fashion'.[13] Thomas Watkins in the 1780s blamed Italians for 'their conjugal infidelity. Before marriage their women are nuns, and after it libertines'.[14] Hester Piozzi, married to an Italian and a fluent speaker of the language, realized the subject was somewhat sensitive to local people. On her asking a young married woman about it, Piozzi was told that the woman loved her husband 'excessively', but, because they were not rich, her *cavalier servente* paid the bills but 'that's all'. She also claimed to detest the custom, and found her *cavaliere*'s attentions wearisome.[15]

There were, of course, Englishmen who were ready to defend the Italians as a nation, even if they disliked some aspects of local life. Despite his views on *cicisbeismo*, Thomas Watkins felt that generally the Italian character 'is often grossly misrepresented by prejudice and ignorance'. While accepting that he might be biased, he declared, 'I have in Italian society passed my time as much to my satisfaction, as in any other whatever. They are infinitely more attentive to us than we are to them, more temperate, less arrogant, and less prejudiced.'[16] By the 1840s, Mrs Shelley was also at pains in her *Rambles* to defend the Italian character, which she considered to have been much maligned in the past by travellers criticizing the Italians in general for effeminacy, and for vice and cowardice among the nobility. She deplored the fact that many English travellers still 'parrot the same, not because these things still exist, but because they know no better'. For her,

> [...] no one can mingle much with the Italians without becoming attached to them [...] Their courtesy, their simplicity of manner, their evident desire to serve, their rare and exceeding intelligence, give to the better specimens among the higher classes, and to many among the lower, a charm all their own.

She felt, too, that the English in particular had an obligation to support the Italians who, living under the tyranny of Austria, lacked the freedoms her countrymen enjoyed.[17]

In 1835, Lady Murray experienced an incident in Verona that gave her a different idea of Italian manners.

> I had occasion for money here, and the banker, a cross old gentleman, was much annoyed at my making him count the zwanzigs he supplied me with, and when I begged him to send the money to the inn, he said '*Avete la*

vettura, è meglio prenderlo adesso' [You have your carriage, so it would be better if you took the money now].

She tried to persuade him, but he would not budge; this might perhaps have been because the banker felt he was being addressed as an inferior.[18] It was true that many English travellers tended to look down on Italians, whose classical past might be thought praiseworthy, but who were now deemed to be somewhat lowly beings, living in a country in various stages of decline. The English, on the other hand, were experiencing a period of economic growth and relative prosperity at home and expansion abroad, allowing them to feel superior to the less fortunate Italians.

Effie Ruskin, writing in 1850, was not one to join in any adverse criticism:

> [...] all that I have yet seen of the Italians makes me come to this opinion that whatever their private morals may be, they respect those who are well conducted, and are themselves extremely good natured, amiable and well-bred and when they find English who sympathize with their tastes and understand them, they will do any thing for them.[19]

Francis Coghlan's 1856 *Handbook for travellers in Northern Italy* provided a lengthy account of the merits and demerits of the Italian character. There was praise, but tempered with a degree of sarcasm and with an attempt to convince the English traveller that he was thought better of than other *stranieri* or foreigners. The Italians

> [...] are of a middle temper, betwixt the starched gravity of the Spaniard and the levity of the French [...] They are ready witted, and of great application, both in study and business. No nation is more scrupulously nice in all the punctilios of civility, more profuse of strained compliments and pompous titles, or more exact in entertaining people according to their quality [...]
>
> These virtues are not without a mixture of vices, which is the case of most nations. Their predominant passions are jealousy and intrigue [...]
>
> They have an extraordinary contempt and aversion for foreigners, whom they slightingly call Oltramontani [from beyond the mountains], though we must except the English, to whom they show much greater marks of respect than to other nations.[20]

Augustus Hare was, for his part, a staunch supporter of the Italian character: writing in the 1870s, he highlighted the different attitudes to class in England and Italy.

A friendly look and cheery word will win almost anything, but Italians will not be driven, and the browbeating manner, which is so common with English and Americans, even the commonest facchino [porter] regards and speaks of as mere vulgar insolence, and treats accordingly. Travellers, however, are beginning, though only beginning, to learn that difference of caste in Italy does not give an opening for the discourtesies in which they are wont to indulge to those they consider their inferiors in the north, and they are beginning to see that Italian dukes and marquises are quite as courteous and thoughtful for their vigneroli [vine-dressers], or their pecorai [shepherds], as for their equals; and that the Italian character is so constituted that a certain amount of friendly familiarity on the part of the superior never leads to disrespect in the inferior. Unfortunately they do not always stay long enough to find this out, and the bad impression one set of travellers leaves, another pays the penalty of!²¹

The likes of Effie Ruskin, Augustus Hare, Edward Hutton and others who had been resident in Italy for long periods had the ability to cast off many of the initial prejudices expressed by visitors, and to value the Italians for what they were.

What kind of reputation did the English visitor to Italy have among the Italians, or those of other nationalities? Horace Walpole expressed strong views about the bad impression left on Italians by members of the Society of Dilettanti, founded in 1732 by young English noblemen who had been on the Grand Tour. He deplored

> [...] the Dilettanti, a club, for which the nominal qualification is having been to Italy, and the real one is, being drunk: the two chiefs are Lord Middlesex and Sir Francis Dashwood, who were seldom sober the whole time they were in Italy.²²

By 1758, Lady Mary Wortley Montagu felt the whole idea of the Grand Tour had fallen into disrepute: 'the folly of British boys and [the] stupidity and knavery of [their] governors [had] gained us the glorious title of Golden Asses all over Italy'.²³ It was not only the young noblemen who were the problem; in 1743, Horace Mann advised Horace Walpole that even 'the reputation of our female travellers is very low'. This was at least in part due to the behaviour of Margaret Walpole, daughter-in-law of Sir Robert Walpole, and later countess of Orford, who spent many years in Italy, allegedly on account of her health. Despite having being married to two different Englishmen, she lived with a number of men there, including Pietro Barbarigo, son of the Governor of Verona, in 1741–2.[24]

Lord Byron was not slow to express dissatisfaction with the increased numbers of his compatriots in Italy after 1815, as they took early advantage of the French defeat; nor did he have a high opinion of his compatriots. 'A man is a fool who travels now in France or Italy, till this tribe of wretches is swept home again. In two or three years the first rush will be over and the Continent will be roomy and agreeable.'[25] In 1830, the German poet Heinrich Heine acknowledged that he made frequent references to the English in his *Italian travel sketches*, but pointed out:

> They are nowadays too numerous in Italy to be overlooked. They stream through the land in great swarms. They camp at all the inns; they run about everywhere, so that it is no longer possible to think of Italian citrus trees without an English woman who inhales its perfumes, or of a gallery without a batch of English who, guide-book in hand, roam about in order to satisfy themselves that everything that is specified in their book as noteworthy is hanging there. The sight of these fair, red-cheeked people, driving over the Alps well groomed and inquisitive, and wandering through Italy with their varnished carriages, smart lacqueys, neighing riding horses, their green-veiled lady's maids, and their other costly appurtenances, gives the impression of an elegant invasion of barbarians.[26]

That was a German's view of the English abroad. Dickens had something to add, about 15 years later. He could not resist using the setting of Verona's Roman Arena – where he had been watching an equestrian performance – to muse upon the spectacle of

> [...] the favourite comic scene of the travelling English, where a British nobleman (Lord John), with a very loose stomach: dressed in a blue tailed coat down to his heels, bright yellow breeches, and a white hat: comes abroad, riding double on a rearing horse, with an English lady (Lady Betsey) in a straw bonnet and green veil, and a red spencer; and who always carries a gigantic reticule, and a put-up parasol.[27]

This caricature of the English abroad might have fitted the nobility, but from the mid-1840s onwards there were many middle-class tourists travelling by the newer method of the railways. They might find fault with Italian hotels, with a lack of cleanliness, or with what they deemed to be overcharging by the locals. To all of this, Augustus Hare would plead that what was 'most necessary – to the pleasure of Italian travel, is not to go forth in a spirit of antagonism to the inhabitants, and with the impression that life in Italy is to be a prolonged struggle against extortion and incivility'. His hope was that 'With every year which an Englishman passes in Italy, a new veil of the suspicion with which he entered it will be swept away [...]' and that he would come to a greater appreciation of both the country and its inhabitants.[28]

# POSTSCRIPT

WHAT CAN NOW be extracted from the range of opinions about Verona expressed by visitors over approximately five centuries? Such a long timescale makes it very difficult to generalize, but it is possible to draw some conclusions about the changing ways in which tourists expressed their views, as well as the subjects they deemed worthy of comment.

Most early travellers visited Italy either as scholars or as pilgrims, categories that rather defined what would be of interest to them. By the time of the so-called Grand Tour, young nobles were undertaking travels designed to expose them to the upper reaches of Italian society, as well as to its art and architecture. Accounts of many of these journeys were later published and widely read. On into the nineteenth century this trend continued; for instance, Samuel Rogers described his 1814 visit in his lengthy poem *Italy*, republished in 1830 to great acclaim, with engravings by Turner that added an extra dimension for the reader. In addition, diaries and letters brought fresh perspectives, with travellers supplying personal details of their journeys; Joseph Spence, for instance, clearly tailored his letters to his mother to provide details of his social life in Verona, rather than merely to inform her of his visits to Roman antiquities.

During the later eighteenth and early nineteenth centuries, the social classes from which travellers came widened, bringing an expanded range of interests. Women, for instance, were now coming to see Italy for themselves, bringing their particular perspectives; they commented freely on the comforts or otherwise of their accommodation, and on the society they saw about them. Men were also becoming more willing to express personal views rather than merely listing the monuments visited. Notions of the picturesque and the sublime meant that someone like William Beckford could admit his feelings on being alone in the Arena at dusk. It became increasingly important to describe local people: how they dressed, how they behaved and how they organized their lives. Goethe was a master at this, writing with enthusiasm about the dress of Veronesi women or the games played by local youths of an evening.

By the nineteenth century, Britain had itself become an increasingly urban society with its cities growing rapidly and having to respond to increasing pressures. Accordingly, the British abroad would be interested in the way a city like Verona functioned, and be ready to comment on what they viewed as its failings, such as dirty streets or lack of lighting. There could be positives as well; Louisa Costello observed in the 1840s that Italian city highways had generally been filthy in the past, but now Verona's streets were as well paved as in other Italian towns. Increasing numbers of American tourists were arriving as well, bringing their enthusiasm for Shakespeare's tale of Romeo and Juliet. By the twentieth century, the city became increasingly well known as a tourist destination of note, with the opera season in the Arena from 1913 onwards becoming a particular draw.

Verona now has so much to offer, from its massive Roman Arena and gates such as Porta Borsari, to the Roman Ponte Pietra. There are also medieval buildings and monuments, such as its unique Scaligeri tombs, and superb Romanesque churches that include the Duomo and the basilica of San Zeno Maggiore. There are innumerable other monuments and churches filled with treasures of art and architecture, some often visited and others still almost unknown even today.

What is now the Castelvecchio museum was originally the palace of the Scaligeri family with its brick-built bridge crossing the Adige; there are also long stretches of the city walls still providing a reminder of Verona's turbulent history. Piazza dei Signori has the Loggia del Consiglio, a Renaissance gem, as well as its rather forbidding statue of Dante. Sixteenth-century palaces such as Palazzo Bevilacqua were built for noble families, many of them designed by Verona's own Michele Sanmicheli, also responsible for the city's imposing gates. There are few baroque buildings here, Palazzo Maffei in Piazza Erbe being the outstanding example. The city's later history embraces its conquest by Napoleon, followed by rule by Austria until 1866, when it became part of the newly formed state of Italy. Changes to the cityscape under French and Austrian government were mainly confined to various military installations, notably the Arsenale built by the Austrians across the River Adige from Castelvecchio.

Verona is now part of the Veneto region of north-east Italy. With the River Adige running through its historic centre, its backing of rolling hills and — on a clear day — its view of the snow-capped Pre-Alpi mountains, the city provides much for tourists to explore. One of its delights is how much of it is still unspoilt, especially if a visitor takes the trouble to explore the back streets and avoids tourist traps such as the so-called house of Juliet. It is a place to wander away from the crowds, and admire tall houses along narrow streets, with their splendid doorways, windows and balconies.

The city now has a population of about 265,000, and is a bustling centre for the local Veronesi as well as for tourists, students and music lovers who come in the summer months to hear grand opera being performed in the Roman Arena, an auditorium unrivalled anywhere in the world. On account of the historic importance of its architectural treasures, UNESCO has declared the city a World Heritage site for the following reasons.

> In its urban structure and its architecture, Verona is an outstanding example of a town that has developed progressively and uninterruptedly over 2,000 years, incorporating artistic elements of the highest quality from each succeeding period. It also represents in an exceptional way the concept of the fortified town at several seminal stages of European history.[1]

The author was lucky enough to spend a year studying at the University of Verona in 2000–1 and, each year since, has returned, with her husband, to visit Veronesi friends. Usually, the first day or so is spent simply wandering the streets, especially the back streets of the old centre, and along the banks of the Adige, visiting favourite churches, and allowing this beautiful city to work its magic once again. It is not hard to understand why the Veronesi do not want to go anywhere else for very long.

 APPENDIX 1

History of Verona Timeline

1st century BC	Under the Romans	*Vitruvius: De Architectura*
4th century AD		*San Zeno bishop*
476–567	Ruled by Theodoric I, Ostrogoth	*Original Castel San Pietro built*
567–774	Ruled by Lombards	
774–*c.*1160	Subject to Holy Roman Empire	
*c.*12th–*c.*13th	Guelph v. Ghibelline wars	
*c.*12th–*c.*13th	Self-governing Commune	
1226–59	Ruled by Ezzelino da Romano	
1259–1399	Ruled by the Scaligeri	
1312–18		*Dante in exile in Verona*
1354–5		*Castelvecchio & bridge built*
1399–1405	Ruled by Visconti or Carraresi	
1405	Came under the rule of Venice	
*c.*1456–60		*Mantegna: San Zeno altarpiece*
1489		*Barduzzi from Florence visited*
1550		*Vasari published his* Lives...
1500s, 1st half		*Michele Sanmicheli architect*
1530s		*England's schism with Papacy*
1535		*Titian's Assumption painted*

Appendix 1

c.1564		*Veronese: Martyrdom, S. Giorgio*
1570		*Palladio's* The Four Books
1608		*Thomas Coryat visited*
1691		*Misson's* ... Voyage ... d'Italie
1732		*Maffei's* Verona illustrata
1786		*Goethe in Verona*
1 June 1796	Occupied by Napoleon	
30 July 1796	Occupied by Austria	
8 Aug. 1796	Occupied by France	
1797	Napoleon takes Venice	
1797	Easter rebellion, or *Pasque Veronesi*	
9 Feb. 1801	Partitioned 'twixt France and Austria	
26 Dec. 1805	Granted to France	
May 1814	Granted to Austria	
1822	Congress of Verona	
1846		*Milan–Venice via Verona rail link*
1849		*Porta Vescovo station opened*
Mid-1800s		*Ruskin's various visits to Verona*
1866	Joined Kingdom of Italy	

# APPENDIX 2

Biographical Notes

These are biographical notes on some of the travellers whose words have been quoted in this book. As far as possible, those travellers who have unwittingly contributed to more than one chapter are included below.

Sources include *Chalmers'* The general biographical dictionary 1812–17; *Chris Beetles Gallery; Christies; the Dulwich Society; Early English Books Online; the Folger Institute; HathiTrust; Ingamells'* A dictionary of British and Irish travellers in Italy 1701–1800; *Julian's* Dictionary of hymnology, 1907; The Oxford companion to Italian literature; The Oxford dictionary of national biography; *Sweet's* Cities and the Grand Tour; *University of Michigan Press; Westminster Abbey; Wikipedia; WorldCat; www.veronanet.it*

Abbot, Charles, 1st Baron Colchester, PC, FRS (1757–1829), was half-brother of Jeremy Bentham by his mother's second marriage. For 12 years he practised as a barrister and then entered parliament, where he had a distinguished career as a reformer and statesman, serving as Speaker of the House of Commons, 1802–17. He travelled in Italy in 1788.

Addison, Joseph (1672–1719), writer and politician, was in Italy as part of a lengthy Continental tour in 1701–2, and there followed his *Letter from Italy*. With Richard Steele, he co-edited and contributed to *The Tatler* and *The Spectator*, and launched successfully into literary criticism. His political career culminated in his being Secretary of State for the Southern Department.

Alford, The Reverend Henry (1810–71), was a biblical scholar and opponent of Ritualism who became Dean of Canterbury. He was a poet, musician, hymn writer and painter in watercolours.

Andersen, Hans Christian (1805–75), was a Danish author, fairy-tale writer and poet particularly noted for his children's stories. However, his book, *The Improvisatore*, an autobiographical novel reflecting his tour of Italy in 1833, was particularly influential in advancing his writing career.

Ascham, Roger (1514/15–68), a Protestant Cambridge classicist, became President of the Fellows of St John's College. He was tutor to Princess Elizabeth in 1548 and from time to time during the reign of Queen Mary, to whom he was Latin secretary. Later in life he wrote an influential book on education, *The Scholemaster.*

Ayscough, George Edward (d. 1779), Guards officer, author and playwright, travelled in Italy in 1769, having obtained leave from the army to do so, on grounds of ill health.

Bacon, Francis (1561–1626), lawyer and politician – he was eventually Lord Chancellor – wrote extensively on Natural Philosophy, for which he remains justly famous, but also on history, religion and education. He worked hard to promote union between England and Scotland in the early 1600s, and survived impeachment for receiving bribes.

Bankes, Henry (1757–1834), politician and parliamentary diarist, of Kingston Lacy, Dorset, was a personal friend and supporter of William Pitt the Younger. He embarked on a Grand Tour in 1779.

Bankes, William John (1786–1855), of Kingston Lacy, Dorset, traveller and antiquary, was a friend of Byron. He collected in Portugal, Spain and, notably, Egypt. He also explored Palestine, Syria and Jordan with James Silk Buckingham, with whom he fell out, and to whom he lost a libel case, perhaps unjustly. A (second) scandalous impropriety with a guardsman resulted in his having to live abroad from 1841, in Venice and elsewhere in Italy, whence he supplied Kingston Lacy with furnishings and artworks, many locally made.

Barduzzi, Bernardino (fl. 1489), was a Florentine friar who preached at the church of San Fermo, Verona, and wrote a letter in praise of Verona (republished in Verona in 1974) to Giovanni Nesi (1456–1506), author of philosophical works and admirer of Savonarola.

Beaumont, Jean François Albanis (1755–1812), tutor to the children of the Duke of Gloucester; engineer and traveller; engraver and landscape painter. He made a trip to Italy in 1786.

Beckford, William Thomas (1760–1844), writer, traveller and collector of art, furniture and books, was heir to a West Indies sugar fortune: he was brought up at Fonthill, which he later developed into a property of architectural importance. He was in the Veneto in 1780 during his Grand Tour.

Bennett (Enoch) Arnold (1867–1931), was a journalist, essayist, travel writer and respected novelist. He was in charge of propaganda in France in World War I and, through his novels and other writing, explored the social revolution following the war.

Bentham, Sarah (née Farr) (1733–1809), widow of The Reverend John Abbot, and mother of Charles Abbot (1757–1829), was the second wife of Jeremiah Bentham, father of Jeremy Bentham (1748–1832), the philosopher and reformer. She wrote descriptions of her time in Italy, 1793–4, in the style of a good travel writer, but was not published.

Blessington, Lady: *see* Gardiner, Marguerite.

Browne, Junius Henri (1833–1902), was an American journalist. As war correspondent for the *New York Tribune* in 1861, he was wounded and imprisoned for nearly two years. He wrote about the American Civil War and also about his trip to Europe in 1871.

Buckingham, James Silk (1786–1855), was an author and journalist who travelled extensively in Egypt, Palestine and Persia, and later in North America. He was a strong critic of the East India Company through a newspaper he established in Calcutta. MP for Sheffield in the 1830s, he was a social reformer of note. He was in the Veneto in 1846.

Burney, Charles (1726–1814), was a musician, composer, music teacher and respected music historian. His publications included *The present state of music in France and Italy* (1771), in which connection he was in Verona the previous year.

Butler, Alban (1709–73), was a Roman Catholic priest and hagiographer, his *magnum opus* being his famous *Lives of the Saints*. He accompanied the Earl of Shrewsbury and his sons the Honourable James Talbot and the Honourable Thomas Talbot on their Grand Tour in 1745.

Byron, George Gordon Noel, 6th Baron Byron (1788–1824), Scottish romantic poet and satirist, undertook a tour of Europe, full of incident, 1809–11; became the talk of Regency London; had a remarkable series of exotic relationships with women in Italy, notably in Venice (1787–1830) and died a hero trying to help free Greece.

Byron, Robert (1905–41), journalist and travel writer, is best known for his book about Persia and Afghanistan, *The road to Oxiana*. He was killed in enemy action when on his way to Cairo as a special war correspondent.

Cadell, William Archibald (1775–1855), was a member of the Faculty of Advocates in Edinburgh but, having private means, did not practise, and spent his time in scientific and antiquarian research at home and abroad. A prisoner in Napoleonic France, he escaped by successfully pretending to be a Frenchman; he visited the Veneto in 1817.

Carter, Nathaniel Hazeltine (1787–1830), was an American lawyer, author and journalist. He travelled extensively in Europe from 1825 to 1827.

Child, Theodore (1846–92), was an American journalist, notably writing for *Harper's Magazine*, but also for the *Cornhill Magazine* and *The Gentleman's Magazine* in England. He was also an author, notably on art and aesthetics, and on Spanish America. He toured Europe in 1886–8.

Clayton, Captain John William (1833–after 1881), served in the 13th Light Dragoons 1850–7, including service at the siege of Sebastopol. Retiring for medical reasons, he took to writing. Works: *Ubique*; *Letters from the Nile*; *Il Pellegrino*.

Cockburn, Henry, Lord Cockburn (1779–1854), Scottish advocate, judge and author, was a zealous reformer of Church and law, being Scotland's Solicitor-General and Lord Advocate in the 1830s. He undertook a Continental tour in 1823.

Colston, Marianne Jenkins (1792–1865), wrote, and illustrated with 50 lithographs from her own drawings, a travel journal of a tour of Europe, 1819–21, undertaken by her and her aristocrat husband shortly after their wedding.

Coryat, Thomas (1577?–1617), traveller and writer, left Oxford with much learning but no degree, and professed a 'curiosity to see the world, and a thirst for personal fame'. *Coryat's crudities* (1611) described his travels in Europe in 1608. He then went to Constantinople, the Levant and the Holy Land, before heading for India via Persia, walking over 3,000 miles and eventually dying of dysentery at Surat.

Costello, Louisa Stuart (1799–1870), poet, historian (especially of the history of France), journalist, painter (especially of miniatures), novelist and travel writer, lived mainly in Paris. Her finely illustrated book on Piedmont and Italy was published in 1861.

Crichton, Kate (fl. 1850s), a young opera singer, who had appeared at Drury Lane Theatre as Princess Isabella in Meyerbeer's *Robert the Devil*, travelled to Milan with a view to learning more of Italian opera. However, an illness which affected her voice put an end to this career and she took, instead, to literature. She spent six years, from 1852, in Italy with her mother.

Da Persico, Giovanni Battista (1777–1845), was mayor of Verona at the time of the Congress of Verona (1822), and author of the comprehensive *Descrizione di Verona e della sua provincia*, published 1820. He initiated major improvements to Piazza Bra.

de Blainville, Henri (fl. 1707), was engaged by William Blathwayt MP (1688–1742), as tutor to his sons William and John, and accompanied them on their four-year Grand

Tour starting in 1707, when William was 16 and John 14. Later, de Blainville was secretary to the embassy of the States-General to Spain.

de Boigne, Comtesse (1781–1866). Adèle d'Osmond, comtesse de Boigne, lived through the French Revolution and much of the Second Empire. Since she was highly educated and, with good contacts in all the upper echelons of society and government, her Paris salon achieved great popularity. In addition to her memoirs she wrote two novels. She visited Verona in 1814.

de Brosses, Charles, comte de Tournay, baron de Montfalcon, seigneur de Vezins et de Prevessin (1709–77), was an eighteenth-century French intellectual who wrote on ancient history and linguistics and was twice exiled for anti-royalism.

de Lalande, (Joseph) Jérôme Lefrançois (1732–1807), was an eminent French astronomer and writer on astronomy; also a mathematician and freemason.

de Montaigne, Michel Eyquem (1533–92), initially a lawyer, became a highly influential French philosopher and essayist. An account of his European tour, including a visit to Italy, in 1580–1, was not first published until 1774.

Dickens, Charles John Huffam (1812–70), journalist and prolific novelist, expressed his outrage with social conditions in England through his novels of the 1850s. Taking his shrewd powers of observation to Italy in the mid-1840s, he produced the strongly anti-Catholic travel book, *Pictures from Italy.*

Dorr, David F. (fl. 1850s), slave, accompanied the Louisiana plantation owner Cornelius Fellowes on a tour of the world's major cities. He was promised freedom on return to America, but the promise was broken; he escaped to Ohio, where he wrote up his experiences.

Drummond, David Thomas Kerr (1805–77), was joint minister of Trinity Episcopal Church, Dean Bridge, Edinburgh, 1838–43, and then minister of St Thomas's English Episcopal Church, Edinburgh, until his death. He visited Switzerland and Italy in 1852.

du Boccage, Anne-Marie Fiquet (née Le Page) (1710–1802), author, poet and playwright, visited Italy in 1770.

d'Uklanski, Baron: *see* von Uklanski.

Eustace, John Chetwode (1761–1815), Roman Catholic priest and travel writer, toured Italy in 1801–2 as tutor and companion to John Cust, later Lord Brownlow, and two other young gentlemen. His *A tour through Italy*, 1813, later retitled *A* *classical tour through Italy*, was highly successful, went through eight editions and became the standard guide for classical tourists.

Evelyn, John (1620–1706), diarist and writer, undertook a Grand Tour in the 1640s. His extensive correspondence on social, cultural and scientific subjects substantially advanced the debate in these areas, and his researches in horticulture and garden design had a major impact on the development of the English landscape garden in the eighteenth century.

Field, Henry Martyn (1822–1907), was an American Presbyterian pastor in Missouri, 1842–7, and in Massachusetts, 1850–4. Between these appointments he travelled in Europe. Subsequently, he edited *The Evangelist* (New York) and wrote books, mainly on travel.

Forsyth, Joseph (1763–1815), from Elgin, Scotland, taught at and then ran an academy in London before embarking on a tour of Italian cities. However, war with France broke out whilst he was returning via Turin in 1803, and he was imprisoned for 11 years; his subsequent ill-health led to his death soon after his return to Scotland.

Fremantle (née Wynne), **Lady Elizabeth** (Betsey), (1778–1857), is best known for her remarkable diaries covering the period between 1789 and the 1850s: from teenage years through courtship and marriage to a naval officer; eight years mostly at sea; social life in Buckinghamshire and motherhood; widowhood. She was in Verona in 1791, before Napoleon's 1796 invasion, and again in 1798.

Friedländer, Ludwig Herman (1790–1851), was a Prussian physician who, from 1823, was Professor of Theoretical Medicine at the University of Halle and wrote three important medical books. He also combined literary and artistic interests, bridged the arts/science divide, and converted from Judaism to Christianity. In 1815, with the painter Philipp Veit, he visited Italy and later wrote his *Ansichten von Italien* …

Frye, Major William Edward (1784–1858), served in Holland, Egypt, India and Ceylon (1799–1814). Then he returned to Europe and was in Brussels during the Waterloo campaign. He visited Western Europe, 1815–19, leaving the army in 1822. He lived much of the rest of his life in France and was a distinguished linguist.

Gailhard, Jean (fl. 1659–1708), writer and religious controversialist, was a Protestant (Calvinist) Frenchman, based in England from about 1660, and undertook various travels as tutor. He encouraged the growth of travel literature with accounts of Italy and Venice in 1668–9.

Galiffe, Jacques Augustin (1773–1853), an historian and genealogist from Geneva, was fluent in six modern languages, and also Latin and Greek. He achieved important positions in various banking houses and worked in a variety of contexts, including military ones, for the independence of Geneva. After the French occupation he reconstituted Geneva's archives. He visited Italy in 1816.

Gallichan, Walter Matthew (1862–1946), British journalist, novelist, writing sometimes under the name Geoffrey Mortimer, and writer on fishing, ornithology and European topography; he is best remembered as a pioneer in sex education.

Gardiner, Marguerite, Countess of Blessington (1789–1849), married the widower Lord Blessington, after recently being widowed herself. She and her husband undertook a Continental tour in 1822–3 and spent two months in Lord Byron's company in Genoa, resulting in the publication *Journal of conversations with Lord Byron*. She was a beautiful and witty hostess, as well as an entertaining novelist and travel writer.

Goethe: *see* von Goethe.

Hare, Augustus John Cuthbert (1834–1903), lived in Italy or on the Riviera for most of his life after his graduation from Oxford in 1857. He wrote guidebooks, biographies and a six-volume 'long tedious and indiscreet' (*DNB*) autobiography. He was also a competent watercolourist.

Hayward, John Samuel (1778–1822), a respected amateur artist, described himself on his business card as 'Floor Cloth and Canvas Manufacturer, House Painter [...] and Supplier of Portable Temples, Ball Rooms, Pavillions, Domes, Treillage Balconies, Awnings and Covered Ways, [...]'. He visited Italy in 1802 and 1816.

Hazlitt, William (1778–1830), essayist, literary critic and journalist, originally wrote *Notes on a journey in France and Italy* as a series of letters in the *Morning Chronicle*; as a book, it was viciously attacked in the *Monthly Review* of 1826 on grounds of ignorance and mediocrity.

Heine, Christian Johann Heinrich (1797–1856), was a German poet, essayist, journalist and literary critic whose *lieder* were set to music by Schubert and Schumann. Born a Jew in Düsseldorf, he converted to Christianity.

Hillard, George Stillman (1808–79), was an American lawyer in Boston, Massachusetts, editor of various Boston journals and also a writer on literature, politics and travel. He spent six months in Italy in 1853.

Hobhouse, John Cam (1786–1869), travelled extensively in Europe with Lord Byron, and was his executor. A politician under Melbourne and, in the cabinet under Lord John Russell, he was an imperialist who promoted railway development in India. He was created Baron Broughton in 1851.

Hogg, Thomas Jefferson (1792–1862), author of a flawed biography of Percy Bysshe Shelley, combined a career as a barrister with unorthodox views – he was an atheist and a vegetarian – and a scandalous life. He toured Europe in 1816 and 1826.

Hume Weatherhead, George (1790?–1853), a Scottish physician, wrote prolifically on medical and other subjects, including his pedestrian tour of France and Italy in 1834.

Hutton, Edward (1875–1969), was an English italophile, travel writer and art historian, who spent many years in Italy, where he was greatly respected and indeed honoured, and was particularly devoted to Verona.

James, Henry (1843–1916), American critic, novelist of distinction and playwright, spent many working years in England and also travelled extensively on the Continent, which led to a period of travel writing.

Jameson, Anna Brownell (née Murphy) (1794–1860), was an Irish writer and art historian, whose writings included art criticism, Shakespearian criticism, travel writing, history, and biography. She visited Italy in 1821.

Keysler, John George (1689–1743), was a learned antiquary of Germany who distinguished himself so much through research on Stonehenge that he was elected a Fellow of the Royal Society. He travelled widely as a tutor to German aristocracy; to Italy, in particular, in 1730, as part of a Grand Tour with the young Barons Bernstorf.

Kotzebue: *see* von Kotzebue.

Latrobe, John Hazlehurst Boneval (1803–91), trained as an engineer and then as a lawyer, in which profession he worked for the Baltimore & Ohio Railroad for over 60 years. A man of wide interests and talents, he involved himself in various institutions and projects in Baltimore. He spent six months in Europe in 1868.

Maffei, Scipione, marchese di Maffei (1675–1755), Italian author, dramatist, art critic, scientist and collector, was sufficiently respected internationally as an antiquarian to receive Fellowship of the Royal Society and a Doctorate of Oxford University when he visited England. His researches on his hometown of Verona were published in his *Verona illustrata*, later condensed into a portable guidebook. His house and museum, where he held court, proved a magnet for visiting aristocracy and intellectuals.

Martyn, Thomas (1735–1825), priest and distinguished botanist, was professor of Botany at Cambridge University for 63 years. He accompanied his pupil and ward, Edward Hartopp, on a two-year tour on the Continent in 1778–9.

Millais (née Gray), **Euphemia** (Effie) **Chalmers** (1828–97), first married John Ruskin, but the marriage was annulled on grounds of non-consummation. She then married Ruskin's protégé John Everett Millais. Her letters throw interesting light on her time in Venice as Mrs Ruskin.

Miller (née Riggs), **Lady Anna** (1741–81), Irish heiress, travelled in Italy with her husband, 1770–1, and her letters home were published and went to a second edition. A range of famous names was associated with the literary salon at her house near Bath, where she was the enthusiastic hostess.

Misson, Francis Maximilian (formerly François Maximilien) (*c.*1650–1722), traveller and author, was a Protestant priest and Huguenot refugee, naturalized English in 1687. As tutor to the grandson of the Duke of Ormond, he undertook a Grand Tour and his journal became the standard travel guide to Italy.

Montaigne: *see* de Montaigne.

Moryson, Fynes (1565/6–1630), traveller and writer, was a Lincolnshire man who was a Fellow and Bursar of his Cambridge college, Peterhouse. Fluent in German, Italian, Dutch and French, he spent four years, 1591–5, travelling in Europe, then heading for Cyprus, Jerusalem and Crete. On his return home, he spent time in Scotland and Ireland before settling to write journals of his well-observed travels.

Pasquin, Antoine Claude (1789–1847), librarian of the Chateau de Versailles, wrote several travel guides, under the pseudonym M. Valéry, including two relating to a visit he made to Italy in 1826–8, updated, depending on the date of publication, by the reports of later travellers.

Patoun, William (fl. 1740s–83), MA 1746, MD 1754, Glasgow University, Library Keeper to the University 1747–50, was a learned Scottish connoisseur and painter who made five trips to Italy, notably with the 9th Earl of Exeter in 1763, which enabled him to write detailed advice, in 1766, to 'the Eldest Son of an English Peer'.

Pennington, Thomas (1798–1852), a fellow of Clare College, Cambridge, made three substantial Continental tours which he then wrote about. Rector of Thorley, Herts, he was also chaplain to the Countess of Bath and to Lord Chief Justice Ellenborough.

Piozzi, Hester Lynch (née Salusbury) (1741–1821), educated well beyond the norm for young ladies, survived 13 pregnancies in a loveless marriage with Henry Thrale. This, however, resulted in an introduction to Samuel Johnson, who was impressed by her and with whom she collaborated on translations and other literary projects. A rich widow in 1781, she married an Italian musician, travelled the Continent and continued writing up to her death at 80.

Raymond, John (fl. 1640s), went on a Grand Tour with a contemporary and Raymond's uncle in 1646: the resulting book, *An itinerary containing a voyage* ... (1648), has been described as 'the first English guidebook to Italy' (Chaney).

Reichard, Heinrich August Ottokar (1751–1828), privy-councillor to the Duke of Saxe-Gotha, travelled in Europe, Scandinavia and Russia. He was celebrated for his travel guides which were among the first to break, in style, from traditional travel narratives.

Rivet, Charles (1800–72), later Baron Rivet, was a childhood friend of the artist Delacroix and accompanied artist Richard Parkes Bonington, his 'atelier comrade', to Italy in 1826. Later, he became 'préfet du Rhone' (Burty).

Rose, William Stewart (1775–1843), poet and translator, held a clerkship in the House of Lords. He spent time in Italy, 1814–18, sometimes in the company of Lord Byron, and translated *Orlando Furioso*, amongst works of other Italian poets.

Ruskin, Effie: *see* Millais, Euphemia.

Ruskin, John (1819–1900), original author of criticism in the fields of art, architecture and political economy, spent much time in Italy, especially Venice, and strongly favoured the early Gothic against the Renaissance. He was appointed Slade professor of Fine Art at Oxford, influenced the Arts and Crafts movement, and championed J.M.W. Turner.

Sala, George Augustus (1828–95), a journalist, notably with the *Daily Telegraph*, was in Italy in 1866–7, witnessing the end of Austrian domination.

Sass, Henry (1788–1844), was an English artist and art teacher: Sass's Academy prepared potential artists for entry to the Royal Academy.

Schottus, Franciscus (1548–1622), was a lawyer from Antwerp whose travels in Italy were published in several editions in Italian and in English, the latter translated by E. Warcupp under the title *Italy, in its original glory, ruine and revival* [...]

Scoto, Francesco: *see* Schottus, Franciscus.

Sedgwick, Catharine Maria (1789–1867), was an American novelist and short story writer from Massachusetts. She was in Verona in 1839 as part of a European tour.

Sewell, Elizabeth Missing (1815–1906), was a novelist, successful in the USA and in Britain, with a particular interest in the education, especially the moral education, of girls.

Skippon, Philip (1641–91), a Cambridge botanist, went on a Grand Tour, 1663–6, with his parson-naturalist tutor John Ray, another of Ray's students Nathaniel Bacon, later to become infamous as a rebel in Virginia, and an ornithologist and ichthyologist Francis Willughby. His remarkable account was eventually published in 1732.

Smith, William (fl. 1880), of Wargrave in Berkshire, travelled in Italy by train, in the autumn and winter of 1880, with his wife, his sister, an Italian courier and a maid.

Soane, John (1753–1837), eminent English architect and antiquary, undertook a tour of Europe in 1778–80 which substantially influenced his architectural career, although he developed a style very much his own. Sir John Soane was later Professor of Architecture at the Royal Academy.

Spence, Joseph (1699–1768), was Professor of Poetry at Oxford and, much later, a prebendary of Durham. He accompanied Lord Middlesex on a Grand Tour, 1730–3, and was in Italy again, with the Earl of Lincoln, 1739–41.

Starke, Mariana (1761–1838), was a playwright, poet and author of travel guides to France and, most notably, Italy, where she lived for a number of years.

Starkie, Walter Fitzwilliam (1894–1976), was an Irish scholar, Hispanist, theatre manager, author and musician. He was in Italy during and just after World War I.

Stevens, Sacheverell (fl. 1740s), was a doggedly Protestant English 'Gent', who gave a full account of his travels in Europe which ran to many editions in English and German.

Stoughton, John (1807–97), was a Congregational minister, theologian and ecclesiastical historian, with many publications to his credit, who travelled in France, Germany, Italy, Spain and Palestine.

Street, George Edmund (1824–81), was a mainly ecclesiastical Victorian Gothic Revival architect of note.

Taine, Hippolyte Adolphe (1828–93), philosopher, critic and historian, was an Anglophile and wrote extensively on English society, literature and culture. He visited Italy in 1866.

Tappen, George (1771–1830), was an architect who was appointed Surveyor to Dulwich College and was responsible for various Dulwich buildings. He enjoyed a tour of Europe, 1802–3.

Valerini, Adriano (fl. 1560–80), was born in Verona. He was one of the first known professional actors in the *Commedia dell'arte* tradition in North Italy, and formed his own company, the *Uniti*.

Valéry, M.: *see* Pasquin, Antoine Claude.

Vasari, Giorgio (1511–74), was an Italian painter, architect, writer and historian, especially famed for his *Lives of the most excellent painters, sculptors and architects*, which provided a foundation for subsequent art history critics and authors.

Vigée le Brun, Marie Élizabeth Louise (1755–1842), was an important French portraitist whose association with royalty made it advisable for her to flee France at the time of the Revolution. Subsequently, she worked in Italy, Austria and Russia, achieving an international reputation.

von Goethe, Johann Wolfgang (1749–1832), writer, artist, scientist and polymath, was a key figure in German literature. His works cover the fields of prose, poetry, drama, philosophy and science. His Italian journey covers his time in Italy in 1786.

von Kotzebue, August Friedrich Ferdinand (1761–1819), a Prussian lawyer, was ambassador to Russia, held important legal posts in Estonia, and was later Russia's consul general in Germany. He was also a novelist, dramatist and journalist, eventually making himself so unpopular to nationalist liberals that he was murdered by one of them in Mannheim. In 1805, he included Italy in extensive travels with his third wife.

von Uklanski, Carl Theodore (fl. *c.*1800–20), was a Prussian traveller whose name appears as 'Baron D'Uklanski' in the English edition of his book about his travels in Upper Italy, Tuscany and 'the Ecclesiastical State'.

Walker, Adam (1730/1–1821), was an itinerant lecturer and writer on 'Natural and Experimental Philosophy' and astronomy.

Webb, William (fl. 1820s), was an Irishman and member of the Royal Irish Academy who lived most of his life in England, expressed loyalty to the King, and was deputy commissary-general to the forces.

Wilson, James (fl. *c.*1815–20), an English tourist travelling to Italy 'in search of health', made two successive journeys on the continent in 1816–18.

Wilson, William Rae (1772–1849), traveller, writer and antiquary, practised as a solicitor before the Supreme Courts of Scotland.

Withrow, William Henry (1839–1908), was a Canadian Methodist minister from Toronto, as well as a journalist and author.

Woods, Joseph (1776–1864), was a geologist, botanist, architect, antiquary and brilliant chess player. He formed the London Architectural Society and was its first president; he was editor of the fourth volume of *Antiquities of Athens* by Stuart and Revett.

Wortley Montagu (née Pierrepont), **Lady Mary** (1689–1762), had already made her mark in intellectual and court society, and had survived smallpox, when her husband was appointed ambassador to Constantinople; she wrote a remarkable series of letters describing this episode and, on her return, championed the Turks' use of inoculation against smallpox. Later, she spent much time in Italy, not without scandal and turbulent family problems.

Wright, Edward (fl. 1720), accompanied George, Lord Parker, son of Thomas, Lord Macclesfield, on his Grand Tour, 1719–22. Lord Macclesfield, appointed lord chancellor in 1718, had just bought Shirburn Castle, Dorset, and Edward Wright, a kinsman, had something of a reputation as an artist and judge of the quality of artworks, so he purchased for Shirburn as well as for himself.

Wylie, James Aitken (1808–90), wrote a three-volume *History of Protestantism* and was joint editor of *The Witness*, based in Edinburgh, for which he wrote many articles, always well researched, against Roman Catholicism and justifying the Reformation.

Wynne, Elizabeth: *see* Fremantle.

Young, Arthur (1741–1820), agricultural reformer and writer, was in Verona in 1789, as part of his European researches into agricultural methods. Later, as secretary to the Board of Agriculture, he was responsible for six of the county reports so valuable in improving agricultural practice in England.

 NOTES

ABBREVIATIONS

DHC   Dorset History Centre, Dorchester
NLS   National Library of Scotland
NRS   National Records of Scotland
ODNB *Oxford Dictionary of National Biography*
SM   The Soane Museum
TNA   The National Archives
V&A   Victoria and Albert Museum, National Art Library

PREFACE, pp. xv–xvii

1   Zorzi, et al., pp. 81–2.

CHAPTER ONE: THE AIMS OF TRAVEL, pp. 1–6.

1   Eustace, 1815, vol. 1, p. 1.
2   Ascham, p. 78.
3   Spedding, vol. IX, pp. 7–13.
4   Spedding, vol. IX, pp. 10–17.
5   Coryat, vol. 1, p. 8.
6   Moryson, 1617, Pt 1, Bk 3, p. 197.
7   Raymond, p. 2.
8   *ODNB*.
9   Nugent, vol. 1, p. xi.
10 Sweet, *Cities*, footnote, p. 264.
11 Klima, p. 82.
12 Colston, vol. 1, p. 284.
13 Eustace, 1815, vol. 1, p. 3.
14 Eustace, vol. 1, p. 10.
15 Eustace, vol. 1, p. 21.
16 Pennington, vol. 2, p. 233.
17 Hale, J. R. ed., p. 62.
18 Murray (pub.), p. x.
19 Sweet, *Cities*, p. 21.

CHAPTER TWO: THE PRACTICALITIES OF TRAVEL, pp. 7–19

1   Clarke, A., p. 263.
2   TNA: PRO 30/9/43.
3   Ingamells, pp. xxxix–lii.

212 *Visitors to Verona*

4 Fall, pp. 7–22.
5 Ayscough, pp. 223–5.
6 Ingamells, pp. xxxix–lii.
7 NLS, MS 8923.
8 Ingamells, pp. xxxix–lii.
9 TNA: PRO 30/9/21, p. 60.
10 NLS, MS 23225, pp. 75–6.
11 Ingamells, pp. xxxix–lii.
12 Ingamells, pp. xxxix–lii.
13 Millard, pp. xliv–liii.
14 Gaze, pp. 8–13.
15 Fremantle, vol. 2, p. 75. A *buona mano* was a tip.
16 Ingamells, pp. xxxix–lii.
17 Baring, pp. 112–14.
18 V&A, RC.K.14–16, MSL/1939/1908–10.
19 Horwitz, pp. 240–1.
20 Buckingham, vol. 2, p. 355.
21 Hare, *Cities*, vol. 1, pp. x–xi.
22 Ingamells, pp. xxxix–lii.
23 Barlow, p. 146.
24 NLS, Adv. MS 50.3.14, ff. 175–210.
25 Lacklustre, pp. 53–4.
26 Keysler, vol. 3, p. 360.
27 Travelling lawyer, p. 90.
28 Moryson, 1908, vol. 1, pp. 376–80.
29 Kotzebue, vol. 1, pp. 45–6.
30 Trease, p. 123.
31 Shelley, vol. 1, pp. 74–5.
32 Ingamells, entry for Cholwick.
33 Taylor, E., p. 374.
34 Browne, pp. 511–15.
35 NLS, Acc. 7551.
36 Latrobe, p. 223.
37 Sedgwick, vol. 2, p. 91.
38 Le Vert, vol. 1, p. 218.
39 Coltro, pp. 42 and 284.
40 Bennett, p. 71.

CHAPTER THREE: ACCOMMODATION AND FOOD IN THE CITY, pp. 20–29

1 Armstrong, pp. 96–7.
2 Simond, pp. 24–7.
3 Black, J., p. 70.
4 Hazlitt, *The works*, vol. 4, pp. 263–7.
5 Dobson, vol. 1, p. 321.
6 Burghley House, EX51/9, pp. 17–20.
7 TNA: PRO 30/9/43.
8 Costello, L.S., p. 255.
9 NLS, MS 23225.
10 W., J., p. 40.
11 Black, J., p. 71.
12 Friedländer, p. 21.

13 NLS, Adv. MS 50 3 14.
14 Misson, *A new voyage*, 1739, vol. 4, p. 395.
15 Lutyens (ed.), p. 256.
16 Kite, p. 188.
17 Wildman, p. 5.
18 Costello, L.S., pp. 255–6.
19 NLS, Acc. 7551.
20 Latrobe, p. 222.
21 Coghill, p. 219.
22 NLS, MS 23225.
23 NLS, Adv. MS 50.3.14, ff. 175–210.
24 Murray (pub.), p. 267.
25 Gaze, pp. 8–13.
26 Barlow, pp. 138–9.
27 Vigée le Brun, vol. 1, p. 255. Transl. by author.
28 Ingamells, pp. xxxix–lii.
29 Fremantle, vol. 2, p. 75.
30 Fremantle, vol. 1, p. 74.
31 SM Soane Notebook 162, f. 158v.
32 V&A, RC.K.14–16, MSL/1939/1908–10.
33 Moryson, 1908, vol. 1, pp. 376–80.
34 Ingamells, pp. xxxix–lii.
35 Young, vol. 2, p. 211.
36 Baring, pp. 112–14.
37 Sedgwick, vol. 2, p. 91.
38 Sala, p. 74.
39 Sala, pp. 79–80.
40 Black, J., p. 76.
41 Beckford, *Dreams*, pp. 137–8.
42 Fremantle, vol. 1, p. 76.
43 NLS, MS 23225.
44 Clarke, A., pp. 263–4.
45 Skippon, vol. VI, p. 548.
46 de Blainville, p. 444.
47 Costello, L.S., pp. 240–1.
48 Drummond, p. 221.
49 Crichton, vol. 2, pp. 209–10.
50 Cambridge, Fitzwilliam Museum, MS 'A Journal to France and Italy'.
51 Moryson, 1908, vol. 1, pp. 376–80.
52 de Blainville, vol. 1, p. 444.
53 Stevens, p. 363.
54 Williams, p. 566.
55 Starkie, p. 119.

CHAPTER FOUR: L'ARENA DI VERONA, pp. 30–39

1 Hale, S., p. 28.
2 Wilson, J., vol. 1, p. 4.
3 Wilson, J., vol. 4, pp. 371–2.
4 Barduzzi, p. 36.
5 Hazlitt, *The works*, vol. 4, pp. 263–7.
6 Moryson, 1908, vol. 1, pp. 376–80.

7   Galiffe, vol. 1, pp. 82–97.
8   Moryson, 1908, vol. 1, pp. 376–80.
9   Coryat, vol. 2, pp. 21–3.
10 Bromley, pp. 216–17.
11 Woods, vol. 1, pp. 225–37.
12 Hazlitt, *The works*, vol. 4, pp. 263–7.
13 Roscoe, p. 141.
14 Mundy, vol. 1, p. 102.
15 d'Uklanski, vol. 1, p. 9.
16 Birch, p. 170.
17 Addison, p. 57.
18 Stevens, pp. 362–3.
19 Burney, pp. 116–18.
20 Friedländer, p. 18.
21 Woods, vol. 1, pp. 225–37.
22 Pasquin, p. 107.
23 A Yankee, pp. 274–5.
24 Wilson, J., vol. 4, pp. 371–2.
25 Eustace, 1815, vol. 1, pp. 115–16.
26 Andersen, pp. 326–7.
27 Sala, pp. 16–17.
28 Kaplan, pp. 41–2.
29 Eustace, 1815, vol. 1, p. 114.
30 Coltro, p. 134.
31 Adolphus, pp. 346–9.
32 Pasquin, p. 107.
33 Coltro, p. 109.
34 Macpherson, p. 212.
35 Murray (pub.), p. 269.
36 Coryat, vol. 2, pp. 22–3.
37 Kotzebue, vol. 4, pp. 261–8.
38 V&A, RC.K.14–16, MSL/1939/1908–10.
39 Sass, pp. 238–9.
40 Simond, pp. 24–7.
41 Pasquin, p. 107.
42 Beckford, *Dreams*, pp. 137–9.
43 Scott, pp. 271–2.
44 Anon., *A classical and historical tour*, vol. 2, pp. 372–7.
45 Baines, pp. 208–10.
46 Klima, p. 82.
47 Walker, pp. 126–8.
48 Trollope, vol. 2, pp. 149–51.
49 Buckingham, vol. 2, p. 361.

CHAPTER FIVE: TRAVELLERS' OPINIONS OF THE CITY, pp. 40–57

1 DHC, D/BKL diary of Henry Bankes, Travels VI.
2 Bloom & Bloom, vol. 1, p. 212.
3 Barduzzi, p. 31.
4 Barduzzi, p. 41.
5 Valerini, p. 109.
6 Moryson, 1908, vol. 1, p. 376.

7   Coryat, vol. 2, p. 17.
8   Dobson, vol. 1, p. 322.
9   Raymond, p. 226.
10 Raymond, p. 227.
11 NLS, Adv. MS 15.2.15.
12 Huguetan, p. 248.
13 Misson, *A new voyage*, 1699, vol. 1, pp. 125–6.
14 Coltro, p. 65.
15 Raymond, p. iv.
16 Wright, vol. 2, p. 490.
17 Stevens, p. 363.
18 Young, vol. 2, p. 210.
19 de Blainville, vol. 1, p. 430.
20 de Blainville, vol. 1, p. 441.
21 Keysler, vol. 3, p. 348.
22 Broderick, pp. 253–5.
23 Bloom & Bloom, vol. 1, p. 134.
24 du Boccage, p. 130.
25 Fremantle, vol. 2, pp. 76–7.
26 Keysler, vol. 3, p. 348.
27 Coltro, p. 102.
28 © The British Library Board, Add. 38837, pp. 25–7.
29 Hogg, vol. 2, p. 231.
30 Colston, vol. 1, pp. 285–6.
31 Sass, pp. 228–9.
32 Costello, L.S., pp. 245–6.
33 Misson, *A new voyage*, 1699, vol. 1, p. 126.
34 Gower, pp. 13–17.
35 Ruskin, *The stones*, 1893, vol. II, p. 248.
36 Coryat, vol. 2, p. 18.
37 TNA: PRO 30/9/43, p. 102.
38 Coltro, p. 220.
39 Walchester, p. 274.
40 Coryat, vol. 2, p. 17.
41 Keysler, vol. 3, p. 360.
42 Hollier, p. 96.
43 Warcupp, pt 1, p. 52.
44 Coltro, p. 299.
45 Cadell, vol. 1, p. 118.
46 Coltro, p. 220.
47 Collins, p. 203.
48 Beaumont, p. 20.
49 Marchand, p. 124.
50 d'Uklanski, vol. 1, pp. 5–6.
51 Galiffe, vol. 1, pp. 82–97.
52 Frye, p. 348.
53 Worcester, p. 830.
54 de Boigne, vol. 1, p. 283.
55 Colston, vol. 1, p. 288.
56 Colston, vol. 1, p. 285.
57 Blessington, vol. 3, pp. 255–6.
58 Hazlitt, *Notes*, pp. 365–6.

59 © The British Library Board, Eg. 1969, f. 208.
60 Buckingham, vol. 2, pp. 367–8.
61 Buckingham, vol. 2, pp. 356–7.
62 Sewell, pt 3, p. 161.
63 Barlow, p. 141.
64 Costello, L.S., pp. 238–40.
65 Dickens, p. 120.
66 Dickens, p. 122.
67 Stoughton, p. 243.
68 Wylie, p. 168.
69 Ruskin, *Letters*, vol. 1, p. 39.
70 Ruskin, *A joy for ever*, para. 76, pp. 85–7.
71 Sewell, pt 3, p. 157.
72 NLS, Acc. 7551.
73 Taine, p. 328.
74 Sala, pp. 75–6.
75 Withrow, p. 172.
76 Child, pp. 155–6.
77 Child, p. 163.
78 Smith, W., p. 9.
79 Coltro, p. 283.
80 Gallichan, pp. 72–3.
81 Bennett, pp. 69–70.

CHAPTER SIX: THE CITY'S CIVIC ARCHITECTURE, pp. 58–66

1 Wildman, p. 4.
2 Child, p. 165.
3 Breval, vol. 2, p. 101.
4 Beaumont, p. 21.
5 Rose, vol. 1, p. 43.
6 Webb, vol. 2, pp. 212–16.
7 NLS, Adv. MS 50.3.14, ff. 175–210.
8 © The British Library Board, Add. 36249, f. 106.
9 Pennington, vol. 2, pp. 233–9.
10 Murray (pub.), p. 275.
11 Starke, pp. 260–1.
12 V&A, RC.K.14–16 MSL/1939/1908–10.
13 Williams, p. 561.
14 Pasquin, p. 108.
15 Murray (pub.), p. 275.
16 Wilson, J., vol. 4, p. 377.
17 Rose, vol. 1, p. 42.
18 Pasquin, p. 107.
19 Child, p. 164.
20 Taine, pp. 328–38.
21 Raymond, p. 232.
22 Butler, pp. 373–6.
23 Coryat, vol. 2, p. 19.
24 Raymond, p. 231.
25 Vasari, *Lives of the most eminent painters*, vol. 4, p. 425.
26 Reichard, p. 240.

27 Woods, vol. 1, p. 237.
28 Woods, vol. 1, p. 237.
29 Vasari, *Lives of the most eminent painters*, vol. 4, p. 436.
30 Buckingham, vol. 2, p. 364.
31 Wilson, W.R., vol. 1, p. 120.
32 Wilson, W.R., vol. 1, p. 120.
33 TNA: PRO 30/9/21.
34 Chaney & Bold, p. 132.
35 du Prey, p. 161.
36 du Prey, p. 202.
37 Wilson, W.R., vol. 1, p. 120.
38 Whitehead, pp. 207–34.
39 Coltro, p. 255.
40 Blessington, vol. 3, p. 271.
41 Sinclair, pp. 71–3.
42 Wilson, W.R., vol. 1, pp. 125–6.
43 V&A, RC.K.14–16, MSL/1938/1908–10.
44 Wildman, p. 3.
45 Wildman, p. 5.
46 Ruskin, *Letters*, pp. 214–15.
47 Child, pp. 164–5.
48 Richards, p. 8.

CHAPTER SEVEN: THE VERONESI, pp. 67–77

1   Anon, *The Geographical Magazine*, p. 180
2   Maffei, *Verona illustrata, Notizie generali*, capo primo, pp. 5–6. Transl. by author.
3   Careri, p. 64.
4   de Blainville, vol. 1, p. 444.
5   Miller, vol. 3, p. 304.
6   Friedländer, p. 20.
7   Wilson, W.R., vol. 1, p. 131.
8   Buckingham, vol. 2, p. 357.
9   Williams, pp. 566–7.
10 Valerini, p. 108. Transl. by author.
11 Aspinall-Oglander, p. 4.
12 Maney, pp. 176–7.
13 Gailhard, pp. 20–1.
14 Maffei, *Verona illustrata, Notizie generali*, capo primo, pp. 5–6. Transl. by author.
15 Broderick, p. 254.
16 Froment, vol. 1, p. 28.
17 d'Uklanski, pp. 5–6.
18 Costello, L.S., pp. 238–40.
19 Sala, p. 16.
20 Shapiro, p. 197.
21 Ruskin, *Letters*, vol. 1, p. 214.
22 Richards, p. 21.
23 Shapiro, p. 196.
24 Goethe, *Goethe's travels*, pp. 37–40.
25 Heine, p. 69.
26 Barlow, p. 141.
27 Costello, L.S., p. 247.

28 Gallichan, pp. 73–4.
29 Bennett, p. 70.
30 Bennett, p. 71.
31 Goethe, *Goethe's travels*, pp. 34–5.
32 Piozzi, *Observations*, vol. 1, p. 129.
33 Bloom & Bloom, vol. 1, p. 214.
34 Vigée le Brun, vol. 1, p. 255. Transl. by author.
35 Coltro, p. 229.
36 Marchand, p. 233.
37 Ingamells, see Hare-Naylor.
38 Manuscripts and Special Collections, The University of Nottingham, Portland Collection, Pw Je 19.
39 NRS, GD/46/15/275.
40 DHC, D/BKL 8C 89.
41 Murray (pub.), *Hand-book*, p. xv.
42 Sweet, *Cities*, p. 287.
43 Beckford, *Dreams*, pp. 160–3.
44 Young, vol. 2, p. 211.
45 Galiffe, vol. 1, pp. 82–97.
46 Pennington, vol. 2, pp. 223–9.
47 Carter, vol. 2, p. 467.
48 NLS, Adv. MS 50.3.14, ff. 175–210.
49 Sala, p. 77.
50 Byron, p. 47.
51 Bennett, p. 74.

CHAPTER EIGHT: THE FRENCH OCCUPATION, pp. 78–82

1 Young English Merchant, pp. 114–15.
2 Ireland, p. 25.
3 Fremantle, vol. 2, p. 217.
4 Tappen, p. 301.
5 Coltro, p. 200. Transl. by author.
6 Hume Weatherhead, pp. 358–64.
7 Wilson, J., vol. 4, p. 373.
8 Da Persico, p. 104. Transl. by author.
9 Coltro, p. 139. Transl. by author.
10 Kotzebue, vol. 1, pp. 118–20.
11 Berrian, pp. 320–4.
12 Da Persico, pp. 84–5. Transl. by author.
13 Wilson, W.R., vol. 1, p. 125.
14 d'Uklanski, vol. 1, pp. 10–11.
15 Young English Merchant, p. 115.
16 Eustace, 1815, vol. 1, p. 124.
17 Kaplan, p. 42.
18 Coltro, p. 198. Transl. by author.
19 de Boigne, vol. 1, p. 283.
20 Costello, L. S., p. 343.

CHAPTER NINE: THE AUSTRIAN OCCUPATION, pp. 83–93

1 Chambers, W., p. 114.
2 Kotzebue, vol. 1, pp. 45–6.

3   http://www.larena.it/home/fu-per-la-santa-alleanza-la-prima-opera-in-arena-1.3023646 [accessed 24 October 2015].
4   Coltro, p. 285.
5   Hobhouse, pp. 66–82.
6   Field, pp. 250-2.
7   Solinas, p. 10.
8   Field, pp. 250-2.
9   Carter, vol. 2, p. 467.
10 Webb, vol. 2, pp. 212–16.
11 Sinclair, pp. 71-3.
12 Barlow, p. 142.
13 Taylor, E., p. 373.
14 Baring, p. 115.
15 Jameson, p. 65.
16 Marsden, p. 91.
17 Crichton, vol. 2, pp. 210–11.
18 NLS, MS 23225.
19 Murray (pub.), p. 126.
20 Wylie, pp. 116–17.
21 Lutyens, p. 220.
22 Lutyens, p. 257.
23 Lutyens, p. 259.
24 von Raumer, vol. 2, p. 333.
25 de Goncourt, p. 15. Transl. by Anthony Earl.
26 Blessington, vol. 3, p. 270.
27 Ruskin, *The stones*, 1893, vol. 3, p. 222.
28 Ruskin, *The stones*, 1893, vol. 3, p. 222.
29 NLS, MS 19455, ff. 95–149.
30 NLS, Acc. 13024/3, p. 122.
31 Alford, pp. 231-2.
32 Drummond, pp. 221-2.
33 Sala, pp. 73–6.

CHAPTER TEN: SHAKESPEARE, ROMEO AND JULIET, pp. 94–100

1   Breval, vol. 2, p. 103.
2   Jameson, p. 66.
3   Hillard, p. 56.
4   Taylor, C., vol. 2, p. 208.
5   Dickens, p. 120.
6   Starkie, p. 116.
7   Child, pp. 158–9.
8   Bennett, pp. 68–9.
9   Clayton, vol. 1, p. 181.
10 Carter, vol. 2, p. 463.
11 Wilson, J., vol. 4, p. 375.
12 Browne, pp. 511–15.
13 Child, p. 161.
14 Latrobe, p. 224.
15 Eddy, pp. 457–8.
16 Pollock, pp. 187–8.
17 Galiffe, vol. 1, pp. 82–97.

18 Champney, pp. 26–9.
19 Carter, vol. 2, p. 468.
20 Fisk, p. 308.
21 Pasquin, p. 105.
22 Eddy, pp. 457–8.
23 Child, p. 160.
24 Walchester, pp. 274–86.
25 Latrobe, pp. 223–4.

CHAPTER ELEVEN: SCIPIONE MAFFEI, pp. 101–106

1 Pasquin, p. 113.
2 Broderick, p. 259.
3 Kotzebue, vol. 4, pp. 261–8.
4 Silvestri, pp. 164–5. Transl. by author.
5 NRS, GD18/4920, p. 82.
6 Piozzi, vol. 1, p. 120.
7 Kotzebue, vol. 4, pp. 261–8.
8 d'Uklanski, vol. 1, pp. 12–13.
9 d'Uklanski, vol. 1, pp. 12–13.
10 Chesterfield, vol. 1, pp. 195–6.
11 Buckingham, vol. 2, p. 369.
12 Buckingham, vol. 2, p. 370.
13 Klima, p. 80. The reference is to *Merope*, first performed in 1712.
14 Silvestri, pp. 164–5. Transl. by author.
15 Halsband, vol. 3, p. 86.
16 Lewis, vol. 17, p. 148.
17 Wilson, J., vol. 4, p. 375.
18 Keysler, vol. 3, p. 353.
19 Pasquin, p. 117.

CHAPTER TWELVE: VERONA'S MANY CHURCHES, pp. 107–114

1 Pasquin, p. 109.
2 Berrian, p. 320.
3 Street, p. 95.
4 Hazlitt, *The works*, vol. 4, pp. 263–7.
5 Woods, vol. 1, p. 236.
6 Friedländer, pp. 18–19.
7 TNA: PRO 30/9/7/10.
8 Blessington, vol. 3, p. 271.
9 Field, pp. 248–9.
10 de la Mottraye, vol. 1, p. 63.
11 Bramsen, vol. 2, pp. 296–9.
12 Pasquin, p. 106.
13 Buckingham, vol. 2, p. 366.
14 Street, p. 104.
15 Chambers, p. 114.
16 Murray (pub.), p. 287.
17 Pasquin, p. 112.
18 W., p. 41.
19 Woods, vol. 1, p. 227.

20 Pasquin, pp. 110–11.
21 Taine, pp. 328–38.
22 Keysler, vol. 3, pp. 362–4.
23 Buckingham, vol. 2, p. 358.
24 Misson, *A new voyage*, 1699, vol. 1, pp. 136–7.
25 de Blainville, vol. 1, p. 433.
26 Pasquin, pp. 114–15.
27 Pasquin, p. 115.
28 TNA: PRO 30/9/7/10.
29 Friedländer, p. 19.
30 Woods, vol. 1, pp. 225–37.
31 Evans, vol. 3, p. 98.
32 Cadell, vol. 1, p. 114.
33 Pasquin, p. 114.
34 Hare, *Cities*, vol. 1, p. 294.
35 Hazlitt, *Works*, vol. 4, pp. 263–7. Montaigne gave the church a different title, but his description seems to fit the same building.
36 Chaney & Wilks, p. 169, both quotations.
37 Pasquin, p. 124.
38 Murray (pub.), p. 298.
39 W., p. 114.
40 Latrobe, p. 222.

CHAPTER THIRTEEN: SAN ZENO MAGGIORE, pp. 115–121

1 Hutton, *Italy*, p. 303.
2 Hutton, *Venice*, p. 303.
3 Woods, vol. 1, pp. 225–37.
4 Hume Weatherhead, p. 358.
5 Street, pp. 120–2.
6 Bennett, p. 74.
7 Misson, *A new voyage*, 1699, vol. 1, p. 128.
8 Buckingham, vol. 2, p. 362.
9 Costello, D., vol. 2, p. 39.
10 Coryat, vol. 2, p. 33.
11 Woods, vol. l, p. 229.
12 Pasquin, p. 105.
13 Evans & Whitehouse, vol. 1, p. 336.
14 Taine, pp. 328–38.
15 Piozzi, vol. 1, p. 123.
16 Buckingham, vol. 2, pp. 362–3.
17 Woods, vol. 1, p. 230.
18 Pasquin, p. 109.
19 Coryat, vol. 2, p. 32.
20 Keysler, vol. 3, p. 366.
21 Stoughton, p. 247.
22 Dorr, p. 149.
23 Pasquin, p. 109.
24 Kaplan, p. 42.
25 Hutton, *Italy*, p. 303.
26 NLS, Acc. 7551.
27 Skippon, vol. vi, p. 542.

28 Woods, vol. 1, p. 231.
29 V&A, RC.K.14–16, MSL/1939/1908–10.
30 de Blainville, vol. 1, p. 434.
31 Pennington, vol. 2, p. 223.
32 Kaplan, p. 42.
33 Alford, pp. 231–2.
34 Willis, p. 12.
35 Costello, D., vol. 2, p. 39.

CHAPTER FOURTEEN: RELIGION THROUGH TOURISTS' EYES, pp. 122–130

1 Cambridge, Fitzwilliam Museum, MS 'Journal to France and Italy'.
2 Brennan, *The origins*, p. 21.
3 Nares, vol. 3, p. 513.
4 Chaney & Wilks, p. 31.
5 *ODNB*.
6 Black, J., p. 166.
7 de Blainville, vol. 1, p. 444.
8 Wright, p. 489.
9 Keysler, vol. 3, pp. 364–5.
10 Klima, p. 81.
11 NLS, MS 9851.
12 Barlow, pp. 138–9.
13 Ruskin, *Works*, Library edition, vol. 33, p. 519.
14 Hume Weatherhead, pp. 358–64.
15 Carter, vol. 2, p. 469.
16 NLS, MS 8923, pp. 82–3.
17 Clayton, vol. 1, p. 181.
18 Hazlitt, *The works*, vol. 4, pp. 263–7.
19 Coryat, vol. 2, pp. 36–7.
20 Skippon, vol. VI, p. 547.
21 Wright, p. 489.
22 TNA: PRO 30/9/43.
23 Murray (pub.), p. 290.
24 Gower, pp. 13–17.
25 Butler, p. 362.
26 Hazlitt, *The works*, vol. 4, pp. 263–7.
27 Coryat, vol. 2, pp. 30–1.
28 de Blainville, vol. 1, p. 440.
29 Veryard, pp. 122–3.
30 NLS, Acc. 7551.
31 Eustace, 1815, vol. 1, p. 24.

CHAPTER FIFTEEN: THE SCALIGERI MONUMENTS, pp. 131–136

1 Williams, p. 565.
2 Coryat, vol. 2, pp. 27–8.
3 Butler, pp. 373–6.
4 Martyn, p. 470.
5 Piozzi, vol. 1, pp. 124–5.
6 Broderick, pp. 259–60.
7 Forsyth, p. 473.
8 Rose, p. 43.

9   Heine, p. 65.
10 NLS, MS 8923, p. 79.
11 Wildman, p. 4.
12 Ruskin, *The stones*, 1893, vol. 3, pp. 53–6.
13 Wildman, p. 22.
14 Buckingham, vol. 2, p. 358.
15 Browne, pp. 511–15.
16 Kaplan, p. 12.
17 Byron, pp. 46–7.
18 Blessington, vol. 3, p. 274.

CHAPTER SIXTEEN: PIAZZA DELLE ERBE, pp. 137–142

1   Murray (pub.), p. 270.
2   Coryat, vol. 2, pp. 29–30.
3   Skippon, vol. VI, p. 542.
4   Coltro, p. 108.
5   Goethe, *Goethe's travels*, p. 40.
6   Heine, p. 63.
7   Pasquin, p. 119. It is not entirely clear what Pasquin meant by an 'arena' in this context.
8   Coltro, p. 60.
9   NLS, Adv. MS 50.3.14, ff. 175–210.
10 Costello, L.S., pp. 240–1.
11 Costello, L.S., pp. 238–40.
12 Wildman, p. 7.
13 Street, pp. 103–4.
14 Smith, pp. 9–10.
15 Tyndale, p. 8.
16 Vincent, p. 78.
17 de Goncourt, pp. 15–18. Transl. by Anthony Earl.
18 Wildman, p. 37.

CHAPTER SEVENTEEN: THE GIUSTI GARDENS, pp. 143–147

1   Hutton, *Italy*, p. 301.
2   Coryat, vol. 2, p. 36.
3   Pona, introduction by Marinelli. Transl. by author.
4   Pona, esp. pp. 69–79.
5   Pona, introduction by Marinelli.
6   Dobson, vol. 1, p. 322. Thomas Howard, Earl of Arundel, had advised Evelyn to visit this garden, 'counted the best in all Italy.' (Hervey, M., p.451).
7   Reresby, p. 58 [a volary is an aviary or flight of birds: volory may be an alternative spelling].
8   Skippon, vol. VI, p. 541.
9   Addison, p. 59.
10 © The British Library Board, Add. 36249, f. 106. Transl. by author.
11 Keysler, vol. 3, p. 368.
12 Gower, pp. 13–17.
13 Piozzi, vol. 1, pp. 130–1.
14 Fremantle, vol. 1, p. 76.
15 Carter, vol. 2, pp. 468–9.
16 Murray, Lady C., vol. 5, pp. 88–9.

17 Pasquin, p. 118.
18 Hare, *The story of my life*, vol. 3, p. 230.
19 Hutton, *Venice*, p. 307.
20 Hutton, *Italy*, p. 301.

CHAPTER EIGHTEEN: LOCAL ARTISTS AND ARISTOCRATIC 'COLLECTIONS', pp. 148–157

1 Goethe, *Goethe's travels*, p. 35.
2 Le Vert, vol. 1, p. 220.
3 Wright, p. 489.
4 Keysler, vol. 3, p. 362.
5 de Lalande, vol. 9, p. 145. Transl. by author.
6 NRS, GD1/616/214.
7 Da Persico, p. 120.
8 Ruskin, *A joy for ever*, pp. 185–6.
9 Mullaly, p. 22.
10 Blessington, vol. 3, p. 274.
11 Hare, *Cities*, p. 267.
12 Murray (pub.), p. xxiii.
13 Murray (pub.), p. 293.
14 Clenche, vol. 1, pp. 472–3.
15 Wright, p. 489.
16 NRS, GD267/35/1/4/30.
17 Bemrose, p. 40.
18 TNA: PRO 30/9/7/10.
19 Wilson, W.R., vol. 1, p. 120.
20 Friedländer, p. 22.
21 de Blainville, vol. 1, p. 433.
22 de Lalande, vol. 9, p. 125. Transl. by author.
23 Colston, vol. 1, p. 287.
24 Pasquin, p. 110.
25 Evans & Whitehouse, p. 334.
26 NLS, MS 8923, p. 86.
27 Bull, p. 243.
28 Pasquin, p. 109.
29 Evans & Whitehouse, p. 335.
30 Pasquin, p. 111.
31 Hutton, *Venice*, p. 301.
32 Keysler, vol. 3, p. 354. Thomas Howard, Earl of Arundel, had visited collections in Verona in the 1640s, including that of 'Dr Mosello' (Dr Muselli) containing works by Veronese and Titian (information supplied by Dr. Edward Chaney).
33 NRS, GD46/15/275, p. 99.
34 Wilson, W.R., vol. 1, p. 122.
35 Colston, vol. 1, p. 288.
36 de Blainville, vol. 1, p. 435.
37 Nugent, vol. 3, p. 122.
38 Piozzi, vol. 1, p. 134.
39 Bloom & Bloom, vol. 1, p. 214.
40 NLS, MS 8923, p. 84.
41 Buckingham, vol. 2, p. 359.
42 Taine, p. 338; these are names used by Taine.
43 Gower, pp. 13–17.
44 Pasquin, p. 119.

45 Murray, Lady C., vol. 5, pp. 81–2.
46 Noon, p. 276.
47 Ritchie, pp. 146–50.

CHAPTER NINETEEN: MUSIC AND THEATRE, pp. 158–165

1 DHC, D/BKL diary of Henry Banks, Travels VI.
2 Paganuzzi et al., p. 71.
3 Paganuzzi et al., p. 129.
4 Keysler, vol. 3, p. 351.
5 Murray (pub.), p. 277.
6 Keysler, vol. 3, p. 351.
7 Silvestri, p. 216.
8 Paganuzzi et al., p. 179.
9 Fenlon, pp. 11–15.
10 Paganuzzi et al., pp. 222–3.
11 Raymond, Introduction.
12 Eustace, 1815, vol. 1, p. 20.
13 Klima, p. 21.
14 D'Amico, p. 1602.
15 Keysler, vol. 3, p. 351. These instruments are still kept today in the Accademia.
16 TNA: PRO 30/9/21.
17 Martyn, p. 387.
18 Miller, vol. 3, pp. 301–2.
19 Butler, pp. 373–6.
20 de Lalande, vol. 9, p. 122. Transl. by author.
21 Burney, p. 118.
22 Kelly, vol. 1, pp. 174–6.
23 The title should read as '*La capricciosa pentita*'. It was by Valentino Fioravanti, first published in 1802.
24 Kotzebue, vol. 4, pp. 261–8.
25 Millard, p. 520.
26 Galiffe, vol. 1, pp. 82–97.
27 Frye, p. 348.
28 Galiffe, vol. 1, pp. 82–97.
29 V&A, RC.K.14–16, MSL/1939/1908–10.
30 Carter, vol. 2, pp. 461–70.
31 Matthews, pp. 287–8.
32 Clayton, vol. 1, pp. 182–3.
33 Goethe, *Goethe's travels*, p. 40.
34 Hale, J.R., p. 170.
35 Ruskin, *Fors Clavigera*, 1873, Letter XXXII, p. 16.
36 Hillard, pp. 58–9.
37 Ruskin, *Complete works*, Library edition 1903–12, vol. 36, pp. 118–19.
38 von Raumer, vol. 2, p. 333.

CHAPTER TWENTY: MATTERS OF HEALTH, pp. 166–170

1 de Blainville, vol. 1, p. 442.
2 Vasari, 1912–14, vol. VI, p. 33.
3 Powell, pp. 120–1.
4 Turner, pp. 9–11.
5 Warcupp, p. 54.

6 Valerini, p. 11. Transl. by author.
7 Beaumont, p. 20.
8 Frye, p. 348.
9 Lewis, vol. 34, pp. 245–7.
10 © The British Library Board, Eg. 1969, f. 215.
11 Hill, pp. 75–6.
12 Ingamells, pp. xxxix–lii.
13 Burgess, p. 101.
14 Burgess, p. 172.
15 Hazlitt, *Works*, vol. 4, pp. 263–7.
16 Ingamells: Cunningham, Alexander.
17 Kotzebue, vol. 4, pp. 261–8.
18 Bessborough, p. 75.
19 Connell, p. 296.
20 Ilchester, vol. 1, p. 112.
21 Hume Weatherhead, pp. 358–64.

CHAPTER TWENTY-ONE: VISITORS' VIEWS ON LOCAL AGRICULTURE AND INDUSTRY, pp. 171–178

1 Piozzi, vol. 1, p. 129.
2 Barduzzi, pp. 33–9.
3 Warcupp, p. 53.
4 Keysler, vol. 3, p. 369.
5 Keysler, vol. 3, p. 359.
6 Beaumont, p. 20.
7 TNA: PRO 30/9/43.
8 Rapelje, p. 172.
9 Tappen, p. 301.
10 Peale, p. 397.
11 Wilson, W.R., vol. 1, pp. 111–12.
12 Warcupp, p. 52.
13 Coltro, p. 110.
14 de Blainville, p. 441.
15 Colston, vol. 1, p. 289.
16 Murray, Lady C., vol. 5, p. 81.
17 Barlow, pp. 138–9.
18 Reichard, p. 243.
19 d'Uklanski, vol. 1, p. 5.
20 Marsden, pp. 91–2.
21 Young, vol. 2, p. 147.
22 Young, vol. 2, pp. 212–14.
23 Young, vol. 2, p. 278.
24 Coltro, p. 150.
25 Pasquin, p. 108.
26 Galignani, pp. 61–6.
27 Cadell, vol. 1, pp. 121–2.
28 See Chapter 2.
29 NLS, MS 23225.
30 Wilson, W.R., vol. 1, pp. 111–12.
31 Thomson, pp. 352–3.
32 de Lalande, vol. 9, p. 132.

33 Beaumont, p. 23.
34 NRS, GD46/15/275, p. 98.
35 DHC, D/BKL HJ3 5.
36 Sebba, p. 221.
37 DHC, D/BKL 8C89.
38 DHC, D/BKL H appendices.
39 DHC, D/BKL 8C89, 11 May 1846.
40 DHC, D/BKL HJ1 866. Transl. by author.

CHAPTER TWENTY-TWO: THE DRESS OF LOCAL PEOPLE, pp. 179–184

1 Murray, Lady C., vol. 5, pp. 81–2.
2 Barduzzi, p. 42.
3 Hazlitt, *Works*, vol. 4, pp. 263–7.
4 Keysler, vol. 3, p. 368.
5 Keysler, vol. 3, p. 385.
6 Bloom & Bloom, vol. 1, p. 134.
7 Goethe, *Goethe's travels*, p. 34.
8 Walker, p. 133.
9 Walker, p. 133.
10 Fremantle, vol. 2, p. 77.
11 Fremantle, vol. 2, p. 217.
12 Ingamells, pp. xxxix–lii.
13 Goethe, *Goethe's travels*, p. 41.
14 Coltro, p. 158.
15 Walker, p. 133.
16 Hobhouse, pp. 66–82.
17 Galiffe, vol. 1, p. 82.
18 Costello, L.S., pp. 238–40.
19 NLS, MS 8923, p. 92.
20 Gardiner, p. 384.
21 Ritchie, pp. 146–50 (*see* Pl. 10).
22 Hillard, p. 57.
23 Devereux, pp. 274–86.
24 von Rochau, pp. 60–1.
25 Butler, p. 376.
26 Bemrose, p. 32.

CHAPTER TWENTY-THREE: ENGLISH VIEWS OF THE ITALIANS, pp. 185–192

1 Broderick, p. 264.
2 Eustace, 1815, vol. 1, pp. 50–1.
3 Cambridge, Fitzwilliam Museum, MS 'A Journal to France and Italy'.
4 Cambridge, Fitzwilliam Museum, MS 'A Journal to France and Italy'.
5 Spedding, vol. 2, p. 17.
6 Halsband, vol. 2, p. 469.
7 Ingamells, pp. xxxix–lii.
8 Cambridge, Fitzwilliam Museum, MS 'A Journal to France and Italy'.
9 Eustace, 1815, vol. 1, p. 50.
10 Jameson, pp. 293–4.
11 Murray (pub.), p. xvii.
12 TNA: PRO 30/9/44.
13 Cambridge, Fitzwilliam Museum, MS 'A Journal to France and Italy'.

14 Watkins, vol. 2, p. 359.
15 Piozzi, vol. 1, p. 100.
16 Watkins, vol. 2, pp. 358–9.
17 Shelley, vol. 1, pp. viii–xii.
18 Murray, Lady C., vol. 5, p. 90.
19 Lutyens, pp. 119–20.
20 Coghlan, p. xxvi.
21 Hare, *Cities*, p. xv.
22 Black, J., p. 132.
23 Hulme & Youngs, p. 42.
24 Black, J., p. 127.
25 Hale, J., p. 60.
26 Heine, p. 75.
27 Dickens, p. 124.
28 Hare, *Cities*, pp. xiv–xvi.

POSTSCRIPT, pp. 193-195

1 http://whc.unesco.org/en/list/797 [accessed 10 October 2014].

BIBLIOGRAPHY

The majority of books listed here are those concerned with the travels of visitors to Verona, some of whose observations were short-listed for reference or possible inclusion as quotations. About 530 other books, not listed here, were consulted and found of no direct relevance, usually because they concerned travellers to Italy who failed to visit Verona or, as in the case of about 40 of them, failed to make any observations likely to be of possible use to the author.

A., F., *The travels of an English gentleman from London to Rome, on foot*, London, 1718
A Yankee, *Old sights with new eyes*, New York, 1854
Adami, M., *La porta bronzea di San Zeno in Verona*, Randazzo, 1984
Addison, J., *Remarks on several parts of Italy* [...], London, 1705
Adolphus, J., *The voyages and travels of her majesty, Caroline* [...], London, 1821
Aglionby, W., *Painting illustrated* [...] *with the lives of the most eminent painters*, London, 1685
Agorni, M., *Translating Italy for the Eighteenth Century* [...], Manchester, 2002
Alford, H., *Letters from abroad*, London, 1865
Allen, A.M., *A history of Verona*, London, 1910
Andersen, H.C., *The Improvisatore*, London, 1869
Anon., *A classical and historical tour* [...] *Italy*, London, 1826
Anon., *The geographical magazine; or, The universe displayed*, London, 1790–2
Armstrong, J., *A short ramble through some parts of France and Italy*, London, 1771
Arundel, T., *Remembrance of things worth seeing in Italy* [...], London, 1987
Ascham, R., *The Scholemaster*, English Reprints, Birmingham, 1870
Aspinall-Oglander, C., *Freshly remembered: the story of Thomas Graham, Lord Lynedoch*, London, 1956
Autori vari, *San Zeno, la figura* [...], Verona, 1988
Ayscough, G., *Letters from an officer in the Guards*, London, 1788
Azzoni, S., *Verona*, Milano, 1999
(Bacon, F.: *see* Spedding, J.)
Baines, E., *Letters from the continent*, Leeds, 1833
Barduzzi, B., *A letter in praise of Verona*, Verona, 1974
Baring, T., *A tour through Italy* [...], London, 1817
Barker, N., *In fair Verona*, Cambridge, 1972
Barlow, T., *A trip to Rome* [...], London, 1836
Bartlett, K., *The English in Italy*, Geneva, 1991
Beaumont, A., *Travels through the Rhaetian alps* [...], London, 1792
Beckford, W., *Dreams, waking thoughts and incidents*, London, 1783

—*Italy*, Paris, 1834
(Beckford, W.: *see also* Melville, S.)
Bemrose, W., *The life and work of Joseph Wright*, London, 1885
Bennassuti, G., *Guida e compendio storico della città di Verona* […], Verona, 1825
Bennett, A., *Journal 1929*, London, 1930
Berrian, W., *Travels in Italy* […], New York, 1819
(Bessborough, Lady: *see* Ponsonby, H.)
Biadego, G., *Verona*, Bergamo, 1909
—*La dominazione austriaca … a Verona …*, Roma, 1899
Biancolinin, G., *Notizie storiche delle chiese di Verona*, Verona, 1749–71
Birch, T., *The life of Henry, Prince of Wales*, London, 1760
Black, A. & C. (pub.), *Black's Guide to Italy*, Edinburgh, 1869
Black, J., *Italy and the grand tour*, London, 2003
(Blathwayt, W. & J.: *see* Hardwick, N.)
Blessington, Countess of, *The idler in Italy*, London, 1840
Bloom, E. & Bloom, L. (eds), *The Piozzi letters*, London, 1989
Bohls, A. & Duncan, I. (eds), *Travel writing 1700–1830*, Oxford, 2005
Borelli, G., *Chiese e monasteri di Verona*, Verona, 1980
Boyd, W.C., *A guide and pocket companion through Italy*, London, 1830
Bramsen, J., *Travels in Egypt*, […] *Italy*, […], London, 1820
Brennan, M. (ed.), *The origins of the Grand Tour* […], London, 2004
—*The travel diary (1611–12) of … Sir Charles Somerset*, Leeds, 1993
Breval, J., *Remarks on several parts of Italy*, London, 1726
Broadbent, E.L., *In and around Verona*, London, 1930
Broderick, T., *The travels of Thomas Broderick, Esq.*, […], London, 1754
Bromley, W., *Several years travels through Portugal* […] *Italy* […], London, 1702
Browne, J.H., *Sights and sensations in Europe*, Hartford, 1871
Buckingham, J.S., *France, Piedmont, Italy* […], London, 1854
Bull, G., *Giorgio Vasari, The lives of the artists*, Harmondsworth, 1971
Burgess, T., *Climate of Italy in relation to pulmonary consumption*, London, 1852
Burnet, G., *Burnet's travels through France, Italy* […], London, 1750
Burney, C., *The present state of music in France and Italy* […], London, 1771
Burty, P., *Lettres de Eugene Delacroix*, Paris, 1880
Butler, A., *Travels through France and Italy*, Edinburgh, 1803
(Byron, Lord: *see* Marchand, L.E.)
Byron, R., *Europe in the looking glass*, London, 1926
Cadell, W.A., *A journey in Carniola, Italy and France* […], Edinburgh, 1820
Caraccioli, L.-A., *Lucidor*, London, 1789
Careri, J., 'Travels through Europe', in Churchill, A., *A collection of voyages* […], London, 1732
Carey, D., *Continental travel and journeys beyond Europe* […], London, 2009
Carter, N., *Letters from Europe*, New York, 1827
Catlow, A. & M.E., *Sketching rambles*, London, 1861
Chalmers, A., *The general biographical dictionary*, London, 1812–17
Chambers, W., *Something of Italy*, London, 1862
Champney, E., *Three Vassar girls in Italy*, Boston, 1886
Chancel, A., *A new journey over Europe*, London, 1714
Chaney, E., *The Grand tour and the great rebellion*, Geneva, 1985
—*The evolution of the Grand Tour*, London, 1998 and 2000
—(ed.), *The evolution of English collecting* […], London, 2003
Chaney, E. & Bold, J., *English architecture public and private* […], London, 1993
Chaney, E. & Wilks, T., *The Jacobean Grand Tour*, London, 2014

Chard, C., *Pleasure and guilt on the Grand Tour*, Manchester, 1999
Chesterfield, Earl of, *Letters written by Lord Chesterfield to his son*, London, 1774
Child, T., *Summer holidays*, New York, 1889
Clarke, A., *Tour in France, Italy and Switzerland* [...], London, 1843
Clarke, J.A., 'A book buying tour in 1645: A note on Ismael Boulliau in Italy', in *The Journal of Library History*, vol. 4, no. 4 (October 1969), pp. 330–6, via JSTOR
Clayton, J.W., *Il Pellegrino*, London, 1863
Clenche, J., 'A tour in France and Italy [...] in 1675', in *A collection of voyages and travels* [...] *compiled from the curious and valuable library of the late Earl of Oxford* [...], London, 1745
Coghill, J., *Abroad*, New York, 1868
Coghlan, F., *Handbook for travellers in Northern Italy*, London, 1856
(Cole, H.: *see* Whitehead, C.)
Collins, L., *Bygone tourist days*, Cincinnati, 1900
Colston, M., *Journal of a tour in* [...] *Italy*, Paris, 1822
Coltro, D., *Il Temporario Diario di una città*, Verona, 1993
Conder, J., *Italy*, London, 1831
Connell, B., *Portrait of a Whig peer*, London, 1957
Cook, T., *Cook's tourist's handbook* [...] *Northern Italy*, London, 1875
Cooke, E.T., & Wedderburn, A., *Works of John Ruskin*, Library Edition, London, 1903–12
Cooper, J.F., *Excursions in Italy*, London, 1840
Coryat, *Coryat's crudities*, Glasgow, 1905
Costello, D., *Piedmont and Italy*, London, 1861
Costello, L.S., *A tour to and from Venice* [...], London, 1845
(Coxe, H.: *see* Millard, J. and also Galignani, A. & W.)
Crawford, E.M., *Gleanings from Venetian history*, London, 1907
(Creed, R.: *see* Thomas, A.)
Crichton, K., *Six years in Italy*, London, 1861
Crowe, J.A. & Cavalcaselle, G.B., *A history of painting in North Italy*, London, 1871
Cust, E., *Records of the Cust family*, London, 1898
Da Persico, G., *Descrizione di Verona e della sua provincia*, Verona, 1820
dal Pozzo, B., *Le vite de' pittori, degli scultori et architetti Veronesi*, Verona, 1718
Dalla Corte, G., *Dell'istorie della città di Verona*, Venezia, 1744
Daly, D., *The Veneto*, London, 1975
D'Amico, S., *Enciclopedia dello spettacolo*, Rome, 1962
Davies, P. & Hemsoll, D., 'Sanmicheli through British eyes', in Bold, J. & Chaney, E. (eds), *English architecture public and private*, London, 1993
de Beer, E.S. (ed.), *Diary* [The diary of John Evelyn], Oxford, 1955
de Blainville, H., *Travels through Holland* [...] *and Italy*, London, 1767
de Boigne, Comtesse, *Memoires of the Comtesse de Boigne*, New York, 1908
de Brosses, C., *Le Président de Brosses en Italie*, Paris, 1858
(de Brosses, C.: *see also* Gower, R.S.)
de Goncourt, E. & J., *L'Italie d'hier*, Paris, 1894
de Lalande, J., *Voyage en Italie* ..., Paris, 1769
de la Mottraye, A., *A. de la Mottraye's travels through Europe* [...], London, 1723–32
(de Montaigne: *see* Trechmann, E.J. and also Hazlitt, W.)
Devereux, W.C., *Fair Italy, the Riviera and Monte Carlo*, London, 1884
Dickens, C., *Pictures from Italy*, London, 1846
Dobson, A. (intro. and notes), *The diary of John Evelyn*, London, 1906
Dorr, D., *A colored man round the world*, privately printed, 1858
Drummond, D., *Scenes and impressions in* [...] *the North of Italy*, Edinburgh, 1854
du Boccage, Madame, *Letters concerning* [...] *Italy*, London, 1770

d'Uklanski, C., *Travels in Upper Italy*, London, 1816
du Prey, P., *John Soane, the making of an architect*, Chicago, 1982
Eastlake Smith, C. (ed.), *Journals [...] of Lady Eastlake*, London, 1895
Eddy, D., *Europa*, Massachusetts, 1852
Eustace, J.C., *A classical tour through Italy*, London, 1815
—*A tour through Italy*, London, 1813
Evans, G., *The classic and connoisseur in Italy and Sicily*, London, 1835
Evans, J. & Whitehouse, J.H. (eds), *The diaries of John Ruskin*, Oxford, 1959
(Evelyn, J.: see de Beer, E.S. and Dobson, A.)
Fall, J., *Memoires of my lord Drumlangrig's [...] travells [...]*, Edinburgh, 1931
Fenlon, I., 'The Mantuan Orfeo', pp. 11–15, in Whenham, J. (ed.), *Claudio Monteverdi: Orfeo*, London, 1986
Ferber, J., *Travels through Italy*, London, 1776
Field, H., *Summer pictures*, New York, 1859
Fisher, D., *Roman Catholic Saints and early Victorian literature*, Farnham, 2012
Fisk, W., *Travels in Europe*, New York, 1839
Flagg, E., *Venice*, New York, 1853
Forsyth, J., *Remarks on antiquities [...] in Italy [...]*, Geneva, 1824
Fremantle, A., *The Wynne diaries*, Oxford, 1940
Friedländer, H., *Views in Italy*, London, 1821
Froment, T., *Oeuvres inédites de Montesquieu*, Paris, 1894
Frye, W.E., *After Waterloo; reminiscences of European travel 1815-19*, London, 1908
Gailhard, J., *The present state [...] of Venice*, London, 1669
Gaiter, D.L. (ed.), *Santuario della Beata Vergine di Campagna [...]*, Verona, 1853
Galiffe, J., *Italy and its inhabitants*, London, 1820
Galignani, A. & W., *Galignani's traveller's guide through Italy [...]*, Paris, 1824
Gallichan, W., *Old continental towns*, London, 1910
Gardiner, W., *Sights in Italy*, London, 1847
Gaze, H., *North Italy and Venetia [...]*, London, 1867
Goethe, J.W., *The flight to Italy*, London, 1999
—*Goethe's travels in Italy [...]*, London, 1885
Gordon, P.L., *A Companion for the visitor at Brussels [...] to which are added notes of a tour to Italy [...]*, London, 1828
Gower, Lord R. S., *Selections from the letters of de Brosses*, London, 1897
Graf, A., *L'Anglomania*, Torino, 1911
Gray, R., *Letters during the course of a tour through Germany, Switzerland and Italy [...]*, London, 1794
Gregory, A.T., *Practical guide to Italy, North and central*, London, 1859
Grove, G., *The new dictionary of music and musicians*, 2nd edition, London, 2001
Guides-Joanne, *Italie du nord*, Paris, 1916
Gwilt, J., *Notitia architectonica Italiana*, London, 1818
Hale, J.R. (ed.), *The Italian journal of Samuel Rogers*, London, 1956
Hale, S., *Verona*, London, 1991
(Hallam, H.: see Rose, W.)
Halsband, R., *The complete letters of Lady Mary Wortley Montagu*, Oxford, 1967
Hardwick, N. (ed.), *The Grand Tour: letters [...] William and John Blathwayt*, Bristol, c.1985
Hardy, S., *Memoirs of [...] Earl Charlemont*, London, 1810
Hare, A., *The story of my life*, London, 1896
—*Cities of Northern and Central Italy*, London, 1876
Hazlitt, W., *Notes of a journey through France and Italy*, London, 1826
—*The works of Michael de Montaigne*, London, 1861
Hearder, H., *Italy: a short history*, Cambridge, 2001

Heine, H., *Italian travel sketches*, London, 1927
Hervey, M.F.S., *The life, correspondence [...] of Thomas Howard, Earl of Arundel*, Cambridge, 1921
Hervey, W., *Journals of the Hon. William Hervey*, Bury St Edmunds, 1906
Heywood, R., *A journey to Italy in 1826*, privately printed, 1826
Hibbert, C., *The grand tour*, London, 1987
Hill, A., *Familiar letters*, London, 1767
Hillard, G., *Six months in Italy*, London, 1867
Hinde, C., *Journal of a tour made in Italy [...]*, Geneva, 1982
Hobhouse, J.C., *Italy: remarks made in several visits [...]*, London, 1859
(Hoby, T.: *see* Powell, E.)
Hogg, T.J., *Two hundred and nine days [...]*, London, 1827
(Holland, Lady E.: *see also* Ilchester, Earl of)
Hollier, R., *Glances at various objects during a nine weeks' ramble [...]*, London, 1831
Horwitz, O., *Brushwood picked up on the continent [...]*, Philadelphia, 1855
Howard, T., *Remembrances of things worth seeing in Italy*, London, 1987
Howell, J., *Instructions for Forreine Travell*, London, 1868
Howells, W., *Italian journeys*, London, 1901
Huguetan, J., *Voyage d'Italie*, Lyons, 1681
Hulme, P. & Youngs, T., *The Cambridge companion to Travel writing*, Cambridge, 2002
Hume Weatherhead, G., *A pedestrian tour through [...] Italy*, London, 1834
Hutton, E., *Italy and the Italians*, New York, 1903
—*Venice and Venetia*, London, 1911
Ilchester, Earl of (ed.), *Journal of Elizabeth Lady Holland [...]*, London, 1908
Ingamells, J., *A dictionary of British and Irish travellers in Italy 1701–1800*, New Haven, 1997
Ireland, T., *Extracts from a journal during a tour in Italy*, Chiswick, 1836
James, H., *Italian hours*, London, 1909
(James, H.: *see also* Kaplan, F.)
Jameson, A., *Diary of an ennuyée*, London, 1826
(Jameson, A.: *see* also Macpherson, G.)
Jefferies, D., *A plain narrative of a journey from London to Rome [...]*, Liverpool, [1750]
Kaplan, F. (ed.), *Travelling in Italy with Henry James*, London, 1994
Kelly, M., *Reminiscences of Michael Kelly*, London, 1826
Keysler, J., *Travels through Germany, [...] Italy, [...]* London, 1760
Kite, S., *Building Ruskin's Italy [...]*, Farnham, 2012
Klima, S. (ed.), *Joseph Spence: letters from the Grand Tour*, London, 1975
Knight, H., *The ecclesiastical architecture of Italy*, London, 1845
Kotzebue, A., *Travels through Italy*, London, 1807
Lacklustre, S., *The wanderings of the body and mind of Simon Lacklustre Esq.: being the notes of a trip from London to Rome [...]*, London, 1848
Lassels, R., *The voyage of Italy [...]*, Paris, 1670
Latrobe, J., *Hints for six months in Europe*, Philadelphia, 1869
Lazise, Conte B., *Saggio d'una statistica della città di Verona*, Venezia, 1823
Le Vert, O., *Souvenirs of travel*, New York, 1857
Lewis, W. et al. (eds), *Horace Walpole: correspondence*, Oxford, 1955
Lorenzoni, G. & Valenzano, G., *Il Duomo di Modena e la Basilica di San Zeno*, Verona, 2000
Lutyens, M. (ed.), *Effie in Venice*, London, 1972
Macpherson, G., *Memoirs of the life of Anna Jameson*, London, 1878
(Macready, W.C.: *see* Pollock, F.)
Maffei, S., *Verona illustrata*, Verona, 1732
(Maffei, S.: *see also* Moroni (pub.))
Magagnato, L., *Arte e civiltà del medioevo Veronese*, Torino, 1962

Maney, H., *Memories over the water*, Nashville, 1854
Marchand, L.E. (ed.), *Byron's letters and journals*, Harvard, 1973–94
Marchi, G-O.A., *Il culto di San Zeno nel Veronese*, Verona, 1972
Marini, P., *Castelvecchio Museum*, Verona, 2003
Marsden, R.C., *Letters illustrative of Italian scenery* […], London, 1821
Martyn, T., *The gentleman's guide through Italy*, London, 1787
Matthews, H., *The diary of an invalid*, London, 1824
Melville, S., *The life and letters of William Beckford* […], London, 1910
Milford, J., *Observations* […] *during a tour through* […] *Italy* […], London, 1818
Millard, J., *Picture of Italy*, London, 1815, 1817
Miller, Lady A.R., *Letters from Italy*, London, 1776
Misson, M., *A new voyage to Italy*, London, 1699, 1714, 1739
—*Nouveau voyage d'Italie*, La Haye, 1731
(Montaigne: *see* Trechmann, E.J. and also Hazlitt, W.)
(Montesquieu, C-L.: *see* Froment, T.)
Monteith, J. (?), *A merchant's holiday*, 1861
Moore, J.H., *A new and complete collection of voyages and travels*, London, 1780
Moroni (pub.), *Compendio della Verona Illustrata*, Verona, 1795
Moryson, F., *An itinerary written by Fynes Moryson*, London, 1617; Glasgow, 1908
Mullaly, T., *Ruskin a Verona*, Verona, 1966
Mundy, P., *The travels of Peter Mundy*, London, 1907–36
Murray (pub.), *Hand-book for travellers in Northern Italy*, London, 1842
Murray, A.H.H. et al., *On the old road through France to Florence*, London, 1932
Murray, Lady C., *A journal of a tour in Italy*, London, 1836
Nares, E., *Memoirs of Lord Burghley*, London, 1828–31
Noon, P., *Richard Parkes Bonington: the complete paintings*, London, 2011
Norwich, J.J., *Venice The greatness and the fall*, London, 1981
—*A traveller's companion to Venice*, London, 2002
—*Paradise of cities*, London, 2002
Nugent, T., *The Grand Tour*, London, 1778
Paganuzzi, E. et al., *La musica a Verona*, Verona, 1976
Parks, G., *The English traveller to Italy, Vol. 1, The middle ages*, Roma, 1954
Pasquin, A., *Historical, literary and artistical travels* […] *Italy*, Paris, 1839
Patuzzo, M., *Verona Romana Medievale Scaligera*, Verona, 2008
Peale, R., *Notes on Italy* […], Philadelphia, 1831
Pennington, T., *A journey into various parts of Europe*, London, 1825
Pesci, F., *Imago urbis*, Verona, 2001
Pine-Coffin, R., *Bibliography of British and American travel in Italy to 1860*, Firenze, 1974
—*Bibliography of British and American travel in Italy to 1860 Additions and Corrections*, Firenze, 1981
Piozzi, H.L., *Observations and reflections made in the course of a journey through France, Italy and Germany*, London, 1789
(Piozzi, H.L.: *see also* Bloom, E. & Bloom, L.)
Pollock, F. (ed.), *Macready's reminiscences* […], New York, 1875
Pona, F., *Il Sileno*, Sommacampagna, 1999
Ponsonby, H., *Lady Bessborough and her family circle*, London, 1940
Powell, E. (ed.), *The travels and life of Sir Thomas Hoby*, London, 1902
Rapelje, G., *A narrative of excursions, voyages and travels*, New York, 1834
Raymond, J., *An itinerary contayning a voyage, made through Italy, in the yeare 1646, and 1647* […], London, 1648
Recordati, L. et al. (eds), *Verona and Lake Garda*, Milano, 2001

Reichard, H., *Itinerary of Italy*, London, 1819
Reitter, P.F. (ed.), *Case, palazzi e ville di Verona* [...], Verona, 1997
Reresby, Sir J., *The travels and memoirs* [...], London, 1813
Richard, Abbé J., *Description historique* [...] *de l'Italie*, Paris, 1769
Richards, B., *Juliet's tomb* [...], Oxford, 2009
Ritchie, L., *Travelling sketches in the north of Italy*, London, 1832
Rognini, L., *Tarsie [...] Santa Maria in Organo*, Verona, 1985
(Rogers, S.: *see* Hale, J.R.)
Roscoe, T., *The Tourist in Switzerland and Italy*, London, 1830
Rose, W., *Letters from the north of Italy*, London, 1819
(Ruskin, E.: *see* Lutyens, M.)
Ruskin, J., *Lectures* [...] *at Edinburgh*, London, 1854
—*Fors clavigera*, Orpington, 1873, 1891
—*The stones of Venice*, London, 1st edition 1851-3; 5th edition, 1893
—*The complete works of John Ruskin LL. D. in 26 volumes*, Brantwood edition, New York, 1894
—*Letters* [...] *to* [...] *Charles Eliot Norton*, Boston, Mass., 1904
—*A joy for ever*, Orpington, 1894; London, 1911
—*Praeterita*, London, 1949
—*Verona e i suoi fiumi*, Verona, 1947
(Ruskin, J.: *see also* Evans, J. & Whitehouse, J.H.; Shapiro, H.I.; Mullaly, T.; Wildman, S.; Richards, B.)
Sala, G.A., *Rome and Venice, with other wanderings*, London, 1869
Sarayna, T., *Le historie e fatti de Veronesi*, Verona, 1542
—*Di origine e amplitidine civitatis Veronae*, Verona, 1540
Sass, H., *A journey to Rome and Naples* [...], London, 1818
Saunders, E., *Italy and her capital*, London, 1868
Savage, C., *Illustrated biography*, Buffalo, 1856
Scolari, A. (intro.), *Dante e Verona*, Verona, 1965
Scoto, F., *Itinerario* [...] *d'Italia*, Padua, 1654
(Scoto, F., *see also* Warcupp, C.)
Scott, J., *Sketches of manners, scenery, &c. in* [...] *Italy*, London, 1821
Sebba, A., *The exiled collector — William Bankes* [...], London, 2004
Sedgwick, C.M., *Letters from abroad to kindred at home*, New York, 1841
Semenzato, C. & Perini, M., *Verona illustrata*, Padova, 1997
Sewell, E.M., *A journal kept during a summer tour* [...], London, 1852
Shapiro, H.I. (ed.), *Ruskin in Italy: letters to his parents*, Oxford, 1972
Shelley, M.W., *Rambles in* [...] *Italy*, London, 1844
Sherer, J.M., *Scenes and impressions in Egypt and in Italy*, London, 1825
Silvestri, G., *Un Europeo del Settecento Scipione Maffei*, Treviso, 1954
Simond, L., *A tour in Italy and Sicily*, London, 1828
Sinclair, J., *An autumn in Italy*, Edinburgh, 1829
Skippon, P., 'An account of a journey through [...] Italy [...]', from Churchill, Messrs (pub.), *A collection of voyages and travels* [...] *in six volumes* [...], London, 1732
Smith, H.F., *American travellers abroad*, London, 1999
Smith, J.E., *A sketch of a tour*, London, 1793
Smith, W., *Journal of a tour in Italy* [...], London, 1881
Solinas, A., *Il congresso di Verona*, Verona, 2003
(Somerset, C.: *see* Brennan, M.)
Spedding, J. (ed.), *The works of Francis Bacon*, London, 1862-76
(Spence, J.: *see* Klima, S.)
Starke, M., *Travels in Europe*, Paris, 1839

Starkie, W.F., *The waveless plain*, London, 1938
Stebbing, H., *Lives of the Italian poets*, London, 1832
Steuart, A.F., *Last journals of Horace Walpole*, London, 1910
Stevens, S., *Miscellaneous remarks made on the spot* [...] *Italy* [...], London, 1756
Stokes, A., *The quattro cento* [...], London 1932
Stoughton, J., *Scenes in other lands*, London, 1853
Street, G.E., *Notes of a tour in Northern Italy*, reissue, London, 1986
Sweet, R., 'British perceptions of Florence in the long eighteenth century', in *The Historical Journal*, vol. 50, no. 4
—*Cities and the Grand Tour, The British in Italy, c.1690–1820*, Cambridge, 2012
Symons, A., *Cities of Italy*, London, 1907
Taine, H., *Italy: Florence and Venice*, New York, 1869
Tappen, G., *Professional observations on the architecture of France and Italy*, London, 1806
Taylor, C., *Letters from Italy*, London, 1841
Taylor, E., *The Taylor papers*, London, 1913
(Taylor, H.: *see* Taylor, E.)
Thomas, A. (ed.), *Richard Creed's journal of the Grand Tour* [...], Oundle, 2002
Thomson, W., *Two journeys through Italy and Switzerland*, London, 1835
(Todd, M.: *see* Trease, G.)
Tothill, M., *Journal of the wanderings of four wanderers, on the Riviera and in North Italy*, Bristol, 1881
Travelling lawyer, *The continental traveller* [...], London, 1833
Trease, G. (ed.), *Matthew Todd's journal*, London, 1968
Trechmann, E.J. (ed.), *The diary of Montaigne's journey to Italy* [...], London, 1929
Trollope, F.M., *A visit to Italy*, London, 1842
Turner, W., *A Booke of the natures* [...] *of the bathes* [...] *Italye*, Collen, 1568
Tyndale, W., *An artist in Italy*, London, 1913
(Uklanski: *see* d'Uklanski, C.)
Valerini, A., *Le belleze di Verona*, Verona, 1586
(Valéry: *see* Pasquin, A.)
Vallardi, G., *Itinerario d'Italia*, Milano, 1815
Vasari, G. (trans. Foster, J.), *Lives of the most eminent painters, sculptors and architects*, London, 1851
—(trans. de Vere, G. du C.), *Lives of the most eminent painters, sculptors and architects*, Medici Society, London, 1912–14
(Vasari, G.: *see* also Bull, G.)
Venturi, G., *Compendio della storia sacra e profana di Verona*, Verona, 1825
Veryard, E., *An account of* [...] *a journey through* [...] *Italy* [...], London, 1701
Vigée le Brun, M.L.E., *Souvenirs of Madame Vigée le Brun* [...], Paris, n.d. (nineteenth century)
Vincent, E., *The Italy of the Italians*, London, 1927
(von Kotzebue, A.: *see* Kotzebue, A.)
von Raumer, F., *Italy and the Italians*, London, 1840
von Rochau, A., *Wanderings through the cities of Italy* [...], London, 1853
(von Uklanski: *see* d'Uklanski, C.)
W., J., *Diary of a tour through Belgium,* [...] *Northern Italy* [...], Manchester, [1863]
Walchester, K., *Our own fair Italy*, Bern, n.d. (c.2007)
Waldie, J., *Sketches descriptive of Italy* [...], London, 1820
Walker, A., *Ideas suggested on the spot in* [...] *Italy*, London, 1790
(Walpole, H.: *see* Lewis, W. and also Steuart, A.F.)
Warcupp, E. (trans.), *Italy, in its original glory, ruine and revival* [...] (a translation of Scoto, F., above), London, 1660
Watkins, T., *Travels through Switzerland, Italy,* [...], London, 1792
Webb, W., *Minutes of remarks on ... Italy*, London, 1827

Whenham, J. (ed.), *Claudio Monteverdi: Orfeo*, London, 1986
Whitehead, C., 'Henry Cole's European travels [...]', in *Architectural History*, vol. 48 (2005), pp. 207-34, via JSTOR
Wiel, A., *The story of Verona*, London, 1902
Wildman, S., *'My dearest place in Italy': Ruskin in Verona*, Lancaster, 2005
Wilkey, E., *Notes of a ramble through* [...] *Italy*, London, 1836
Williams, C., *The Alps, Switzerland and the North of Italy*, London, 1854
Willis, R., *Remarks on the architecture of the Middle Ages especially of Italy*, Cambridge, 1835
Wilson, J., *A journal of two successive tours upon the Continent* [...], London, 1820
Wilson, W.R., *Notes abroad and rhapsodies at home* [...], London, 1837
Wilton, A. & Bignamini, I. (eds), *Grand Tour* [...] *Lure of Italy in the Eighteenth Century*, London, 1996
Withrow, W.H., *A Canadian in Europe*, Toronto, 1881
Woods, J., *Letters of an architect from France, Italy* [...], London, 1828
Worcester, J.E., *A geographical dictionary* [...], Boston, 1823
(Wortley Montague, Lady Mary: *see* Halsband, R.)
Wright, E., *Some observations made in* [...] *Italy* [...], London, 1730
(Wright, J.: *see* Bemrose, W.)
Wylie, A.J., *Pilgrimage from the Alps to the Tiber*, Edinburgh, 1856
(Wynne, E.: *see* Fremantle, A.)
Young, A., *Travels during the years 1787, 1788 and 1789*, London, 1792
Young English Merchant, *A tour through some parts of* [...] *Italy* [...], London, 1815
Zorzi, R.M., Gery, J., Bacigalupo, M., & Casella, S.F., *In Venice and the Veneto with Ezra Pound*, Università Ca'Foscari di Venezia, 2007

ELECTRONIC RESOURCES

(University of Chicago), *British and Irish women's letters and diaries, from 1500–1900*, Chicago, 2001–
Oxford Dictionary of National Biography (*ODNB*)

REFERENCE WEBSITES

www.ancestry.co.uk
www.archive.org
www.books.google.com
www.copac.ac.uk
www.HathiTrust.org
www.jstor.org
www.larena.it
www.wikipedia.org

MANUSCRIPTS

Burghley House archive
EX 51/9 (Culpepper Tanner re John, 5th earl of Exeter)

Dorset History Centre, Dorchester (DHC)
The Bankes Collection, D/BKL: Box 8C/75; 8C/89; HJ1; HJ3; Diary of Henry Bankes; H appendices

Cambridge, Fitzwilliam Museum
MS, The Honourable William Fitzwilliam, A Journal to France and Italy 1769–70

College Archives, Eton College
The diary of Major General Sir Arthur Brooke, 1816, MS 487
Travels of the late Henry Chichester Esq., 1838–9, MS 488
Sketchbook (anon.) 1825, K.MSS

Lincoln Record Office
1WORS 10, 16, 24 and 44 (Correspondence Worsley & Macartney)

Manuscripts and Special Collections, The University of Nottingham
Mellish Collection Me 2 L 4/1; Me C 8/3/9
Portland Collection Pw Je 19–21 (Albertini to Lord William Bentinck)
Portland Collection PwM 383 and 385 (Prudence Bentinck to Albertini)

National Library of Scotland (NLS)
Acc. 13024/3 from *Edinburgh Evening Courant*, 1860 and 1862
Acc. 7551 (Anon., Memorandum of tour in France, Switzerland and Italy ..., 1864)
Adv. MS 50.3.14, ff. 175–210 (Anon., Description of Italy, 1841)
Adv. MS 15.2.15 (Anon., Description of Italy, c.1600–50)
MS 39/89 (Richardson, 1823)
MS 2598 (Anon., 1838)
MS 5785 (Kerr, Sir W., 1625)
MS 8923 (Anon., 1830)
MS 9851 (Hay, A., 1825)
MS 19455 (Journal of Lady Melgund (?), Minto family, 1853)
MS 20014 (Haldane, 1868)
MS 23225 (Cockburn, H., 1823)

National Records of Scotland (NRS)
GD1/616/214 (Anon., 1770)
GD18/4920 (Adam, J., 1761)
GD46/15/275 (Stewart, J./Seaforth, 1815)
GD267/35/1/4/30 (Home, P., 1773)
GD477/442 (Makdougall, H., 1776–7)

Sir John Soane Museum
SM Soane Notebooks 39 and 162

The British Library Board
Add. 36249, ff. 2–246 Harwicke papers, vol. DCCCCI, Continental Travels of William Freman
Add. 38837 (Robson)
Add. 39790 Flaxman XI
Eg. 1969 (Henry, Duke of Gloucester)
Eg. 1970 (Martyn, T.)

The National Archives (TNA)
PRO 30/9/7/10 (Gibbes, Elizabeth)
PRO 30/9/21 (Abbot, Charles)
PRO 30/9/43 and 44 (Bentham, Sarah)

Victoria and Albert Museum, National Art Library (V&A)
RC.K.14–16, 3 vols, MSL/1939/1908–10, Hayward, J.S., Journal and memoranda

INDEX

Index of People

Abbot, Charles 8, 10, 63, 159, 198, 200, 238
Adam, James 102, 238
Addison, Joseph 33, 145–6, 198, 229
Adolphus, J.H. 36, 229
Aglionby, William 167, 229
Aguiari, Lucrezia (La Bastardina) 160
Alberti, Valentino 79
Albertini, Alberto 74, 238
Alexander I, Tsar 84–5
Alford, Henry 91, 121, 198, 229
Andersen, Hans Christian 35, 198, 229
Arundel, Earl of 223-4, 233
Ascham, Roger 1, 185, 199, 229
Ayscough, George 9, 199, 229

Bacon, Francis 2, 186, 199, 229
Baines, Edward 39, 229
Balestra, Antonio 149
Bankes, Henry 40, 158, 199, 237
Bankes, William xi, 51–2, 74, 177–8, 199, 235, 237, Plate 3
Barduzzi, Bernardino 30, 40, 171, 179, 196, 199, 229
Baring, T. 12, 26, 87, 229
Barlow, Thomas 14, 24, 52, 72, 125, 173, 229
Barry, Charles 63

Bartlett, William Henry xii, 167, Plate 14
Bassano 155
Beaumont, Albanis 48, 58, 167, 172, 176, 199, 229
Beckford, William 26, 38, 67, 75, 193, 199, 229
Bellini 127, 154
Bellotto, Bernardo xi, 157, Plate 7
Bennett, Arnold 19, 57, 73, 77, 96, 116, 200, 230
Bentham, Jeremy 8, 198, 200
Bentham, Sarah 8, 19–22, 29, 46, 128, 172, 187, 198, 200, 238
Berrian, William 80, 107, 230
Bertola, Abate 73
Bessborough: *see* Spencer
Bevilacqua, Count 159, 161
Bibiena, Antonio Galli xii, 159, Plate 11
Birkett Foster, Miles xi, 157, Plate 8
Blathwayt, William senior, William junior and John 27, 43, 201, 230, 232
Blessington, Countess of 5, 50, 65, 90, 108, 110, 136, 150, 204, 230
Bonifazio 156
Botticelli, Sandro 141
Bozza, Vincenzo 155
Bramsen, John 109, 230
Breval, John 58, 95, 230
Briotolo 118

Broderick, Thomas 44, 69, 102, 133, 185, 230
Bromley, William 32
Browne, Junius 17–18, 97, 135, 200, 230
Brusasorzi, Felice 149–50
Buckingham, James Silk xi, 13, 39, 51–2, 54, 63, 68, 104, 109, 111, 116, 118, 135, 155, 199, 200, 230, Plate 2
Burgess, Thomas 168, 230
Burghley, Lord 123, 234
Burney, Charles 33, 82, 161, 200, 230
Butler, Alban 62, 129, 132, 160, 184, 200, 230
Byron, George, Lord 5, 48, 74, 84, 191, 199, 200, 204, 207, 234
Byron, Robert 77, 135, 200, 230

Cadell, William 47, 113, 175, 200, 230
Caius, John 122
Caliari, Paolo: *see* Veronese, Paolo
Can Grande, Cangrande 61, 131, 134–5
Can Signorio 134
Callow, William 157
Careri, Giovanni 67, 230
Caroline, Queen 36, 229
Caroto, Giovanni 59, 149
Carter, Nathaniel 18, 76, 85, 97, 99, 126, 146, 163, 201, 230
Castelbarco, Guglielmo da xi, 22, 157, Plate 9
Catullus 58, 62
Cavazzuola, Paolo 150
Chambers, William 83, 110, 230
Charlemagne 60
Charles (Karl) Ferdinand, archduke of Austria 89
Charles, king of Sardinia 84
Chesterfield, Earl of 103, 231
Child, Theodore 18, 56, 58, 62, 66, 95, 97, 99, 156, 201, 231
Cholwick, Thomas 17

Cignaroli, Giambettino 149
Clarke, A. 8, 27, 231
Clayton, Captain J.W. 97, 127, 163, 201, 231
Clenche, John 151, 231
Cockburn, Henry 10, 21, 24, 27, 29, 87, 175, 201, 238
Coghill, J. Henry 24, 231
Cole, Henry 64, 237
Collins, Laura 48, 231
Colston, Marianne 4, 45, 50, 152, 154, 157, 173, 201, 231
Conder, Josiah 231
Cooke, Edward William 157
Coryat, Thomas xvi, 2, 31, 33, 37, 41, 46–7, 62, 117–19, 128–9, 132, 143–4, 197, 201, 231
Costello, Dudley 117, 121, 231
Costello, Louisa 23, 27, 45, 52, 70, 72, 82, 139, 157, 182, 194, 201, 231
Coxe, Henry: *see* Millard, J.
Cranborne, Lord 114
Creed, Richard 236
Crichton, Kate 27–9, 87, 201, 231
Crivelli, Carlo 156
Cunningham, Alexander 169
Curtoni, Domenico 65
Curtoni Verza, Contessa Silvia 73

Da Persico, Giovanni Battista xii, 79, 81, 84, 101, 110, 149, 152–3, 201, 231, Plates 16–18
da Porta, Louis 94
da Verona, Stefano 112
da Vinci, Leonardo 156
dai Libri, Girolamo 148–50
dalla Corte 94, 231
Dante Alighieri xv, 61, 77, 109, 131, 194, 196, 235
Davison, Francis 122
de Blainville, Henri 27–8, 43, 67, 111, 120, 123, 129, 152, 154–5, 166, 173, 201–2, 231

Index

de Boigne, Adèle, comtesse 50, 82, 202, 231
de Brosses, Charles 46, 128, 145, 156, 202, 231–2
de Goncourt 90, 141–2, 231
de la Mottraye, Aubrey 109, 231
De Lalande, Jérôme 149, 152, 160, 176, 202, 231
de Montaigne, Michel 21, 31–3, 44, 107–8, 113, 127, 129, 169, 179, 202, 232, 236
della Scala 61, 114, 131, 134–5
Devereux, William 47, 100, 184, 231
Dickens, Charles 53, 95, 187, 191, 202, 231
Dorr, David 119, 202, 231
Drumlangrig, Lord 9, 232
Drummond, David 27, 92, 202, 231
du Boccage, Anne-Marie 44, 202, 231
d'Uklanski: *see* von Uklanski

Eddy, Daniel 98–9, 232
Elizabeth I, Queen 122, 186, 199
Eustace, John 1, 4, 35–6, 81, 102, 130, 149, 159, 186–7, 202, 232
Evans, G.W.D. 113, 232
Evelyn, John 21, 41, 144, 203, 223, 231
Ezzelino da Romano 60, 196

Falconetto, Giovanni Maria 156
Farinati, Paolo 149–50
Ferrari, Luigi 74
Field, Henry 18, 85, 108, 203, 232
Fioravanti, Valentino 161, 225
Fisk, Wilbur 99, 232
Fitzgerald, Lady 170
Fitzwilliam, The Honourable William 9, 28, 122, 186, 188, 237
Forsyth, Joseph 48, 133, 203, 232
Fortescue, Lady Henrietta xii, 60, 157, Plate 19
Fracastoro, Girolomo 62
Francis I, Emperor 84–5
Frederick III, King 84
Freman, William 59, 145, 238

Friedländer, Herman 22, 34, 68, 108, 112, 151, 175, 203, 232
Frye, Major William 49, 162, 167, 203, 232
Fuseli, Henry 157

Gailhard, Jean 69, 203, 232
Gaiter, Luigi 178, 232
Galiffe, Jacques 31, 49, 75, 98, 162, 182, 203, 232
Gallichan, Walter 56, 72, 204, 232
Gardiner, William 183, 232
Garibaldi 91
Gaze, H. 12, 24, 232
Gibbes, Elizabeth 108, 112, 151, 238
Giocondo, Fra' 62, 149
Giolfino, Niccolò 150, 156
Giorgione 154
Giotto di Bondone 61
Giovanni da Verona, Fra' 112
Gloucester, Duke of 51, 167, 199, 238
Goethe: *see* von Goethe
Goff, Robert xi, 157, Plate 9
Goodwin, Albert 157

Hallam, Henry: *see* Rose, William
Harding, James Duffield 157
Hare, Augustus 13, 113, 146, 150, 189–90, 192, 204, 232
Hare-Naylor, Georgiana 74
Hay, Adam 124, 238
Hayward, John 12–13, 25, 37, 60, 66, 120, 157, 162, 204, 238
Hazlitt, William 51, 204, 232
Heine, Heinrich 71, 133, 138, 141, 191, 204, 233
Hillard, George 95, 164, 183, 204, 233
Hobhouse, John Cam 84–5, 182, 204, 233
Hoby, Sir Thomas 166, 234
Hogg, Thomas 45, 205, 233
Hollier, Richard 47, 233
Home, Patrick 151, 238

Horwitz, Orville 13, 18, 233
Howard, Thomas: *see* Arundel, Earl of
Howells, William Dean 18, 59, 233
Huguetan, Jean 42, 233
Hume Weatherhead, George 115, 125, 170, 205, 233
Hutton, Edward 115, 119, 143, 147, 153, 190, 205, 233

Ireland, T.J. 78

James, Henry 18, 35, 82, 119, 121, 135, 205, 233
Jameson, Anna 36, 87, 95, 187, 205, 233
Jefferies, David 233
Joseph II, Emperor 36

Kelly, Michael 161, 233
Keysler, John 15, 43, 45, 47, 106, 111, 118, 124, 145, 149, 153, 158-9, 172, 179, 205, 233
Kinnoull, 9th Earl of 69
Knight, Henry Gally xii, 157, 233, Plate 20
Kotzebue: *see* von Kotzebue

Lacklustre, Simon 14, 233
Lassels, Richard xvi, 233
Latrobe, John 18, 33, 98, 100, 114, 205, 233
Le Vert, Octavia 19, 148, 233
Liberale di Verona 148, 150
Little, Thomas 157
Longfellow, Henry 66
Lucius III, Pope 109

Macready, William 98, 234
Maffei, Scipione xi, xii, 3, 44, 69, 79, 101-6, 110, 119, 136-7, 159, 162, 177, 197, 205, 233, 235, Plates 1, 11, 12
Magli, Giovanni 158
Malenza, Giovanni Battista 75
Maney, Henry 69, 234
Mann, Horace 105, 190

Mantegna, Andrea 79, 116, 120-1, 150, 152-3, 156, 196
Marsden, Robert 87, 174, 234
Martinelli 11, 88
Martyn, Thomas 132, 160, 205, 234, 238
Mastino 134
Matthews, Henry 163, 234
Metternich, Prince 84
Millard, J. 11, 162, 166, 175, 234
Miller, Lady Anna 68, 160, 162, 206, 234
Misson, Francis 3, 22, 42-3, 46, 111, 116, 197, 206, 234
Monga, Andrea 59
Monsignori, Francesco 166
Montaigne: *see* de Montaigne
Montesquieu, Charles-Louis 70, 232
Monteverdi, Claudio 158, 232, 237
Montmorency, Duke of 84
Montresor, Michelangelo 74, 177
Morando, Paolo 156
Morone, Domenico 149-50
Moryson, Fynes xvi, 2, 15, 19, 25, 28, 31, 41, 122-3, 206, 234
Moscardo, Count Ludovico 154
Mosconi, Countess 73
Mozart, Leopold 160
Mozart, Wolfgang Amadeus 160
Mundy, Peter 32, 234
Murray, John 5, 12, 24, 36, 59, 60, 74, 88, 110, 114, 128, 137, 149-50, 153, 187, 234
Murray, Lady 146, 156, 173, 179, 188, 234
Muselli, 224

Napoleon Bonaparte xvi, 5, 8, 33, 35, 48-50, 60, 78, 80-4, 90, 93, 103, 109-10, 112, 128, 155, 164, 194, 197
Nugent, Thomas 3, 154, 234

Palladio 63-4, 81, 112, 197
Palmerston, Lord and Lady 21, 88, 170

Pasquin, Antoine 6, 34, 36–7, 60–1, 99, 101, 106–7, 109–14, 117–19, 138, 146, 149, 152–3, 156, 175, 206, 234
Patoun, William 8, 10–12, 14, 25, 168, 181, 186, 206
Peale, Rembrandt 172, 234
Pegrassi, Salesio 74, 177–8
Pelacani, Antonio 110
Pelavicini, Mabilia 110
Pennington, Thomas 4, 59, 75, 120, 206, 234
Pepin 60
Petrarch 110
Piccinni, Niccolò 162
Pindemonte, Ippolito 73–4
Piozzi, Hester xi, 5, 40, 44, 67, 73, 102, 118, 132, 145, 155, 171, 179, 188, 206, 230, 234, Plate 6
Pisanello 111, 153, 157
Pius VI, Pope 36
Pliny 28, 32, 62
Pomfret, Countess 26
Pona, Francesco 144, 146, 234
Pope, Alexander 105
Prout, Samuel 157

Radetzky, General 89
Rapelje, George 172, 234
Raphael 155
Raymond, John 2, 41–2, 62, 159, 207, 234
Reichard, Heinrich 62, 174, 207, 235
Reresby, Sir John 144, 234
Riccio, Andrea 79, 110
Ritchie, Leitch 157, 183, 235
Rivet, Charles 157, 207
Robson, James 45, 238
Rogers, Samuel 92, 164, 193, 232
Romano, Giulio 152, 155
Rose, William 59, 61, 133, 207, 235
Rossi, Gaetano 84
Rossini, Gioachino 49, 84, 162
Rushbury, Henry 157

Ruskin, Effie 22–3, 66, 89, 189–90, 206, 233
Ruskin, John xi, 22–3, 46, 54–5, 58, 66, 70, 89–91, 115, 117, 120, 125, 132, 134–5, 140, 149–50, 152–3, 157, 164–5, 197, 206–7, 231–5, 237, Plate 5

Sala, George 26, 35, 56, 70, 76–7, 92, 160, 207, 235
Saraina, Torello 102
Sarti, Giuseppi 160
Sass, Henry 37, 45, 207, 235
Scaliger(i) xiii, 6, 21, 61, 81, 131–6, 194, 196
Schottus: *see* Scoto
Scoto, Francesco 47, 167, 171, 173, 207, 235–6
Scott, John 38, 235
Seaforth 154, 176, 238
Sedgwick, Catharine 18, 26, 50, 207, 235
Serlio, Sebastiano 30
Sewell, Elizabeth 52, 55, 207, 235
Shakespeare, Talbot 100
Shakespeare, William 4, 6, 50, 77, 94–100, 194
Shelley, Mrs 16, 188, 235
Simond, Louis 20, 37, 235
Sinclair, J. 65, 86, 235
Skippon, Philip 27, 119, 128, 138, 144, 208, 235
Smith, William 56, 140, 208, 235
Smyth, Edward 122
Soane, John 25, 63, 208, 232
Spence, Joseph 3, 39, 104–5, 124, 193, 208, 233
Spencer, Henrietta, Lady Bessborough 170
Stanfield, William Clarkson 157
Stanhope, Philip 103
Starke, Mariana 5, 59, 208, 235
Starkie, Walter 28, 208, 236
Stevens, Sacheverell 28, 33, 43, 208, 236
Stoughton, John 53, 119, 208, 236
Street, George Edmund 108–9, 116, 140, 208, 236

Taine, Hippolyte 55, 62, 110, 117, 156, 208, 236
Tanner, Culpepper 3, 21, 237
Tappen, George 78, 172, 208, 236
Taylor, Catharine 95, 236
Taylor, Sir Herbert 17, 86, 236
Theodoric 60, 66, 116, 196
Thomson, William 176, 236
Tintoretto 151, 153
Titian 69, 79, 109, 140, 148, 150–2, 154–5, 196
Todd, Matthew 16, 236
Turner, J.M.W. xii, 93, 157, 193, Plate 13
Turner, William 167, 236
Turodi 156
Trollope, Mrs 39, 236
Tyndale, Walter 140, 157, 236

Uklanski: *see* von Uklanski

Valerini, Adriano 40, 69, 167, 209, 236
Valéry: *see* Pasquin
Vasari, Giorgio 62–3, 112, 149, 152, 166–7, 196, 209, 230, 236
Verdi, Giuseppe 165
Veronese, Paolo 79, 111–12, 148, 150–1, 153–6, 197
Veryard, Ellis 129, 236
Victor Emanuel II, King xvii, 93
Vigée le Brun, Marie Elizabeth Louise 24, 29, 73, 157, 209, 236
Vincent, Eric 140, 236
Vitruvius 60, 62, 196
Vivaldi, Antonio xii, 105, 159
von Goethe, Johann Wolfgang xi, 6, 71, 73, 138, 148, 164, 180–1, 187, 193, 197, 209, 232, Plate 4
von Kotzebue, August 16, 37, 80, 83, 101–2, 161, 169, 209, 233

von Raumer, Friedrich 89, 165, 236
von Rochau, August 184, 236
von Uklanski, Baron Carl Theodor 32, 48–9, 70, 81, 102–3, 174, 209, 232

W., J. 21, 236
Wales, Henry, Prince of 33, 230
Walker, Adam 39, 180–1, 209, 236
Walpole, Horace 105, 190, 233, 236
Watkins, Thomas 188, 236
Webb, William 59, 86, 209, 236
Wellington, Duke of 84
White, William 142
Williams, Charles 28, 60, 68, 131, 237
Willis, Robert 121, 237
Wilson, James 30, 35, 61, 79, 97, 105, 237
Wilson, William Rae 63–5, 68, 81, 151, 154, 173, 175, 209, 237
Withrow, William 31, 56, 210, 237
Woods, Joseph 32, 34, 63, 108, 110, 112, 115, 117–19, 210, 237
Wortley Montagu, Lady Mary 44, 103, 105, 186, 190, 210, 232
Wright, Edward 42, 128, 149, 151, 210, 237
Wright, Joseph 151, 184, 230
Wylie, James 54, 88, 210, 237
Wynne, Elizabeth 12, 25–6, 44, 78, 145, 180, 203, 232

Yankee, A 34, 229
Young, Arthur 25, 29, 43, 75, 174, 178, 210, 237
Young English Merchant 78, 81, 237

Zenobrio 44

General index

Accademia di Filotimi 158–9
Accademia Filarmonica 85, 158–60
accommodation 10, 17, 20–9, 86, 193
Acqua Morta 47
amphitheatre: *see* Arena
Arco dei Gavi xiii, 58, 60, 81
Arco di Gallienus: *see* Porta Borsari
Arena xii, xiii, xvi, 3–4, 6, 18, 30–9, 41, 44, 52–4, 58, 64–5, 67, 73, 75, 81, 84, 87, 95, 103, 114, 128, 138, 141, 162, 165, 191, 193–5, Plates 13, 14, 21
Arsenale xiii, 64, 194

Baldo, Monte 172
balloon 36
baths 24, 54, 166–7, 187, 236
Biblioteca Capitolare 106, 109–10
birboni 49
Bolca 63, 155
Bologna 1, 17, 40, 122, 179
bread 10, 24, 27, 29, 61

Caldiero 166–7
Cambridge 2, 31, 122, 140, 163, 199, 205–6, 208
campanile 64, 112, 115, 121, 137, 139
carnevale 45
Castel San Felice 61
Castel San Pietro xii, 59, 61, 64, 76, 79–80, 86, 143, 196, Plate 15
Castelvecchio xiii, 60–1, 64, 74, 79, 81, 131, 134, 194, 196
castrati 129–30, 158–9
Catholic xvi, 1, 3–4, 120, 122–7, 129–30, 132, 139, 176, 185, 200, 202, 210
(Il) Cavalletto 21
cicerone 5, 17, 74–7, 97, 108, 136
cicisbeo 187–8

clean(liness) 20–1, 29, 45, 52, 54, 70, 129, 180, 182, 187, 192
(La) Colomba d'Oro 24, 26, 76
Congress of Verona 64, 84–6, 146, 197, 201, 235
conversazione 73, 103, 160, 181
Corso 44–5, 49, 59–60, 68, 81, 114, 157
Culloden 124

dirt(y)/filth(y) 1, 17–18, 20–1, 27, 29, 37, 42, 44, 46, 49–50, 54, 56, 63, 70, 72, 95–6, 98, 109, 116, 138, 140, 151, 163, 187, 194
dress 12–13, 28, 34, 57, 68, 72, 96, 126–7, 140–1, 154, 179–84, 186, 191, 193
Due Torri 16, 21–6, 29, 47, 51, 78, 89, 140, 153, 165, 175
Duomo xiii, 41, 71, 79, 85, 107–9, 114, 125, 127, 130, 148, 151–2, 182, 194

(La) fida ninfa xii, 105, 159, Plate 11
(La) fiera 106
foglia 175
fresco 66, 91, 98, 111–13, 135–6, 141–2, 149, 152–3, 156–7
friar 124, 128, 180
fruit 26, 72, 98, 137–40, 143, 153, 171–2, 175

ghetto 129
Ghibelline 131, 196
Giardino Giusti xiii, 114, 143–7
Gothic 6, 54–5, 61, 107, 110, 112, 115–16, 118–20, 126, 131–5, 139, 142, 150, 207–8
Gran Guardia 64
(Il) Gran Parigi 24
Grand Tour xvi, 1–4, 41, 58, 67, 103, 114, 123, 132, 159, 185–6, 190, 193, 199–200, 203, 205–8, 210, 230–4, 236–7

Holy Roman Empire/Emperor 8, 60, 131, 196
Huguenot 27, 42, 206

Jesuit 51, 123, 127–9, 168, 170
Jew; Judaism 43, 108, 129, 203–4

Kingdom of Italy xv, xvii, 56, 76, 80, 87, 92–3, 138, 194, 197
Kingston Lacy 41, 51–2, 74, 177–8, 199

lazzaretto 17, 63, 169
leather 11, 70, 174, 182
Liston 64, 73
Loggia : *see* Palazzo del Consiglio
Lombard (architecture) 54, 116, 119–20
Luneville, Treaty of 79

Madonna Verona 81, 85, 138
marble 21, 32, 45–6, 50, 64, 66, 95, 97, 99, 101, 109–11, 113, 115, 118, 120, 132, 134, 137, 141, 145, 162, 176–7
market xiii, 27, 53, 64, 72, 76, 86, 137–42, 182
Mass 107–8, 120, 127, 130, 182
Merope 105, 220
mill xi, 47–8, 174, Plate 7
monk 78, 111–12, 118, 126–9, 147
Mont Cenis 7–9
mulberry 79, 171–3, 178
municipio 56
music xii, 5, 30, 33, 36, 65, 72–3, 84, 104–5, 129–30, 158–65, 195, 198, 200, 204, 206, 208, 230, 232, 234

Naples xv, 41, 67–8, 91, 93, 147, 181, 235
naumachia 59, 76
nun 127–8, 179, 188

olive 55, 164, 171–2
opera 35, 85, 105, 127, 158–9, 161–5, 170, 194–5, 201
Oxford 1, 3, 39, 102, 105, 201, 204–5, 207–8

Padua 1, 7–8, 12, 55, 69, 122, 129, 131, 184
Palazzo Albarelli 154

Palazzo Bevilacqua 63, 81, 153, 158, 194
Palazzo Broilo 185
Palazzo Canossa 45, 63, 82, 84
Palazzo del Consiglio xiii, 62, 64, 144, 155, 194
Palazzo della Ragione xiii, 60, 157
Palazzo Giusti 90, 144–6
Palazzo Maffei xiii, 106, 194
Palazzo Mocenigo 63
Palazzo Pompei 63, 156
Palazzo Sparavieri 63
Pasque Veronesi 79, 197
passeggiata 50, 64, 184
passport 12, 15–16, 18, 54, 88, 91–2, 169
Pellegrini chapel 110, 112
Piazza Armi: *see* Piazza Bra
Piazza Bra xiii, 30, 58, 64–5, 71, 93, 101
Piazza Dante: *see* Piazza Dei Signori
Piazza dei Signori xiii, 6, 60–2, 64, 76–7, 131, 137, 157, 194
Piazza delle Erbe or Piazza Erbe xii, xiii, 27, 56, 60, 81, 106, 129, 137–42, 156–7, 194, Plate 18
Piazza Sant'Anastasia xi, xiii, 21–2, 89, 157, 165, Plate 9
plague 17, 42, 52, 144, 167, 169
play (drama) 33–5, 59, 69, 82, 85, 94, 105, 129, 163
Ponte Emilio 59, 76
Ponte Navi xii, Plate 17
Ponte Nuovo 48
Ponte Pietra xi, xiii, 47, 58, 66, 112, 194, Plate 8
Porta Borsari 58
Porta Palio xiii, 62
Porta Leoni xiii, 59
Porta Nuova xiii, 19, 62, 71
Porta San Giorgio 51
Porta San Zeno 62
Porta Stupa 62
Porta Vescovo 17, 19, 55, 62, 92, 175, 197
Porto San Pancrazio 63, 169
Pressburg, Treaty of 80

priest 4, 14, 76, 108, 125–7, 129–30, 132, 151, 153–4, 171, 199–200, 202, 205–6
Protestant 1, 3, 111, 122–5, 130, 185, 199, 203, 206, 208, 210

rail(way) xiii, xv, xvi, 4, 12, 17, 18, 55, 90, 191, 197, 204–5
Reformation xvi, 1, 122, 130, 185, 210
Renaissance 54–5, 62, 64, 73, 153, 194, 207
rice 174–5
Romeo and Juliet xiii, 4, 6, 23, 50, 53, 69, 77, 94–100, 182–3, 194, 235

Sala Maffeiana 160
San Bernardino xiii, 112, 149–50, 153, 156
San Fermo Maggiore xiii, 30, 79, 107, 110, 114, 153, 199
San Giorgio xiii, 47, 51, 63, 66, 79, 107, 112, 128, 148–51
San Lorenzo xiii, 114
San Sebastiano 114
San Tommaso xiii, 47, 92, 114
(San) Zeno xii, xiii, xv, 49, 60, 62, 64, 77, 79, 107, 110, 114–21, 123, 148, 152–3, 194, 196, 229, 233–4, Plates 16, 20
Sant'Anastasia xi, xiii, 23, 41, 107, 110, 114, 126, 140, 153, Plate 9
Sant'Elena 114
Sant'Eufemia xiii, 79, 114
Santa Maria Antica (della Scala) 114, 131, 136
Santa Maria in Organo xiii, 107, 111, 123, 125–6, 153, 156, 235

Santi Nazaro e Celso xiii, 113, 153, 156
Santo Stefano 114
Santuario della Madonna di Campagna 113, 232
scorpion 22
silk 43, 68, 79, 121, 164, 171–4, 178–9, 181
Simplon 7–8
spinning 70, 79
Stuart 34, 124

tea 10–11, 24, 27, 29, 103
Teatro Filarmonico xii, 84, 101, 159, 163, 165, Plate 11
Teatro Ristori 163
Torre dei Lamberti xiii, 60
(La) Torre di Londra 24, 27
(Le) Tre Corone 79

Veronetta 16, 19, 47, 63, 80, 112–13, 143, 151, 157
via Mazzini 66, 184
vine 41, 96, 98, 171–2, 174, 178, 190

wine 9–10, 24–6, 28, 37, 142, 170–1
woodpecker 141
wool 146, 173–4, 178

yellow fever 169

Plate 1. Scipione Maffei (1675–1755), by Giuseppe Ghislandi

Plate 2. James Silk Buckingham (1786–1855), attributed to Clara S. Lane, *c.*1850

Plate 3. William John Bankes, MP (1786–1855), by George Sandars, 1812

Plate 4. Johann Wolfgang von Goethe (1749–1832), by Johann Heinrich Ramberg, 1791–2

Plate 5. John Ruskin (1819–1900), by George Richmond, *c*.1837

Plate 6. Hester Lynch Piozzi (1741–1821), by an unknown Italian artist

Plate 7. The River Adige at Verona, showing floating watermills, by Bernardo Bellotto, (1720–80)

Plate 8. Ponte Pietra, engraved by J. Godfrey, after Myles Birket Foster, c.1870, published in *Picturesque Europe*, 1875, hand coloured

Plate 9. Castelbarco tomb and gate, next to Sant'Anastasia, by Robert Charles Goff, *c.*1900

Plate 10. Female costume and hairstyle in Verona, 1825, from an anonymous sketch book

Plate 11. A rehearsal for *La fida ninfa*, with text by Maffei and music by Vivaldi, in the Teatro Filarmonico, 1732, pen and ink wash by the architect Francesco Galli-Bibiena and the set designer Jean-Joseph Chamant

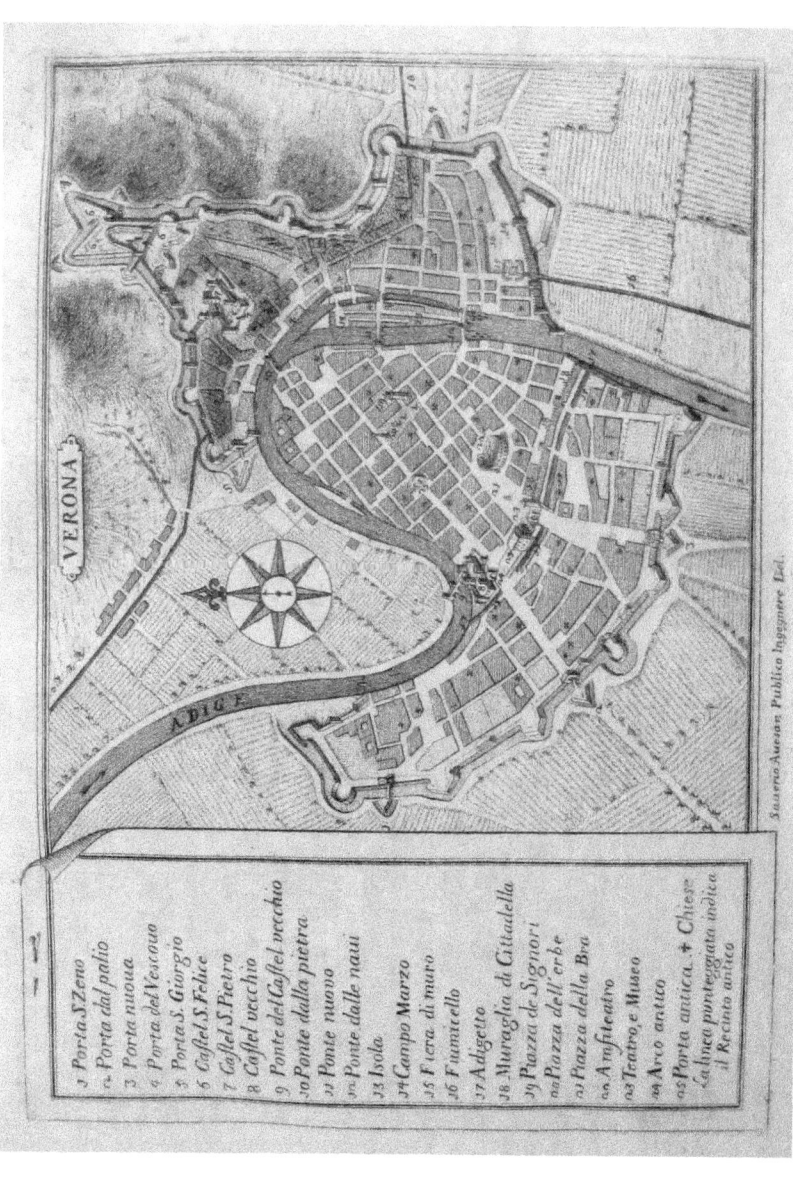

Plate 12. Map of Verona by Saverio Avesan, published in Scipione Maffei's *Verona illustrata*, 1732

Plate 13. The Arena, Verona, engraved by W. Miller, after J.M.W. Turner, c.1833, published in *Drawing and engraving* by P.G. Hamerton, 1892

Plate 14. The interior of the Arena, Verona, engraved by J. Sands after W.H. Bartlett, c.1840, published in *Fisher's drawing room scrap book for 1845*

Plate 15. Verona, with Castel San Pietro in the foreground, engraved by Mattheus Merian, from Martin Zeiller's *Itinerarium Italiae...*, 1640; edition of 1688

Plate 16. 'Lungadige alle Regaste di S. Zeno', engraving, published in Da Persico's *Descrizione di Verona e della sua provincia*, 1820

Plate 17. 'Ponte delle Navi caduto l'anno 1757', showing the flood damage that year; engraving, published in Da Persico's *Descrizione di Verona e della sua provincia,* 1820

Plate 18. Piazza delle Erbe, etching, published in Da Persico's *Descrizione di Verona e della sua provincia*, 1820

Plate 19. 'Porta di Borsari', drawn by Lady Henrietta Fortescue, 1821

Plate 20. San Zenone (San Zeno Maggiore), lithograph from *The ecclesiastical architecture of Italy* ... by Henry Gally Knight, 1844

Plate 21. 'The amphitheatre at Verona', woodcut by Edward Whymper published in *Italian pictures drawn with pen and pencil* by The Reverend Samuel Manning, *c.*1885

Plate 22. 'The war – Austrian lancers passing the tombs of the Scaligers, *Verona*'; wood engraving after T.R. MacQuoid, published in *The Illustrated London News*, 1859

www.ingramcontent.com/pod-product-compliance
Lightning Source LLC
Chambersburg PA
CBHW060946230426
43665CB00015B/2078